THE LAST
OF THE
TASMANIANS

David Davies

FREDERICK MULLER

First published in Great Britain in 1973
by Frederick Muller Limited, London NW2

Printed in Great Britain
by Ebenezer Baylis and Son Ltd.
The Trinity Press, Worcester, and London
Bound by Webb Son & Co., Ferndale, Glamorgan
ISBN 0 584 10151 1

THE LAST OF THE TASMANIANS

Contents

Illustrations

Introduction

When, in 1642, the Dutchman, Abel Tasman, was sailing along the then known Southern Ocean that lies between Australia and the South Pole, he came across a rocky wooded island. This he called Van Diemen's Land, later to become known as Tasmania.

The aboriginals who inhabited the islands, like the aboriginals of New Guinea, believed themselves alone in the world, and had numerous legends about their origins. The Tasmanian aborigines, dark of skin, brilliant in eye, had massive and immense jaws with receding chins. They had woolly hair and the men curly beards. Their dark skin was scarified according to tribal custom, yet they had shapely feet and small hands. These interesting people wandered about in many little tribes and until the end of their sojourn on this earth, very rarely were they united. Apart from colour, they were unlike their neighbours of "New Holland", now Australia. In hair, nose and limb they differed markedly. But both races were wandering hunters, neither cultivating the land nor taming bird or beast for food supply. The chase gave no chance of settled habitation or form of government. The wooden pointed spear stayed the kangaroo and the wallaby in its leap, and the boomerang brought down the winged fowl. The friction of two pieces of wood produced fire in whose embers food was roasted. Without garments, save for the raw skin that they wore on the upper parts of their bodies, and using only windbreaks for shelter, they had no homes—and needed none.

To nineteenth-century Europeans they represented the deepest depths of barbarism. But they were neither stupid nor miserable and they were still men and women. Isolated those thousands of years, they had no need to advance beyond the rudest state; all they needed was around them. Yet they had sense and feeling. An expansive, and often lofty, forehead betrayed their gorilla look. A language, albeit with no ordinary grammatical niceties, proved their human kind: though, as with all primitive people, it was complicated and difficult to understand, for they had so much time to compose it while squatting round their camp fires. The merry laugh in that evening firelight, the ready joke, the boisterous fun, the play of mother and child, must have made the camp a lively place. Their wants were few and easily supplied. Without regrets for past good, and no desire for any future except a fair day's sport on the morrow, they lived, like the Eskimaux, entirely in the present. They made no stores in any way for the future. They foraged on what was around for the day, and let the morrow take care of itself.

If, like their changing skies, the smile was quickly followed by a mood of gloomy rage, the cloud of anger soon melted into peace. In this way they were so related to the inhabitants of the highlands of New Guinea. A hasty tumult was raised, and the little tribal gathering would begin to sing, shake the limb into the sensuous dance, and stir the forest with their shouts of merriment. If wanting little for the body, they required even less for the soul. With no gods, no form of worship, their vague fears were due only to the wild, dread voices of the constant storms, the darkness and the eyes of the Tasmanian Wolf and the Devil peering at them out of the blackness beyond the fire. With these fears life must have been all the more terrible because they did not have the slightest understanding of the laws of the universe. They were of the earth, content with one day's food and gladness; so they lived, so had their fathers lived.

Another wanderer came, another claimant of the bounding kangaroo. The aborigine saw a man like himself, but white of skin, clothed and armed with thunder stolen from the skies. But, far worse, the intruder brought mistrust and gloom to the island so long owned by the darker race. Henceforth the scene is changed: the men and women find another heaven spread over them.

To tell the tale of sorrows flowing from this arrival, how the war between the weak and strong brought all-prevailing power to one, but eventual extinction to the other, is the object of this present book.

PART ONE

Prologue

chapter 1

The Earliest Records

The discoverer of Van Diemen's Land, Abel Jansen Tasman, never saw the original inhabitants. However, he detected the notches put in tree trunks by which they climbed the trees looking for, he thought, birds' nests, though later evidence showed that it was for opossums. He often saw smoke, and heard a noise like a trumpet (the blowing of the conch shell). Tasman was satisfied with hoisting the Dutch flag, and then he sailed on to discover New Zealand, much more welcome to an explorer.

A Frenchman, Captain Marion, made the first contact with the wild men of Van Diemen's Land, in 1772, 140 years after Tasman's landing. Rienzi, the historian, speaks of the kind reception the natives gave his countrymen. Women and children were present to greet the strangers, which indicated that they did not have war on their minds. But a little later there was bloodshed:

"About an hour after the French fleet had landed, Captain Marion landed. Advancing in front of him, one of the aborigines offered him a lighted firebrand, indicating that he should set alight a heap of wood heaped up just above the waterline.

"Marion took it, believing it to be a formality that would go on to give friendship between the parties; but hardly had the pile of wood been lighted, when the aborigines retired *en masse* towards a little height on the foreshore, from which vantage point they threw a volley of stones, which wounded the two Captains on the beach below. The French sailors accompanying the Captains, discharged several of their muskets, and as a result they killed one of the aborigines and wounded several of the others. The others fled howling towards the woods."

From another chronicle on the voyage we learn other particulars. A party of thirty aborigines came down, the women carrying their children behind their backs, held with ropes of rushes. The men were said to be carrying stakes, that had been hardened in the fire, and stone axes. Presents of useful pieces of iron, looking glasses, and even handkerchiefs, were laid down before them, but these were rejected with sulky disdain. Some ducks and geese were also offered to them, but were angrily thrown back again. The firebrand was presented to a sailor first of all, and then afterwards to Captain Marion. But evidently the act, supposed to be friendly, was taken in another spirit. They might have regarded it as a proof that the strangers intended an encroach upon their own hunting grounds. The chronicler adds:

> "This was no sooner done, than they retired quickly to a small hill, and threw a shower of stones, by which Captain Marion and the Commander of the Castries were both wounded."

Shots, of course, replied to the stones and the Frenchmen returned hurriedly to their boats. The aborigines sent their women back to the shelter of the forest, and then ran along the shore after their foes. The sailors pulled back from the shore to stop the pursuit (as they were still afraid for their captain). At this moment an old chief assumed the leadership, and raised a hideous warcry, and then a storm of spears was rained on the sailors. Fifteen sailors now chased the assailants, and with their destructive fire killed and wounded several of them.

It appears, from the presence of women and children, that the aborigines had no intention of aggression at the outset. Other primitive tribes in New Guinea, the Australian aborigines, and peoples in islands near Tasmania do not have their women and children around when they intend to do battle, or have aggressive intentions. It seems rather symbolic that the first whites to arrive on the shore were given a firebrand and with it made a conflagration! Probably nothing more than another of the misunderstandings that have marred relations between whites and native peoples, it might just have been premonition.

The unfortunate Marion met his death in New Zealand. A French author describes his countryman as being fattened for thirty-two days, and being eaten on the thirty-third. However, it is known that the New Zealanders (Maoris) treated him well, until sailors under his command polluted their sacred places, forced them to cook food with tabooed wood and put two chiefs in irons. Might they not have also conducted themselves badly in Tasmania, so creating animosity among the aborigines there? Such circumstances could well have been omitted in their journals, which were, after all, for the benefit of their superiors, wives and friends at home.

Captain Furneaux preceded Captain Cook to Tasmania by nearly four years, but storms drove him off the island. Captain Cook, arriving in the *Adventure* in 1777, saw much of the race on one of the offshore islands, Bruni Island, and has left us his observations:

"They were quite naked, and wore no ornaments, unless we consider as such some large punctures in different parts of their bodies, some in straight and others in curved lines. The men were of the middle stature, but rather slender. Their skin and hair were black, and the latter as woolly as that of any native of Guinea; but they were not distinguished by any remarkably thick lips, nor flat noses. On the contrary, their features were far from being disagreeable. They had pretty good eyes and their teeth were tolerably even, but very dirty. Most of them had their hair and beards smeared with a red ointment, and some of them also had their faces painted with the same form of composition. When some bread was offered them, as soon as they understood that it was to be eaten, they either returned it or threw it away, without tasting it."

A couple of pigs were brought ashore to turn loose, but the aborigines seized them by the ears and carried them off, doubtless to eat them. A musket was fired and the party fled in great disarray. However, one little girl returned, and brought several families back with her. Of these it was remarked that they "wore kangaroo skin fastened over their shoulders, the only use for which seemed to be to support their children on their backs, for it left those parts uncovered which modesty directs us to conceal. Their bodies were black and marked with scars like those of men; from whom, however, they differed, in having their heads shaved —some of them, in fact, being completely shorn, others only on one side, while the rest of them had the upper part of their heads shaved, leaving a very narrow circle of hair all round. They were far from being handsome; however, some of our gentlemen paid their addresses to them but without the usual effect. That the gallantry of some of our people was not very agreeable to the men was certain; for an elderly man, as soon as he observed it, ordered the women and children to retire, which they all did, but some with a little reluctance." He adds: "They wander about in small parties from place to place in search of food, which is the chief end of their existence and, from what we are able to judge, they are altogether an ignorant wretched race of mortals though at the same time the natives of a country capable of producing every necessity of life, with a climate the finest in the world."

It is interesting to note here that the women of the highlands of New Guinea often have the same lack of hair; theirs is shaved to provide substance for their husband's wig. (See plate A5.

Cook was also surprised at their indifference to presents and disregard of iron, fishhooks, and goes on to say "they lived like beasts of the forest, in roving parties, without arts of any kind, sleeping in summer like dogs, under the hollow sides of trees, or in wattled huts made with low branches of evergreen shrubs, stuck in the ground at small distances from each other, and meeting together at the top". The great navigator was struck by "the superior virtue of the Tasmanian women" over the more polished Polynesians. His remarks upon the conduct of Europeans towards the women of primitive tribes are worthy of mention. He describes it as "highly blamable", as it creates a jealousy in their men, that may be attended with consequences fatal to the success of the common enterprise, and to all callers at the islands, without advancing the private purpose of the individual, or enabling him to gain the object of his wishes. In regions where uncivilized people are found, where the women are easy for the stranger to obtain, the men of the tribe are the first to start the negotiations and in regions where this occurs there is little, or no, animosity occurring through the strangers having contacts with the women of the tribe. But where this is not the case, neither the allure of presents nor the opportunity of privacy will be likely to have the desired effect.

The most important contemporary accounts of Tasmania are those of the famous French naturalist Labillardiere and Péron. The former was a companion of Admiral d'Entrecasteaux on his visit in 1792; and the latter went there with Admiral Baudin in 1802.

Here is an extract of what Labillardiere had to say about his experiences on the island:

"We got ready a few cartridges as fast as we could, and set out towards the place where we had seen the aborigines. It was now only nine o'clock. We had gone only a few steps before we met them. The men and the youths were ranged in the front, nearly in a semicircle; the women, the children and then the older girls, were a few paces behind. As their manner did not indicate any hostile design, I hesitated not to go up to the oldest, who accepted, with a very good grace, a piece of biscuit that I offered him, of which he had seen me eat. I then held out my hand to him, as a sign of friendship, and had the pleasure of seeing that he understood my meaning very well, he gave me his hand also, at the same time inclining himself a little sort of bow, at the same time as he did this he raised his left foot, which he carried backward in proportion as he bent his body forward. All these motions were accompanied by a very pleasant smile.

"My companions seeing this, also advanced up to the other males of the tribe, and immediately the best understanding prevailed. They received with a show of great joy the neckcloths that we offered to them. Then the young people approached nearer to us, and one of them had the generosity to give me a few small shells, of the welk kind, pierced near the middle, and strung like a necklace. This ornament, that he seemed to call 'canlaride', was the only one that he appeared to possess, and it had been worn round his head. A handkerchief supplied the place of this present, gratifying the utmost wishes of his savage heart, when he advanced towards me I tied it round his head for him, and his countenance expressed the greatest joy, as he lifted up his hand to feel it again and again. We wore an abundance of clothes, on account of the coldness of the nights; and we bestowed the greater part of these upon our new found island friends.

"The women were very desirous of coming nearer to us: and though the men made signs to them to keep at a distance, their curiosity was ready every moment to break through all other considerations. The gradual increase in confidence, however, that occurred, eventually overruled the warnings of their menfolk and then they came up to us. It appeared very astonishing to us that at that high latitude, where, at a period of the year so little advanced as the present, we needed all the clothing that we could wear, that they did not feel the necessity for wearing clothes. Even the women for the most part were entirely naked, as well as the men. Some of the women only had the shoulders, or part of the back, covered with a kangaroo's skin, worn with the hair next to the body, only two had this form of a covering, and each of these had an infant at the breast. The sole garment of another was a strip of kangaroo skin, about two inches broad, which was wrapped six or seven times around the waist. Another had a collar of skin round the neck, and some had a slender cord bound several times round the head. I afterwards learned that most of these cords were fabricated from the bark of a shrub of the Spurge family, very common in this country.

"I had given several things to them without thinking, or expecting, anything in return; but I wished to get a kangaroo's skin. Among the aborigines that were around us I could see only one girl who had one. I made signs that implied that if she gave it to me she could have a pair of pantaloons instead, but she ran away to hide herself in the woods. The other aborigines appeared truly hurt at her refusal to give it to me, and called several times for her to come back. At length she yielded to their entreaties, and came to bring me the skin. Perhaps it was from timidity only that she could not prevail on herself to part with the 'garment'. In return she received the pantaloons, less useful to her, according to the customs of the ladies of this country, than the skin, which served to cover the shoulders, which are the particular part, at least among the females, that have to be hid. We showed her the manner of wearing the pantaloons; but notwithstanding this, it was necessary for us to put them on for her ourselves. To this she yielded with the best grace in the world."

It appears from this account that it is not always the genitals that mankind is nervous about showing to the common gaze.

In the party mentioned above there were seven men, eight women and seven children. The French sailors tried the earliest known means of "civilizing" the wild men, by giving them grog. But it was promptly rejected by the unsophisticated palate. I have seen similar scenes in New Guinea where the Australians have tried the same tactics with rum, with the same result. The Frenchmen, however, got the girls of the little band together and induced them to run races with each other. Any attempts by the Frenchmen to go beyond this were resisted at once by the girls, though in a good-tempered way. One girl, more rudely assaulted, fled to a rock overhanging the sea, being prepared to plunge in if her pursuer advanced any further towards her. One cannot, now, tell whether it was a show put on for the benefit of their menfolk, or if they would have behaved differently had they not been present, as was often the case in meetings between European men and the aborigine women described later on.

In 1798, Captain Flinders and Bass fell in with the aborigines near the River Derwent. It was in consequence of a report of this visit that the island became colonized by the British Government, the first stage in the extinction of the aboriginal inhabitants, and the account told by

Captain Collins, afterwards appointed to be the founder of the colony at Hobart Town, makes interesting reading. After speaking of the run of the H.M.S. *Norfolk* up the beautiful River Derwent, he goes on:

"In their way up, a human voice saluted them, coming from the hills; on which they had landed along with one of several swans that they had just shot. Having nearly reached the summit, two females, with a short covering hanging loose from their shoulders, suddenly appeared at some little distance before them; but, each snatching up a small basket, scampered off. A man then presented himself, and suffered them to approach him without any sign of fear, or distrust. He received the swan joyously, appearing to esteem it a treasure.

"His language was unintelligible to them, as was theirs to him, although they addressed him in several of the dialects that they knew from New South Wales, and some few of the most common words of the South Sea Islands. With some difficulty, they made him understand that they wished to see his place of residence. He pointed over the hill, and proceeded onwards; but his pace was slow and wandering, and he often stopped in pretence as it were that he had lost the track, which led them to suspect that his only aim was to amuse and tire them out. Judging, then, that in persisting to follow him they must lose the remaining part of the flood tide, which was much more valuable to them than the sight of his hut could be, they parted from him, but in great friendship." [Little knowing that within 80 years there would be none left.]

The most probable reason for his unwillingness to be their guide, seemed to be his fear that if he took them to his women their charms might induce elopement—a jealousy very much shared with the Australian aborigines.

"He was a short, slight man, of middle age, with a countenance more expressive of benignity and intelligence, than of the ferocity or stupidity which generally characterized the other aborigines of Tasmania; and his features were less flattened, or negro-like, than theirs. His face was blackened, and the top of his head was plastered with red earth [ochre]. His hair was either naturally short and close, or had been made so by burning, and, although short and stiffly curled, they did not think it woolly. He was armed with two spears, very badly made and of solid wood only. Only the red silk handkerchiefs round their necks attracted his attention enough to comment. Their firearms were to him neither objects of curiosity, nor fear."

But by far the most pleasing stories from those early years of Tasmania's exploration are told by the Frenchman, M. Péron, who was there also in 1802, a naturalist as well as an explorer and, therefore, a keen observer.

"To the signs of friendship that we made to the aborigines, one of them precipitated himself from the top of a rock, rather than descend it, and in the twinkling of an eye was in the midst of us. He was a young man, of from twenty-two to twenty-four years of age, of an apparently strong constitution, having no other defect than a slenderness of legs and arms that seems to characterize his nation.

"His face exhibited neither austerity or ferocity; his eyes were quick and sparkling, and his looks expressed at the same time benevolence and surprise. M. Freycinet having embraced him, I did the same. But the air of indifference with which he welcomed this evidence of our interest made it easy to observe that it had no significance for him. [It appears that kissing, etc., was not a practice of the Tasmanian aborigines as with many other primitive peoples.]

"What appeared to affect him more was the whiteness of our skins. Wishing to assure himself, without doubt, if the colour was the same all over the body, he opened our waistcoats and shirts, and his astonishment was manifested by his loud cries of surprise, and above all, by extremely quick stamping of the feet.

"Yet our cutter appeared to occupy him more than our persons, and, after having gazed a few moments, he rushed down to the landing place. There, without disturbing himself about the sailors whom he found there, he seemed quite absorbed in his new observation. The thickness of the ribs and the panels, the solidity of its construction, its rudder, its oars, its masts, its sails, he observed with all that silence and the profound attention which are the least equivocal signs of a reflective interest and admiration. In a moment one of the sailors, wishing without a doubt to add to his surprise presented him with a wine bottle filled with the grog that formed part of the rations of the ship. The brightness of the glass called forth a cry of astonishment from the aborigine, who took the bottle and examined it for some few moments; but the interest in this bauble was most short lived and his curiosity again led to the direction of the vessel. He threw the bottle into the sea, without appearing to have any intention, other than to relieve himself of an indifferent object of the fancy, and from then on went on with his research. Neither the cry of the sailor, who was now troubled at the loss of his grog, nor the entreaty of one of his comrades to throw himself into the water to catch it, appeared to move him. He made several attempts, however, to push the cutter free, but the cable which held it attached to the shore, rendered all his attempts in vain; he was then constrained to abandon it and to return to rejoin us, after having given us the most striking example of reflection and attention that we had ever seen in primitive people."

Another very lucid passage runs:

"The old man, after having examined both of us with as much surprise and satisfaction as the first, made signs to two women, who had hitherto been unwilling to approach. They hesitated some moments, after which the elder of the two came to us. The younger then followed her, more timid and fearful than the first. The first one appeared to be about forty years of age, as the large furrows upon the skin of the abdomen announced, and also indicated that she had mothered several children. She was absolutely naked, and appeared like the old man, to be kind and benevolent. The young woman was of from twenty-six to twenty-eight years of age, and of a pretty robust build. Like the preceding woman she also was entirely naked, with the exception of a kangaroo skin, in which she carried a little girl, which she continued to suckle. Her breasts, a little withered already, appeared otherwise to be pretty well formed, and of the pendulous type, and were sufficiently furnished with milk. This young woman, like the older man and woman, who we presumed to be her mother and father, had a most interesting face and expression. Her eyes were the most expressive part of it, and there seemed to be even something spiritual, and this surprised us, and which since then we have been unable to find in any other female of that nation. She appeared also to cherish her child much; and her care for it had that affectionate and gentle character which is exhibited among all races, as the particular attribute of maternal tenderness."

Another family group excited the most romantic ravings of the French explorers. These consisted of a father and mother, a young man, a little boy about five years old, a girl of younger years, and a most beautiful savage of sixteen or seventeen, such as one will occasionally come across amongst the New Guineans or Australian aborigines today. Such beauty appears even more outstanding in contrast to the general ugliness of the other women. This is one of the peculiarities of the people found in these regions. Upon the Frenchmen making the acquaintance of this distinguished little party, Péron, like a true man of gallantry, drew off his glove, while bowing to this beauty, preparatory to his offering the salutation of refined society. The fair one of the forest was struck with horror and alarm at the facility with which her admirer could peel off his skin at a moment's notice.

The old man, in primitive simplicity, invited the visitors to his evening meal of cockles and mussels. Péron sang, for his supper, the Marseillaise. The effect he describes:

> "The young man of the party tore his hair and scratched his head with both hands, agitated himself in a hundred different ways, and repeatedly iterated his approving clamour."

Other, more tender airs, followed from Péron, which doubtless touched the young lady, and he describes what happened:

> "The young girl whom I have noticed made herself more and more conspicuous every instant, by the softness of her looks, and the affectionate and sparkling expression in her eyes. Oura Oura (for that was her name), like her parents, was perfectly naked, even to lack of adornment of a necklace, but there appeared nothing immodest or indecent about this lack of dress. Of a weaker constitution than her little brother and sister, she was though more lively and impassioned than they, with a most slender waist which is rare in these people. M. Freycinet, who seated himself beside her, appeared to be more the object of her most agreeable attentions, and the least experienced eye might have been able, in the look of this innocent child of nature, to distinguish that delicate shadow which gives to simple playfulness a more serious and reflective character. Coquetry, that all women know how to use, appeared to be called forth to the support of the natural attractions and attributes that Nature had endowed her with.
>
> "Oura Oura introduced us for the first time to the natural rouge of these regions, as well as the details of its application. After having put some charcoal in my hands she crushed it, and reduced it to a

very fine powder; then, keeping this dust in the left hand, she took some with the right, and rubbing at first the forehead, then the two cheeks, in an instant her countenance was frightfully black: that which above all appeared singular to us was the complacency with which the young girl looked at us after the operation, and the air of confidence which this new ornament had spread over her features. Thus then, the sentiment of coquetry, the taste for ornament, are wants, so to speak, innate in the heart of women."

In New Guinea this sort of rouge is also used by the mountain people, even today, and takes its place in the daily toilet. M. Péron then proceeds to describe a little bit of vanity on the other side:

"Oura Oura carried a reed bag, of an elegant and singular construction, which I much desired to obtain. As this young girl evidenced for me some more amicable distinctions, I ventured to ask for her little bag. Immediately and without hesitation, she put it into my hand, accompanying the present with an obliging smile and some affectionate phrases, which I regretted not being able to understand."

The gallant Frenchman gave her his handkerchief and a tomahawk in return; but when M. Breton, another member of the party, bestowed a long red feather on her, "She leaped for joy. She called her father and her brothers. She cried, she laughed; and altogether was intoxicated with pleasure and happiness."

But the best of friends must part. The gentlemen prepared for the loneliness of the life on the ocean wave, grieving at the thought of giving up the delights of the Arcadian simplicity, and pure pleasures of aboriginal innocence. Yet these primitive people were too polite to permit their guests to depart unattended. The civilities of the civilized were not wanting.

"M. Freycinet gave his arm to Oura Oura; the old man was my mate. Our way lay through briars and undergrowth, and our poor savage friends, being wholly naked, suffered greatly. Oura Oura, in particular, was sadly scratched. But heedless of this, she boldly made her way through the thickets, chattering with Freycinet and vexed at her inability to make herself understood; at the same time, accompanying her discourse with sportive wiles and smiles, so gracious and expressive, that the most finished coquetry could not have rendered them more so, offering him flowers from the wayside as they went."

How affectionate must have been that parting! We know that the Frenchmen entered their boats with profound despondency and the feeling was reciprocated: "The aboriginals manifested their sorrow in the most affecting manner."

The naturalist adds:

"Our good friends did not leave us for an instant; and when we pushed off from the shore, their grief showed itself in a most touching manner. They made signs for us to return to see them."

They lit a large fire upon a neighbouring hill, and even when the winds had driven the vessel miles away, the column of smoke could still be seen, a memorial to peace and friendship. (The people of the highlands of New Guinea today are also singularly expressive in regard to demonstrations of emotion: they sob grievously when a visitor leaves them.) No wonder that poor Péron, thoroughly smitten, closes that day's journal with the words: "The whole of what I have related is minutely exact; and assuredly it were difficult to resist the soft emotion which similar incidents inspire."

The following passage shows what a master of detail he was:

"On a wide swarth of verdure [at Maria Island], beneath some antique caruarinae, rose a cone, formed coarsely of the bark of trees, inserted at the bottom in the ground, and terminated at the top in a large band of similar materials. Four long poles stuck in the earth, sustained and served for all the pieces of bark to lean against; these four poles seemed also calculated to ornament the building; for instead of uniting all their upper extremity like the bark, and forming a simple cone, they crossed each other about the middle, and then extended without the roof of the ornament. From this disposition resulted a sort of inverted tetracdic pyramid in the upper part opposed to the cone below. This contrast of form in the two parts of the building had a somewhat graceful effect, which was increased by the following additions: With each of the four sides of the pyramid corresponded a wide strip of bark, the two bent extremities of which were at the bottom bound together by a large band, which united all the pieces of bark at the top of the cone; it follows that each of these four strips formed a sort of oval, least rounded at its inferior extremity, and widest and most rounded above; and as each of these ovals corresponded with one of the sides of the inverted pyramid, it is not difficult to conceive the elegance and picturesque effect of the plan." [When Péron first saw it, he felt that he had made an important discovery, and wanted to know the reason for the structure and set to work to find out. He raised some upper layers of turf, he saw below some white ashes. He thrust his hand into these, and felt something hard and withdrew it, and he found it to be the jawbone of a man with threads of flesh still adhering to it.]

But, sadly, not all the contacts in the early days were of this nature, visits of peace and friendship were the exception, not the rule.

Another French crew landed on Bruni Island. On this occasion they encountered no Oura Oura. A fine athletic aboriginal had been showing off his wrestling powers when a French midshipman engaged him in a wrestling match and, with superior knowledge of the science, threw him. The sulky brave got up, and threw a spear at the victor. At another time, three young men by the name of Petit, Leschenault and Hamelin went ashore at Bruni. Petit, an artist, began to draw what he saw of the aborigines around him. This liberty was resented by one man, who rushed forward and seized the portraits, which were only saved with difficulty. Blows fell thick and fast on both sides, and a shower of stones closed the *entente cordiale*. The practical Leschenault wrote of the incident: "I am surprised to hear persons of sense still affirm that man in a natural state is not of a bad disposition, but worthy of confidence." Had Péron received a stone to his head instead of a basket from the pretty Oura Oura, his views, too, might have been similar.

This is another extract from Péron's journal. While wandering among the bush flowers of Tasmania, and admiring the sylvan charms of the "Isle of Beauty", he encountered a company of Diana's forest maidens, to whom in the distance, the French officers waved their handkerchiefs.

"At these demonstrations of friendship the troop hesitated an instant, then stopped, and resolved to wait for us. It was then that we recognised that we had a company of women; there was not a male individual among them. They were a bit apprehensive about us coming too close to them and it seemed to be the arms that we carried that caused the concern. For one of the oldest among them disengaged herself from her companions, and made signs for us to stop and to sit down, crying at the same time 'Medi, Medi' (sit down, sit down). She also indicated that we should lay down our arms, the view of which alarmed her. These preliminary conditions having been complied with, the women squatted on their heels, and from that moment abandoned themselves, without reserve, to the vivacity of their character, speaking all together, questioning us all at once, making a thousand gestures and a thousand contortions, as singular as varied. M. Bellefin, who was a doctor, began to sing, at the same time accompanying himself with very lively and animated gestures. The women kept silent, observing with much attention his actions, as if by these alone to interpret his singing. Hardly had one couplet been finished, than some of them applauded with loud cries, others laughed to the echo, while the young girls, more timid without a doubt, kept silent, showing, however, by their quick little movements and by the expression on their faces, their surprise and satisfaction at the songs.

"All the women were naked with the exception of kangaroo skins that only a few of them wore upon their shoulders but, without appearing to think anything of their nudity, they so varied their attitudes and their postures, that it would be difficult to describe the bizarre and the picturesque effects presented to us by that meeting. Their skins so black and made disgusting by the rancid fat of seals, their hair, short, crisp, black and dirty, reddened in some with the dust of ochre; the forms, all bedaubed with charcoal that had merged with the fat, their whole physique, generally thin and faded; their breasts, long and pendulous. In fact, all the details of their physical constitution were repulsive. We must always exempt from this general tableau two or three young girls of from fifteen or sixteen, in whom we distinguished forms agreeable enough, contours sufficiently graceful, and of whom the breast was really firm and well placed, although in our opinion the nipple was a little too large and too long, when comparing with the European girl. These few young girls had something also in the expression of their features, the most ingenuous, the most affectionate, and the most gentle, as if the better qualities of the soul could exist, even in the midst of the most primitive of the human species, the more particular the gift of youth, of grace, and of beauty.

"Among the more aged females, some had a gross and ignoble figure; others, much fewer in number, had a fierce and sombre look; but in general, one remarked in all of them inquietude and depression, which misfortune and slavery imprint on the features of all beings who bear the yoke. Almost all were covered with scars, sad fruits of the ill-treatment doled out to them by ferocious husbands. One only in the midst of all her companions had preserved a dignified aspect, with much enjoyment and joviality, and it was she who had imposed the conditions of which I have spoken before. After M. Bellefin had ended his song, she began to mimic with her gestures and her tone of voice in a very original and pleasant manner, which much diverted the Frenchmen and her companions. Then she began to sing herself, in so rapid a way, that it would be difficult to apply such music to the ordinary principles of our own types of song. Their song, nevertheless, is here in accordance with their language, for such is the volubility of speech of these people, that it is impossible to distinguish any precise sound in their pronunciation: it is a sort of trilling sentiment, for which we cannot find any terms of comparison or analogy in our European languages."

It is most interesting that the observations of the naturalist, Péron, touch on two points that have been found to be common to those primitive peoples in the world today, though with the possible exception of the "People of the Yellow Leaves", it might be difficult to find a race or a tribe as primitive as the extinct Tasmanians. One is that the more primitive a people the more complex their language. The Australian aborigines and the New Guinea highlanders, the Aleuts and the Eskimaux, all have complicated languages. It is as if with so little to do, they fill their time making their language as difficult as possible as they squat round the camp fire. The other point is that most of the extremely primitive people have little of our regard for love. Instead there is usually some form of bride price in operation, which values the female, not on her love-making, or personal qualities, but on her ability as a worker. After many generations of this emphasis, when good looks are unneccessary to attract the male, there is a marked lack of feminine beauty. Indeed, the females are ugly. A few throwbacks to happier times do, occasionally, appear, the rest suffer by comparison. But even in the most primitive of tribes there are a few months in the lives of the young girls when they have a definite bloom about them. This is especially so among the Eskimo and the Samoyed girls, at the age of about fourteen.

But, to continue with M. Péron's accounts of the primitive Tasmanians:

"This woman, excited, so to speak, by her own singing, which we had not failed to applaud with warmth, and wishing, without a doubt, to deserve our sufferages on other accounts, our jovial companion commenced to execute various dance movements, many

of which would have been regarded as excessively indecent, if that
state of human society were not foreign to all that delicacy of sentiment and action which is for us but a fortunate product of the
perfection of social order.

"While all this passed, I employed myself accurately to collect and
note the details that were presented, and which I now describe. It
was remarked, doubtless by the same woman who was dancing; for,
hardly had she finished her sensuous dance, than she approached
me with an obliging air, took from a reed bag some charcoal which
she found there, crushed it in her hand and began to lay on me a
plaster of the rouge of those regions. I willingly lent myself to this
obliging caprice. M. Hierisson, who was also with me, had the same
complacency, and received a similar mask. We appeared then a great
object of admiration to these women; they seemed to regard us with
even more sweet satisfaction, and to felicitate us upon the new
adornments which we had just acquired."

It appears that they now felt more "at home" with the Frenchmen of
the party whom they liked. But in their timidity or coldness they were
the true nymphs of the chaste Diana, and were frightened at any
approach made to them by the Frenchmen. If any advances were to
be made then the aboriginal women had to make them!

"The deference which we paid to these women, and perhaps also
the new charms which we owed to their attentions (the charcoal,
etc.), seemed to add to their kindness, to their confidence in us, but
nothing could induce them, however, to allow themselves to be
approached nearer, let alone be touched. The least movement
which we made, or appeared to make, to pass the prescribed line,
caused them to spring up from their heels and seek safety in flight.
Any longer to enjoy their presence, we were constrained to conform
ourselves entirely to their wishes. After having lavished presents on
them, and the caresses from their direction, we considered it proper
to retake our route towards the anchorage, and our companions also
appeared to have the intention of walking the same way as ourselves."

The companions left.

"But we were again obliged to come to terms with these inexorable
women, who condemned us to follow the shore, while they walked
along the sand-dunes parallel to it."

The French gentlemen were doubtless not used to such prudery in the salons of Paris. But the next extract exhibits a more prosaic sequel to this romantic adventure:

"They were returning from fishing when we had perceived them, being laden with large crabs, lobsters, and different shell fish, all which looked as if they had been half-grilled upon ashes, and which they carried in baskets of reed (the aborigines of the island would not touch scaled fish—they were tabu). These baskets were tied round the front of their persons by a circle of cord, and hung behind the back; some of these were very heavy, and we very sincerely pitied these poor women, in their carrying of such burdens.

"Our journey all the while was nonetheless gayer than our interview, and from the top of the sand-dunes they gave us many pleasantries, and many playful compliments, to which we endeavoured to reply as expressively as it was possible.

"Without a doubt we should have continued for a much longer time these innocent amusements, when all at once one of the women uttered a great cry, and all the others repeated it with fright. They had discovered our landing place and our comrades. We sought to calm their fears and excitement, assuring them that so far from experiencing any injury from our friends, they were going to receive new gifts. But all was in vain, and already the troop were hiding themselves in the woods, when the same woman who, almost alone, had made our interview so agreeable, seemed to change her mind. At her call there was a moment of hesitation; but not being able, as it appeared to us, to induce them to follow her, she leapt down alone from the top of a sand-dune, and walked along the shore at no great distance before us with much confidence and, even with a sort of pride, she derided the timidity of her companions. The others then appearing ashamed of their weakness; little by little increased their courage, until they decided at length to return to the beach. Accompanied by this numerous and singular escort, we arrived at the place of embarkation, near which, by an accident that no one could have foreseen due to the lie of the land, all the husbands of these poor women, had been gathered together for some time.

"In spite of the least equivocal evidence of the benevolence and the generosity of our countrymen, they [the husbands] exhibited a restless and dour front to their womenfolk, and their looks were also ferocious and threatening towards them, and in their attitude we distinguished a constraint, malevolence and perfidy which they

sought to dissemble in vain. At this inauspicious meeting, all the
women that had followed us appeared much concerned. Their
furious husbands cast upon them glances of anger and rage, which
were not likely to comfort them. After having laid the products of
their fishing at the feet of these men, they seated themselves on the
other side of a large sand-dune, a little distance off. The men
immediately set to on the food, without offering any to the women,
and there during the meal these unfortunate creatures dared neither
to raise their eyes, nor to speak, or to smile."

After this unfortunate termination of a happy meeting, the Frenchmen
took their departure. But the effect of this visit upon the sensitive
nature of the naturalist is very clear in the closing words of his journal:

"Thus ended our interview with the inhabitants of Van Diemen's
Land. All the descriptions that I have given, are of the most rigorous
exactitude, and without a doubt it would have been difficult to deny
oneself the sweet emotions which similar circumstances ought to
inspire. This gentle confidence of the people in us, these affectionate
evidences of benevolence which they never ceased to manifest
towards us, the sincerity of their demonstrations, the frankness of
their manners, the touching ingenuousness of their caresses, all
concurred to excite within us sentiments of the tenderest interest.

"The intimate union of the different individuals of a family, the
sort of patriarchal life of which we had been spectators, had strongly
moved us. I saw with inexpressible pleasure the realization of those
brilliant descriptions of the happiness and simplicity of the state of
nature of which I had so many times in reading felt the seductive
charm."

Such were the sentiments entertained of a people almost universally
regarded by the English colonists, only a few years later, as tigers and
demons, whose destruction was an act of merit, as well as an act of
necessity. Smile as we may at the simplicity of Péron, had our faith in
the poor creatures been more like that of the Frenchman we would
have been spared that further blot upon our nation—the loss of the
Tasmanian race.

It was unfortunate that the island was colonized when slavery and
blackbirding were still current, and certain men, because of the colour
of their skin, were considered at best as chattels. By the time a more
kindly feeling was developing towards the coloured people the Tasma-

nians were already on their way out. Also at the time of the contact, the English race was at its most smug. In particular the Tasmanians were ridiculed for their ineptitude with figures. It would have been salutary for the complacent colonizers and exploiters to have remembered the words of advice given to Atticeis by Cicero: "Do not obtain your slaves from Britain," wrote he, "because they are so stupid, and utterly incapable of being taught, that they are not fit to form a part of the household of Athens."

chapter 2

The Tasmanians under British Rule

Whatever sorrows arose from mixing Europeans and aboriginals in Tasmania, it cannot be affirmed that the government of the day was ignorant of the usual effects of such contacts, nor was it careless of its duty to protect the aboriginal inhabitants. Warned by the consequences of such neglect on the mainland of New Holland (Australia) and shocked at the cries reaching England from the newly formed province of New South Wales, Lord Hobart, the then Secretary for the Colonies, sent a despatch to Captain Collins in Tasmania at the close of 1803. Collins was to make some form of a settlement with the aborigines to be found in Tasmania. The meeting was to be held on the banks of the Derwent, not far from Hobart Town.

"You are to try," wrote Lord Hobart, "by every means in your power, to gain contact with the aborigines, and to conciliate their good-will, asking all parties under your government to live in friendship and show kindness towards them; and if any person does any act of violence against them, or shall wantonly give them any interruption in the exercise of their several occupations, you are to cause such an offender to be brought to punishment, and according to the degree of the offence you are to deal with him."

However, before Captain Collins, the first Governor of Van Diemen's Land, established his office in Hobart Town, the unhappy collision between the Whites and the "Blacks" had taken place on the banks of the River Derwent. Just before the arrival of Collins, a party had been sent down from Sydney after the abortive attempt to settle Port

Phillip, and camped at Restdown (later to be called Risdon), five miles from Hobart. It was there, really, in 1804, that the sad story of the "Black War" begins.

The story of this first conflict between the races is rather obscure and, as we shall see, the accounts, even of "eye-witnesses", differ. The first colonial Chaplain, the Reverend Robert Knopwood, was only a few miles from the scene of the incident. He inquired into it of the parties concerned, but all he could get to put in his journal was the following:

> "Had heard different opinions, that they wanted to camp on the site of Burke's hut, half a mile from where the soldiers were camping, and ill-used his wife, that the hut was not burnt or plundered, that the Tasmanian natives did not attack the camp, that our people went from the camp to attack these natives, who remained in the vicinity of Burke's House."

At Risdon in 1804 Burke had set up a hut in the middle of an aboriginal sacred ground, where the people who were going to take part in a kangaroo drive (for this was the method of their hunting) would congregate. It showed total lack of understanding of the aborigines, as one would expect from an ignorant ex-convict. This is the reason why they menaced him, and was the cause of him running to the soldiers to ask for protection.

It appears from this, that the stage was all set for a fateful clash between these soldiers who were spoiling for a fight and the poor blundering aborigines, and the excuse for the confrontation was Burke's exaggeration of what the aborigines were doing on what, after all, was their own ground, and a place moreover where it was convenient to corral and trap kangaroos when they were hunting. (Such places exist in Lapland today, for the collecting or the corralling of the reindeer. Often established for many generations.)

All that is positively known about the first encounter of large groups of Europeans and the aborigines in 1804 is that one day there appeared on the heights a large body of the aborigines, not very far from the spot where Bass and Flinders had held a friendly parley with one of the tribe. Nor was there any reason to suspect hostile intentions, as the women and children were present. The officer in command ordered his men to fire upon the advancing hunters, and many were slain. One person states that the event took place while Lieutenant-Governor Bowen was on a tour, and that the aborigines came down from a hill

shouting and singing happily in full pursuit of some kangaroos. Another
eye-witness mentions the fact that Burke, living just outside the camp-
site chosen by the soldiers, ran with great alarm to the soldiers at the
sight of the five hundred or so aborigines, plus their women and
children. The same source of evidence records the death of at least
fifty men, women and children of various ages. It is also mentioned that
these aborigines came almost in a semicircle down the hill, making
loud cries as they came, and driving a herd of kangaroos before them
into the valley bottom, evidently the better to despatch them in the
enclosed area in which was also the camp. It would have been far
better had the soldiers destroyed the kangaroos rather than the poor
aborigines, for the area was apparently regularly used for trapping
kangaroos. Similar methods of hunting were used for other game,
including young swans, all at certain times in their hunting year.

A body of gentlemen, the Aborigines' Committee, was appointed by
the benevolent Governor Arthur to watch over the interests of these
unhappy people. The Committee, engaged in investigating the causes
producing the hostility of the dark race, took certain evidence that
bore upon this question. One witness, Edward White, who had been a
servant to W. Clark and had erected a crude hut that was inhabited
by the commanding officer, Lieutenant Bowen, stated before the
Committee, that, on May 3rd, 1804, he was engaged in hoeing turnips
on some ground near the creek at Risdon. Hearing some shouting, he
looked up and saw what he estimated as about three hundred aborigines, men, women and children, coming down the hillside in a circle,
with a herd of kangaroos enclosed in the circle. White then continues:

"They looked at me with their eyes. I went down to the creek, and
reported them to some soldiers, and then went back to my work.
The Natives did not threaten me in any way, and I was not afraid
of them. Clark's house was near where I was at work, and Burke's
house near Clark's house. The Natives did not attack the soldiers.
They could not have molested them. The firing commenced about
eleven o'clock. There were many Natives slaughtered and wounded.
I don't know how many. But some of their bones were sent in two
casks to Port Jackson (New South Wales) by Dr Mountgarrett, to
be studied. They went in a ship called the *Ocean*. A boy was taken
from them. This was three or four months after we had landed. They
never came so close again after that. They had no spears with them,
only the waddies [clubs for killing kangaroos]. They were hunting
and came down into the bottom where the soldiers were."

This is the first mention of a child being taken from the aborigines, but it is mentioned frequently later on. No reason for the removal was ever given, but it appears that it was for no good purpose, as we never read of any being brought up by the settlers or receiving any education.

Another witness, Robert Evans, belonging to the Risdon hamlet, was examined by the Committee. He had not been present at the massacre, but had learned the news soon afterwards. He was told that when the aborigines came on in a large body, they did not make any attack on the soldiers, but they brought a large number of kangaroos with them for the corroboree. He never heard that they disturbed any-one, but were nevertheless fired upon. He did not know who had given the order to fire, or how many were killed, though he had heard that there were men, women and children, that some of these were killed by the firing and that some of the children were taken away by the soldiers. It appears, therefore, that the tribe was going to have a corroboree, followed by a feast, in the same hollow as the soldiers were camped, and the kangaroos were going to provide food for the feast.

One of the settlers present said that the officer in charge of the soldiers, a Lieutenant Moore, saw double that morning due to an overdose of rum. Several said that before the event, which became known as the Black War, there was good feeling between the Europeans and the aborigines. However, the soldiers of the New South Wales Corps (later the 102nd regiment), were well known for their drinking, and their officers for spirit dealing. This led many to think that the whole incident was a half-drunken spree, and that the firing arose from a brutal desire to see the "niggers" run.

A Captain Holman heard the following story when he went through the area in 1831, twenty-five years after the affair:

> "It is said to have originated in the following manner. A small stone house had been erected for a gardener, and he had just started the cultivation of the ground that was immediately round it. While in the middle of his work one morning, he was surprised at the appear-ance of some aborigines advancing towards him, and ran off in a very much frightened frame of mind, to the camp to 'give the alarm'. Lieutenant Moore, who commanded a party of the 102nd, drew up his men to resist the expected attack, and upon the approach of the aborigines, the soldiers were ordered to fire upon them. The result of this volley terrified them to such a degree, that those that could run, fled, without attempting the slightest resistance. From this moment on, a deep rooted hatred sprang up among the aborigines

for any strangers, and since that time in 1804 all endeavours at
friendship had hitherto proved ineffective."

From an Australian newspaper, *The Sydney Gazette* (founded in 1803)'
we can gain some further information. On March 18th, 1804 (before
the terrible slaughter on the banks of the Derwent), it carried the following report brought back by the boat that conveyed Lieutenant
Bowen, the Government representative in Tasmania.

> "The Natives are very numerous, and undaunted even by the
> explosion of our muskets; but were very friendly to small parties
> that they met accidentally, though they cannot be prevailed upon to
> visit the encampment. During the stay of the Lady Nelson, a large
> kangaroo was taken in the woods by Henry Hacking, who also had
> a Sydney aborigine with him; but being waylaid by a tribe of the
> sooty inhabitants of this neighbourhood, the kangaroo, being fifty
> or sixty pounds weight, was for a moment, considered as lost. The
> aborigines made use of every policy to wheedle Hacking out of his
> booty; but, as they did not offer or threaten violence, he, with
> counteracting policy, preserved it. Although they treated him with
> much affability and politeness, they regarded his companion as an
> object of jealousy and indignation; and the poor fellow, sensitive to
> his critical and precarious position, appeared very thankful when
> safely delivered from their unwelcome presence."

Such a story surely leaves the military without excuse for their barbarous onslaught upon the aborigines at Risdon. They must have
known, by experience of the aborigines, that though too shy to approach
the camp, or rather, too fearful to place themselves, their wives and
children within reach of the armed soldiery, they were gentle in their
manners, and, in circumstances where numbers and forest freedom
could have made them audacious, they merely became more confident.

The Sydney printer put "politeness" in small capitals. No wonder
the Tasmanians were jealous of the stranger from New Holland who
looked so much like them yet was "not of them". They must have been
indignant that a Black should appear in their presence with two front
teeth knocked out, with an improper collection of cicatrices and with
flowing hair, instead of the approved crisp and corkscrew ringlets, and,
nonetheless, having the confidence of a "White"—savages can make the
best conservatives.

A letter from Port Dalrymple (afterwards Launceston) appeared in

The Sydney Gazette on December 23rd, 1804, showing how tragically unnecessary the "Black War" really was.

"On the 14th of November, one of our small parties in the bush was surprised at the appearance of the first body of the Natives to be seen; and they, with a hideous shout, expressed an astonishment scarcely to be conceived at the sight of the visitants so opposite to themselves in habit and complexion. About two hundred approached our small party with impetuous fury, they prudently retired, and were pursued into camp, near which the Natives were prevailed upon to enter into parley. Signs were then made of a more friendly disposition towards them, and, appearing to gather confidence, they accepted trifling presents, expressing extreme surprise at every object that occasionally attracted their attention; but their apparent reciprocal inclination towards a more friendly understanding was now and then interrupted by an indignant clamour, which, beginning with some individual, ran rapidly through the throng, accompanied with gesticulations menacing and ferocious and at the same time biting at their arms either as a token of vengeance or defiance. They afterwards peacefully withdrew, having from us experienced no other than a courteous and conciliatory treatment; but were positive in forbidding us to follow them."

How different was the treatment of the aborigines by these settlers to that by the soldiers at Risdon. Although only a small party in the bush, they were not unduly alarmed by the sudden presence of two hundred really wild men of the woods. Though the settlers retired, they managed to go into conference with the aborigines, and there was no trembling at the war-shouts and the spear rasping that they carried out when agitated, thus throwing an even worse light on the confrontation at Risdon between the unarmed aborigines and armed soldiers. By giving presents and kindly words (the tones, if not the actual words, could well have been understood) instead of oaths and bullets, these settlers achieved a real victory. The little northern settlement had peace when other districts experienced fire and bloodshed. Twenty years after this meeting, the women of Launceston were able peacefully to do their laundry at the Basin on the river bank above the Falls, while the aborigines of the forest looked down curiously from the heights above.

An old lady, in 1870, told of her experiences when she and her parents arrived at Hobart Town with the first batch of the free settlers 1804. She had heard people express fear of the wild blacks and her mother frequently cautioned her against venturing far into the bush because she "might be killed and eaten by cannibals". At that time her family lived on their farm about three miles from Hobart. She was a bold and enterprising child and she had long wished to get a closer view of the magnificent Mount Wellington, whose snowy cap had caught her imagination. Accompanied by her younger brother, she set off one day while her parents were absent, and they hiked through the bush until they were lost amidst the dense foliage of the mountain gullies. There she had her wish and fell in with some aborigines. The spirited girl showed no alarm, and the children were kindly treated by the wild-looking bunch. She does not say how she returned home, or whether she ever reached the mountain. But she does say that she often met groups of aborigines at "The Camp", as the district where the aborigines were to be found in Hobart was called, and there they always seemed quiet and well behaved.

There seemed to be no government or official record for the first six years after the settlement at Hobart. The explanation of this seems to lie in the story that, upon the sudden death of the first Governor, Captain Collins, who was found dead in his chair, two of the leading officers of the government placed a marine outside the door so that they would not be disturbed, and proceeded to burn every document in the office.

James Bonwick, who wrote at the time when the aborigines had just disappeared, states:

"I must acknowledge my gratitude to Mr. Hull, Clerk of the Tasmanian Council, and son of my old and esteemed neighbour, Mr. Commissary Hull, through whose kindness I obtained access to the last remaining document, and for its preservation he is to be credited. This is the Muster Book of 1810, that was kept at the barracks, in which the commanding officer entered the countersign of the day, and in which, also, occasional notices of the day's happenings were written. The previous Muster Books, which for safety had been conveyed to the Governor's Office, all disappeared in the fire as mentioned above on that one dark night of destruction. In this interesting note book is an entry for January 29th, 1810, dealing with a Government Order about the 'Black War'. It declares the sentiments of the authorities as to its origin, and their resolution to protect the 'poor creatures who were the objects of civilized cruelty".

This is the entry:

"There being great reason to fear that William Russell and George Gelley will be added to the number of unfortunate men who have been put to death by the Natives, in revenge for the murders and the abominable cruelties which have been practiced upon them by the white people, the Lieutenant-Governor, aware of the evil consequences that must result to the settlement if such cruelties are continued, and abhorring the conduct of those evil people who perpetrate them, hereby declares that any person whomsoever who does violence to a native, or who shall in cold blood murder, or cause any of them to be murdered, shall on proof being made of the same, be dealt with and proceeded against as if such violence had been offered, or murder committed on a civilized person."

This was studiously carrying out the instructions of the minister, Lord Hobart, at least so far as declarations went; but history gives no instances of the issuing of the decree or of anyone being brought to anything like a trial. The man who wrote the order died shortly afterwards and a disorderly time followed. So, when the new Lieutenant-Governor arrived from England, the island was in such a chaotic state that there was even some excuse for further neglecting to protect the aborigines. The aborigines were in fact fair game and more interesting than kangaroos to chase. When the Governor of a British Colony sank so low as to hold correspondence with an outlaw, as Governor Sorrell did, noted for his ferocity and refined tortures of the aborigines, and permit his use of the euphemistic term "Bushranger", and allow him to visit the capital, Hobart, unmolested, it cannot be expected that the order of January 29th, 1810, would carry much weight. *The Sydney Gazette* of April 10th, 1813, in an article describing the life of Tasmanian society of the time, also describes the progress of the "Black War" and, seemingly, gives a true picture.

"The Natives of Van Diemen's Land," reads the *Gazette*, "continue to be very hostile. This is mostly attributed to the constant ill-treatment that they get at the hands of the Bushrangers, who have taken themselves to the woods in order to avoid punishment for the numerous crimes that they have committed. Escaped convicts are there also. They exist miserably there on what the woods can offer them. Acts of cruelty are constantly reported committed by these desperadoes upon the Native population; and the latter seldom let an opportunity slip by for wreaking their vengeance upon all persons of the same colour as that of the lawless wanderers of the woods."

It was to control these same Bushrangers that, on June 26th, 1813, the Government from Hobart issued a proclamation against them, after the aborigines had attacked a herd of cattle at the Coal River. The Governor pointed out the real cause of the attack:

"The resentment of these poor uncultivated beings has been justly provoked by a most cruel and inhuman mode of proceeding acted toward them, viz., the robbing of their children."

The Governor then expressed his horror at such shameful behaviour, and exclaims in most unofficial language:

"Let any man put his hand to his heart and ask the question, which is the savage—the white man who robs the parent of his children, or the black man who boldly steps forward to resent injury, in order to recover his stolen offspring; the conclusion, alas! is too obvious."

The end of the proclamation pledges the Government to punish all offenders with the utmost rigour of the law.

Before the confrontation at Risdon many of the explorers could go about without fear only accompanied by their dogs, but afterwards few of the colonists were safe from attack. In a people so gentle and affable as confronted the first explorers, it is difficult to recognize the race afterwards covered with sores, wasted by want and vice, or animated with revenge, who filled the colonists with disgust and terror.

Sometimes the Whites were punished for the wanton cruelty towards the Blacks—a man was severely flogged for exhibiting the ears and other parts of a boy he had mutilated alive and another for cutting off the little finger of a native and using it as a tobacco stopper.

Mr. Knopwood remembered that in 1813 and 1814 the natives fed at his door, but a number of children were taken for prostitution among the sex-starved convicts and they did not return for food again. Often if they saw a mother they would run after her until she dropped her children and these would also be used eventually for slavery.

An interesting account is given in the Hobart Town *Gazette* of August 20th, 1814, about a visit of some of the aborigines to Hobart and the valuable service of a courageous and benevolent ex-convict.

The account shows that the Tasmanian aborigines differed from the Australian aborigines in their disinclination to approach the Whites, for it records an important tribe living on the South Arm of the Derwent, a peninsula at the junction of the Derwent and Storm Bay, and only really a few miles from the Hobart, that had had no acquaintance with the white people even after they had been on the island for at least ten years.

As these people were either the same as, or neighbours of, those kangaroo hunters who were so wantonly attacked by the soldiers under Lieutenant Moore in 1804, there could be some reason for their apparently retiring nature, as well as some apology for attempts at outrage. The passage appearing in the Hobart Town *Gazette* runs:

"We mentioned some time ago of several Natives being brought to town from the woods at the South Arm of the Derwent. After receiving certain articles of clothing from His Honour the Lieutenant-Governor and other humane gentlemen of this settlement, they were conducted through the streets by A. Campbell (a prisoner). Their curiosity, which had never been gratified before with such a sight, prompted them to examine everything with wonder and amazement, without bestowing their attention longer than a moment on any single object.

"The Lieutenant-Governor having expressed a desire to see the remainder of the Natives left at the South Arm, Campbell accompanied with 2 other persons again returned to that place. The party spent 3 days in fruitless search after them, when they discovered 2 Natives who informed them that the rest were on Betsy's Island.

"Next morning, Campbell and party went in a boat to that island, accompanied by a native woman of one of the neighbouring islands, and who has lived with Campbell for some years; this woman has been of considerable service to the party, by representing the humane treatment she herself had received from the white people. On landing on the island they saw a number of Natives sitting round the fire, and on their perceiving the children clothed they were greatly astonished, and felt their dresses. When the Natives informed them of their reception in town, they all expressed a wish by Campbell's woman to see Hobart, and it was with difficulty the party prevented the boat from sinking, so eager were they to get in."

Campbell brought thirteen to town, who received every kindness and humanity from the Lieutenant-Governor, who clothed them likewise. They were afterwards landed on the Island of Le Bruni, at their own request.

"We trust that the exertions of Campbell and his party will be a prelude to more friendly intercourse with the Native tribes, and by the means of such humane treatment endeavour to reclaim them from a savage life."

The kindness of the Hobart townspeople to a few visitors from the wilds told favourably afterwards; for from another account from the same newspaper, we learn that Campbell was indirectly the means of saving the life of one of his own countrymen.

"A few days ago," reports the Hobart Town *Gazette*, "upwards of a 100 natives surrounded a house at South Arm, and knocked at the door; on the person within opening it, and perceiving the Natives, he was in great terror, and after shutting the door tried to escape by a back window, but seeing it in vain, he again opened the front door, when several Natives came in, to whom he offered food, but they refused to eat. After they had surveyed the premises, an elderly man led the person by the arm, who lived in the house, nearly half a mile into the woods, and there placed him in the middle of them, and at the moment when the natives were about to throw their spears at the unfortunate victim a native man, whom A. Campbell had brought to Hobart Town some time ago, addressed them. Then they all walked away, leaving the person to return to his own residence once more.

"Thus by humanity already shown to these natives the life of a fellow creature has been preserved."

The actions of the aborigines described in this passage are remarkably similar to those often shown among the highland tribes of New Guinea, with whom the extinct Tasmanians had much in common. The elderly men often take into their own hands some form of action or directive and the tribe follows their lead. These elderly men, or Laopoons as they are called, are frequently the tribe's executioners, and often, before an execution, there is much vigorous discussion about the pros and cons of the punishment, as a result of which the intended victim may be abandoned, as was the Tasmanians'.*

James Bonwick, who lived contemporaneously with the last of the Tasmanians, writes:

"A gentleman whose station was in the centre of the island, spoke to me of the Natives occasionally coming down to his hut, and there bartering a kangaroo's tail for a bit of mutton. Others have told me that they were able to travel about the Bush in perfect security between 1814 and 1822.

"Several elderly ladies (who were young during the above period) have narrated to me circumstances showing that much banter and friendly intercourse was carried on between the white people of those times and, for instance, their children played with those of the aborigines, their boys going to hunt with the dark skins. These ladies had the conviction that such a happy state of things would have continued but for the conduct of the Bush prisoner servants [who were employed as stockmen by the early settlers], towards the native females.

"An old man, who had been assigned as servant to a Mr. Wedge, gave me the story of falling in with a company of 200 aborigines, in 1819. They were quietly camping on Mr. Archer's Run [ranch], and after seeing that same year a score of 'Blacks' assisting at Mr. Bonner's

* There are so many similarities between these peoples that it would be impossible to enumerate all of them. Some of the most apparent are as follows:

In both New Guinea and Tasmania the women's hair is taken from them, giving them a shared bald appearance. Both peoples are afraid of the dark, and both suspend bones from their ears. Constant conflicts with other tribes are common to both races. The Tasmanians would break twigs when passing through forest in order to mark their way, in the same fashion as the New Guinea people today.

The dances are very similar. The thunder and lightning dance, which consists merely of stamping on the ground, was identical with that of the modern New Guineans, except for the fact that with the latter it is accompanied by shouting.

The Tasmanians had a dog complex, developed after the arrival of the Europeans, similar to the pig complex of the New Guineans. Women suckled puppies, often at the expense of their own infants. In fact, children were often abandoned, since it was thought that the puppy would bring a quicker return: in but a short time it would be able to assist in the hunting of game, whereas a child would take several years to mature.

The explorer Labillardiere (French) said that they welcomed visitors by raising hands over their heads, shouting and stamping on the ground. I have seen a very similar practice in the highlands of New Guinea.

farm, in harvest-time, they receiving in return potatoes and damper for payment."

The Hobart Town *Gazette*, even as late as 1824, contemplated the quiet times:

"Perhaps taken collectively, the sable natives of this colony are the most peaceful creatures in the world."

They had a great deal of native intelligence, and tried to pass this on to the New Tasmanians as the following story shows—but for what reward?

The English were seen by some friendly natives to catch a toad fish, which is poisonous, and by which several people had perished: the natives, perceiving its preparation for food, endeavoured to show, by gestures, that it was not to be eaten, and exhibited its effects by the semblance of death. Not very long after, a native was shown a pistol, which the white man snapped at his own ear; and who, after it had been loaded with one shot, encouraged him to perform the same manœuvre. He was then murdered by his own hand. Similarly a miner in New Guinea, having a surfeit of dynamite, would light the fuse to a stick and give it to a native. He thought it huge fun when the New Guinean blew himself up, and disposed of 27 in this fashion before being apprehended.

But even from early days there took place occasional outbreaks of retaliation against the ill-treatment meted out. The difference, however, between these and the outrages the aborigines carried out at later times lay in the fact that, while most of the former were confined to petty thieving, the latter were more frequently from motives of hatred and revenge, and part of a combined movement of real aggression due to their many grievances, a last kick before death.

The ceasing of friendly relationships was due, as already mentioned, to interference with the gins [wives] and the stealing of children; usually, it seems, for the sexual pleasure of the frustrated and isolated white ex-convict stockmen, or, at best, for slavery in the house and fields. They never seemed to live very long, but whether that was due to their captivity or a naturally short lifespan, we cannot be sure.

Too often we prefer to associate kidnapping with the rogues and vagabonds of this world, rather than with people of our own land and language. Yet the very proclamations of the government of this time attest to the truth of the indictment that the kidnapping of female children was constant. The first chaplain took some interest in the aboriginal people; he often had a festive and happy gathering at his house, and described them as being always well behaved. They did not come in twos and threes to his cottage but up to twenty at a time. But, after 1814, the numbers gradually dropped off, until his visitors came no more. On seeking the cause of the change, he was told by the aboriginals themselves that they would not go to the town again because there were so many bad men about who stole their female children.

When Governor Macquarie returned to Sydney, the seat of Government for the whole region of Australia, after his memorable tour through the islands of his dependency he issued a public notice, on June 18th, 1814, thanking all the settlers of Van Diemen's Land for their loyal attention, and praising them for their enterprise and progress; but the conditions of the aborigines of the little colony filled his heart with much consternation and despair, and stirred him to action. It was the constant brutality towards them that aroused his anger, and called forth a strongly worded proclamation:

"Although it was not sufficiently clear and satisfactory to warrant the institution of criminal prosecution, it was enough so to convince any unprejudiced man that the first personal attacks were made on the part of the settlers and their stockmen. Several years have elapsed since anything like a principle of hostility has been acted upon, or even in the slightest degree exhibited in the conduct of the Natives. It must be evident that no deep rooted prejudice exists in their minds against the British subjects or white men."

An amusing, though tragic, story is told of an affront once given by the tribes when Governor Sorrell had invited a number of them to Hobart Town. They were gathered in the Government paddock, a large reserve outside the town, equivalent to the racecourse of these days, and the aborigines were exercising themselves before the Whites. One young and very beautiful girl aborigine snatched one of the braves' spears, and threw it at Captain Hamilton, the most dashingly handsome of the young officers, no doubt as some form of rapport. Although the weapon never struck him, nor had it ever been intended to strike him, the son of Mars, being indignant, and with no sense of humour to match his beauty, and unable to laugh at the liberty taken by a young girl, complained to the Governor and insisted that the natives be cleared from the precious Government paddock. Governor Sorrell, to appease the now excited soldier, requested his visitors (the aborigines) to withdraw from the scene. So indignant were they at the treatment meted out, for so trifling an incident, that they never accepted another invitation from the Governor.

This was just one of the many unfortunate incidents which marked the path of the relationship between the two races. Naturally, Tasmania was such that the lives of the primitive peoples were precarious and difficult. Indeed, with the arrival of another and more sophisticated race, the stage seemed perfectly set for what was to come. The Tasmanian aborigines were a doomed race from the first arrival of a white man upon their shores.

In 1816, the interior of the island was again disturbed. The Hobart Town *Gazette*, in its own inimitable style, gave the first account.

> "The Black Natives of this colony have for the last few weeks manifested a stranger hostility towards the Up-country settlers and in killing and driving away their cattle, than has been witnessed since the settlement of the colony. And since their visit to New Norfolk, they have been at the herd of Mr. Thomas McNeelance near Jericho and killed two beautiful cows."

This New Norfolk affair arose from a quarrel between three convict stock-keepers and a score of aborigines over the running of stock through the Tasmanians' camp. Actions followed words and, on the aborigines' side, forty spears were thrown; though evidently from a distance, as none of the convicts were hurt. The shots of the convicts told more harshly, mortally wounding three aborigines and wounding another, whom they took away. The stockmen considered the Blacks, as they were called, quite as much a nuisance as kangaroos to the successful grazing of livestock.

In 1817, a disastrous relationship between a settler and a native had great impact on relations between the two groups. An ex-convict, turned Bushranger, Michael Howe, had been the terror of the whole colony for many years, although this had not prevented him from being a party in a treaty with the Governor of the Island. He had formed a liaison with a young aborigine girl, Mary Cockerell, living with her for some months in a retreat in the forest not far from Oatlands, which is 51 miles from Hobart in the county of Monmouth, but had to move on as people were too hot on his trail. They went further inland, to a place of great beauty high in the mountains of the Shannon country. Even there he was constantly chased, for there was a great reward for his capture, since even the Governor could no longer shield him from the angry populace. Mary, who was now pregnant, constantly irked him by her inability to keep pace with him through the scrub in his efforts to keep ahead of his pursuers. He tried to kill her, bungled it and only succeeded in wounding her. The Bushranger escaped, but the girl was found. Mary was now indignant at his cruelty, and promised to show where his hideouts were: this would lead, eventually, to his discovery and death. Mary was taken to Hobart Town Hospital where she lingered for some time, and many people went to visit her there, even some of the dignitaries of the town, but eventually she died of her wounds.

Michael Howe continued at large for some time and would amuse himself by torturing those natives that happened to come his way. The remains of these mutilated corpses helped people to track him down, and he was eventually found at one of the huts that he had shared with Mary when she was with him.

There is a reference to Mary in one of the letters sent about this time by Governor Macquarie to his Lieutenant-Governor at Hobart (remember that Mary was now quite an invalid, though it seems that she could get about):

> "In co-operation with your humane feelings in regard to Mary, the native girl whom you sent hither some time since as a witness respecting the Bushrangers, I had a private decent lodging provided for her here, where she has ever since remained, out of the way of bad connections or improper intercourse, and she is now about to get some decent apparel. His Excellency the Governor has deemed it expedient to detain her here for some little time further, lest she should renew her intercourse with Howe, and be the means of protracting the term of his submission, or more desirable, apprehension."

Lieutenant-Governor Sorrell issued a proclamation on May 19th, 1817, against the perpetrators of base outrages upon the persons of some inoffensive aborigines. After mentioning the plea of the perpetrators that the shots were fired at the natives in a sportive spirit,* the official paper proceeds:

> "The Lieutenant-Governor thus publically declares his determination that if, after the promulgation of this announcement, any

* This viewpoint still exists in modern South America, where a party in July 1972 were apprehended for the killing of some Indians at Villavicencio in southern Colombia. They considered it sport rather than a punishable crime, and were acquitted by the court.

person or persons shall be charged with killing, firing at, or committing any act of outrage or aggression on the native people, the Offender or Offenders shall be sent to Port Jackson [near Sydney] to take their trial before the criminal court."

In the year 1818, fewer crimes and attacks upon the aborigines are reported in the papers. Perhaps there were less aborigines now to carry out crimes upon, but a burst of philanthropic feeling does seem to have permeated the colony. A real sermon is given to the settlers in the Hobart Town *Gazette* of April 25th, 1818. In this an affecting appeal is made on behalf of the denizens of the forests.

"Notwithstanding the hostility which has so long prevailed in the breast of the Natives of this island towards Europeans, we now perceive with heartfelt satisfaction, that that hatred in some measure is now gradually subsiding. Several of them are to be seen about the town and its environs, who obtain subsistence from the charitable and the well-disposed. The more that we contemplate the peculiar situation of this people, the more are we impressed with the great debt of justice that is due to them. Are not the aborigines of this colony the children of our Government? Are we not all happy but they? And are they not miserable? Can they raise themselves from this sad position? Or do they not claim our assistance? And shall the assistance be denied? Those who fancy that 'God did not make of one blood all the nations upon the earth' must be convinced that the Natives of whatever matter formed can be civilized, nay, can be christianized. The moral Governor of this world will hold us accountable. The aborigines demand our protection. They are the most helpless members, and being such, have a peculiar claim upon us all, to extend every aid in our power, as well in relation to their necessities as to those enlightening means which shall at last introduce them from the chilling rigours of the forest into the same delightful temperature which we enjoy."

It surely indicates that if there was sufficient sympathy for such an article to be accepted, there must have been some good people in Hobart. But probably many of those who lived in the town were not properly aware of what was going on in the countryside.

Most of the aborigines lived in the country and it was their heartland. The culture that was starting up in it, and thriving, was entirely alien to their way of life. They were as opposed to each other as fire to water, and could never have mixed. The only thing that could have been done was to have had vast areas of reserve for the aborigine and his kangaroo game. They were used to vast distances, but this new way of life was one of agriculture and domesticated animals, with sharply defined territories and restrictions. That of the aborigine was that of the hunter-fisher-foodgatherer, and for this way of life to continue, great areas of land were needed. The arrival of the European brought so much that was alien to the aborigine culture: their freedom was not the much vaunted European freedom and was doomed at the first European footfall upon the shore. The firebrand given to the first Frenchmen as they landed was a significant foreboding of the fate to come. So there was a confrontation, not only of the greatly contrasting peoples, but also of cultures.

It would be interesting to know if these people had the attribute of telepathy found in so many other primitive peoples from Lapland to India. It is often stated, in the old records about these people, that they had something rather strange about their eyes. People were most disturbed when a Tasmanian looked at them for any length of time, as with the settler who recalled: "They looked at me with all their eyes, so I ran to the soldiers."

The calmness and serenity of 1818 was followed by a storm of violence in the following year. It was the usual tale of provocation and revenge. Early in March, 1819, the Oyster Bay Eastern Tribe, or the Oyster Bay Mob as they were colloquially called, speared John Kemp and another man. But the "Journal of the Day" gives the provoking cause in these words:

"It is well known that for some time before Kemp was killed many natives were provoked by the Whites and a Native man was shot in the woods by some of the stockmen to the east, and that the women had also been deprived of their children in that quarter."

It certainly does appear as if the ex-convicts, who had been ill-treated themselves, worked off their spite and passion upon the aborigines that came their way, and the feeble weapons that the latter used in their resistance to the often formidable armoury of the bushrangers merely added to the fun of the sporting occasion. Even the spears of the aborigines were merely wooden stakes hardened in the fire, a pathetic retort to powder and shot.

In 1819, one Jones was employed as stock-keeper on the station of Messrs. Morris and Stocker, near Relief River (later known as the

Macquarie). His fellow-servant, M'Candless, had gone to look after the sheep on the nearby plains. A neighbour's man, James Forrest, had called in at the hut, when M'Candless burst in breathlessly, declaring that he had run for his life from "the Blacks", who were spearing the sheep. The stockmen decided that this was not to be taken lying down, and resolved to chase the culprits, taking two infirm muskets with them for the battle. The light of day was fast departing when the men came in sight of about two hundred aborigines on a hill-top. They sought to frighten them from the hill with their muskets. The men of the forest, who dreaded Europeans' "fire sticks", did not come down to attack, but were content with making hideous and blood chilling noises, with some of the bolder spirits among them coming forward and shaking their spears in defiance. But the stock-keepers, to their horror, realized that they had mislaid the powder horn in their hurry, and that they had only enough powder for one shot. All they could do was retreat; and this they accomplished in deepening gloom, with the best show of courage they could maintain.

At daybreak, Jones (who must have been a very brave man), set off for the sheep fold, leaving his mates in bed. He had only gone a few hundred yards, when, hearing voices, he looked back and saw a crowd of aborigines descending the hill towards the hut, with the evident intent of firing the bark roof, and murdering the men inside. Jones ran hastily back, aroused the men, and prepared the defence. Standing outside the door and facing their dark foes, the Europeans again presented their guns, and ordered the party off. But some endeavoured to get round another way with lighted torches to fire the hut from the rear, while others stood on the hill-side and answered the challenge with shouts of derisive laughter. Spears, waddies, and stones were thrown at the three, but so far with little effect. One, evidently the leader and apparently of gigantic size, was armed with a huge spear, unlike the rest of the mob. He stood erect, leaning on his weapon, calmly giving orders to his tribe.

Again and again did the stockmen pull the triggers of their muskets without producing any fire. The aborigines now observed their rather helpless position, and motioned them to leave the hut. The bushmen hoped this might be their chance and the aborigines would be happy with the good stores that they found in the hut and allow them to escape. They could see that further stay would be hopeless as the Blacks obviously wanted to wear them down: hours had already passed in this bloodless warfare and any sudden rush would have destroyed them. So they fled rapidly towards a gully. But the aborigines followed

ignoring the hut and throwing their spears as they came. A wild cow
and several of the kangaroo dogs, used by the stockmen to destroy
kangaroos, were speared. But the pursued only received one slight
wound. At last they were hemmed in at the end of the gully and their
retreat blocked by two hundred naked red-ochred wild men. The crude
guns still would not go off, much to the amusement of their opponents.

Jones now received three spears at once. One passed through his
right cheek, another through the muscles of his right arm and a third
embedded itself in his right side. One of his mates pulled out the
weapons and as he did so he received a spear in the back. The third
man was as yet untouched. For seven hours since their waking had the
terrible stuggle continued. The stockmen were now exhausted and
stood like the sheep they had so often killed, waiting, shivering, for the
slaughter. The aborigines saw that the time had come to finish them off.
The chief had already given the word for them to charge in with "the
waddy", to dash the brains out of the three men as if they were killing
their kangaroos. "At this moment," says Jones, "a most fortunate
accident occurred, which I have ever to consider an act of Providence."
One of the guns went off. Suddenly, and unexpectedly, it discharged.
The shot struck the chief who fell dead on the spot. His tribesmen could
not understand this at all, trying desperately to lift him on to his feet to
see if he could stand; while others shouted, shook their spears and beat
their breasts in their extreme emotion. Finding their efforts to revive
him all in vain, they were seized with panic and fled, leaving the three
Europeans to struggle back to civilization and tell their tale.

A very interesting and remarkable Government Order that appeared
from the pen of Colonel Sorrell, dated March 13th, 1819, from Hobart
Town, marked the culmination of the first part of the "Black War".
In content it is humane and judicious, and so particularly enters into
the whole question relative to the conduct of the two races as to be
considered one of the best state-papers ever to be drawn up in the colony.
This is the full text of the document which was headed "The Public
Order":

"From information received by His Honor the Lieutenant-
Governor, there seems reason to apprehend that outrages have been
recently perpetrated against some of the Native People in the remote
country adjoining the River Plenty, though the result of the en-
quiries instituted upon these reports has not established the facts
alleged, further than that two Native Children have remained in the
Hands of a Person resident above the Falls District of Hobart: Upon

this subject which the Lieutenant-Governor considers of the highest Importance, as well to Humanity as to the Peace and Security of the Settlement, His Honor cannot omit addressing the Settlers.

"The Lieutenant-Governor is aware that many of the Settlers and Stock-Keepers consider the Natives as a Hostile People, seeking provocation, opportunities to destroy them and their stock, towards whom any attempts at Forbearance or Conciliation would be useless. It is, however, most certain that if the Natives were intent upon Destruction of this kind, and if they were incessantly to watch for opportunities of effecting it, the Mischief done by them to the Owners of Sheep or Cattle, which are now dispersed for grazing over so great a part of the Interior Country, would be increased one hundredfold. But so far from any systematic Plan for Destroying the Stock or People being pursued by the Native Tribes, their Meetings with the Herdsmen appear generally to be accidental; and it is the opinion of the best informed Persons who have been longest in the Settlement, that the former are seldom the Assailants, and that when they are, they act under the Impression of recent Injuries done to some of them by White People. It is undeniable that in many former Instances, Cruelties have been perpetrated repugnant to Humanity and disgraceful to the British Character, while few attempts can be traced on the part of the Colonists to Conciliate the Native People, or to make them sensible that Peace and Forbearance are the objects desired. The Impressions received from earlier Injuries are kept up by the occasional Outrages of Miscreants whose sense of Crime is so remote as to render detection difficult, and who sometimes Wantonly set fire to and kill the Men, and others pursue the Women for the purpose of compelling them to abandon their children. This last Outrage is perhaps the most certain of all to excite in the Sufferers a strong Thirst for revenge against all White Men, and to incite the Natives to take Vengeance indiscriminately, according to the General Practice of an Uncivilized People wherever in their Migrations they fall in with the Herds and Stockmen."

(The women were considered ugly and were often left alone at the expense of their children, who were considered more attractive.)

"It is not only those who perpetrated such Enormities against a People comparatively Defenceless that suffer; all the Owners of Stock and the better Stock-keepers are involved in the Consequences brought on by the wanton and criminal Acts of a few.

"From the conduct of the Native People, when free from any feeling of Injury, toward those who have sought friendship with them, there is a strong reason to hope that they might be conciliated. On the North-East Coast, where Boats occasionally touch, and at Macquarie Harbour, where the Natives have been lately seen, they have been found Unsuspicious and Peaceable, manifesting no disposition to Injure; and they are known to be equally Inoffensive in other Places where the Stock-keepers treat them with Mildness and Forbearance.

"A careful Avoidance, on the part of the Settlers and Stockmen, of conduct tending to excite Suspicion of Intended Injury, and a strict Forbearance from all Acts and Appearances of Hostility, except when rendered indispensable for position of Self-defence, or the Preservation of the Stock, may yet remove from the Minds of the Native People the Impressions left by past Cruelties: so that the Meetings between them and the Colonists, which the Extension of the Grazing Grounds and Progressive Occupation of the Country must render yearly more frequent, may be injurious to neither; and that these Mischiefs, which a Perseverance in Cruelty and Aggression must lead to, and which must involve the Stock in perpetual Danger, and the Stockmen in Responsibility for the Lives that may be lost, may be prevented.

"To effect this Object, is no less the Interest than the Duty of the Settlers and Stockmen; to bring to condign Punishment any one who shall be open to proof of having destroyed or maltreated any of the Native People (not strictly in Self-defence), will be the Duty and is the Determination of the Lieutenant-Governor, supported by the Magistracy, and by the Assistance of all the just and well-disposed Settlers.

"With a view to prevent the Continuance of the Cruelty before mentioned, of depriving the Natives of their Children; it is hereby Ordered that the Resident Magistrates at the District of Pittwater and Coal River, and the District constables in all the Other Districts do forthwith take an account of all the Native Youths and Children which are Resident with any of the Settlers and Stock-keepers, stating from whom, and in what manner, they were obtained.

"The same Magistrates and the District Constables are in future to take an Account of any Native Person or Child which shall come or be brought into their Districts, or County adjoining, together with the circumstances attending it. These Reports are to be transmitted to the Secretary's Office, Hobart Town.

"No Person whatever will be allowed to retain Possession of a Native Youth or Child, unless it shall be clearly proved that the Consent of the Parents had been given; or that the Child had been found in a state of Demanding Shelter and Protection, in which case the Person into whose Hands it may fall, is immediately to report the circumstances to the nearest Magistrate or Constable.

"All Native Youths and Children who shall be known to be with any of the settlers or Stock-keepers, unless so accounted for, will be removed to Hobart Town, where they will be supported, and instructed at the Charge and Under the Direction of the Government."

END OF PROCLAMATION

It appears from the first part of the proclamation that Governor Sorrell regretted his hasty action of coming too quickly to the aid of the gallant captain and the Tasmanian girl. From the second part it appears that the convicts in those days were in the habit of perpetrating outrages of various kinds, then blaming them on the black population.

PART TWO

War

chapter 3

The Tragedy within the Race

Who can give a true picture of the terrible wrongs done to the Tasmanian aborigines? We are horrified at the attempts by various races at extermination of Jews, the extermination by the Spaniards of in Incas and the Caribs, and more recently the Indians of the Amazon Forests.

Should we not equally regret the causes that led to the annihilation of the tribes of Tasmania? It was not the result either of a contest between rival nations or civilizations. No senator uttered a "Carthage must be destroyed", to incite the faltering energies of a struggling people. No Thermopylae, which witnessed the expiring effort of its Greek sons of freedom, remains in Tasmania's mountain fastnesses. No Welsh bard has sung the deeds of heroism. But it was a long series of misfortunes and cruelties that gradually wrought the destruction of these primitive inhabitants of Tasmania.

They would not, could not, be reduced to slavery. They would not, could not, be assimilated into the community of the intruders upon their soil. As their own brilliant Waratah flower, when torn from the rocky crest of its mountain home, refuses to expand its crimson petals in an artificial bed, and pines to death for the loss of its free and bracing native airs, so could they never assume the rigid robe of the civilization that was offered them in the Victorian era, with all its inhibitions and hypocrisies, nor forsake their wild and wooded ridge for the tenements of the shanty town.

We Europeans came upon them as evil dragons, blasting them with the breath of our presence. We broke up their home circles, the only real unit of their society. We arrested them at their corroborees, which, in their turn, were considered evil and taken from them. Even in this one facet of their lives we destroyed their community as much as possible. Yet with what was it replaced? Reading and knitting, most passive and introverted of pastimes, can in no way substitute for something as extroverted as singing and dancing, in which young and old partake.*

We, the Europeans, turned their song into weeping, and their mirth into sadness. We were without the simple faith of the French explorer, who discovered a nymph of grace and beauty in the dark and luscious Oura Oura, and in her nakedness, as also in the patriarchal government of the tribes, beheld primeval innocence. In arrogance and blindness, too many failed to see that social graces and virtues could flourish in a gum-tree's shade; that maternal joy sparkled in the eyes of a woman, clad in the least of an opposum's skin, as she joined in the gambols of her little child; that honest friendship united hands and hearts of brother hunters; that soft glances, sweet smiles, told that love could dwell equally well in clematis bowers as in the woodbine's shade.

When the white man entered this peaceful scene the hunter ceased his roaming among the hills, resorting to stealth even upon his ancestral lands. The mother hushed her child and checked her own maternal emotions, lest the slightest noise brought the dreaded stranger to take away a mother's joy. And silenced was the talk of love; for deeds of wrong to maid and matron chilled the heart, and eyes that could flash with love now flashed with hate and rage.

The story of the Tasmanians' sufferings would be like that written by the benevolent padre, Las Casas, in his *Short Account of the Destruction of the Indies*, which is thus described by the historian Prescott: "It is a tale of woe. Every line of the work may be said to have been written in blood." Yet it is true that in that case also the government had cherished proper sentiments towards the native Indians, for the historian observes again: "The history of Spanish colonial legislation is the history of the impotent struggles of the Government on behalf of the Natives, against the avarice and the cruelty of its subjects."

In other words, the good intentions a government proposes can, too easily, be ignored by certain sections of the populace. Too often a colonial government is very weak and can be formed to a large extent by "dark" personalities, if not of the black populace, not to mention blackmail from some of its more influential citizens: with the poor Indians it was the avarice of a few that caused their oppression.

But it was not so much so with the Tasmanian aborigines, who had nothing to give. They were merely in the way! The behaviour of their

ᵎ In the art of reading, some Tasmanians excelled sufficiently to read a newspaper.

oppressors was brutal, indeed primitive and animal in its ferocity. As a cow, caught helplessly by its horns, is gored to death by the rest of the herd, so were the defenceless Tasmanians brutalized, raped and killed by the more powerful Europeans: it was the law of the jungle at its worst.

One great cause of mischief was the liberty given to the prisoners, about the year 1806, to disperse themselves in search of kangaroos during a season of famine. The effect on the convicts of this sudden release, after the rigours of prison discipline, can easily be imagined. At first they were kindly treated by the dark children of the forest, but they repaid their hosts by frightful deeds of violence and wrong for no apparent reason. They drank "firewater", and their drunkenness accentuated the outrages. Fear and terror entered the hitherto peaceful vales of Tasmania with the convicts who, too often, left the remains of the tortured humanity that had provided their night's pleasure rotting by some lone hut.

One is not surprised by the Rev. John West, quoted in the *Derwent Star* of 1810: "The Natives who have been rendered desperate by the cruelties that they have experienced from some of our people, have now begun to distress us by attacking our cattle."

Another extract in the same year (1810), painfully illustrates the subject:

> "The unfortunate man, Russell, is a striking instance of the Divine Agency, which has overtaken him at last, and punished him by the hands of those very people, who have suffered so much from him; he being known to have exercised his barbarous disposition in murdering or torturing any of them that came within his reach."

These outrages aroused the indignation of Governor Davey, and in 1813 he wrote the following:

> "That he could not have believed that British subjects would have so ignominiously stained the honour of their country and themselves, as to have acted in the manner as they did towards the aborigines."

Another governor, Governor Arthur, was also much shocked at the barbarity of his people, but was unable to prevent the evil. Immediately after his arrival in the colony, a tribe applied to him for protection. It was readily granted and the governor gave his personal attention and kindness to their well being and protected them from insult and injury.

They settled at Kangaroo Point, a tongue of land separated from the town by the broad estuary of the Derwent. There they stayed quietly and happily for a few years, until one of the number was savagely murdered by some of their white neighbours, although it was difficult to put the blame on any particular person. The aborigine camp broke up immediately and made for their old haunts in the wildness of the interior. Governor Arthur's kindness could not prevail over the savagery of his own compatriots.

What is so amazing is that from what we can glean from newspapers and letters of the times, the people of the town considered themselves most highly respectable and civilized; they were a strong church- and chapel-going community, and on a par with any English country town of the time. There was no need to walk about with guns for protection from the Indians, as often happened in the first settlements of New England.

But this respectability hardly stands up when the Whites' treatment of the unfortunate female aborigines is considered. As they wore no clothes they were considered fair game by all the white males, who considered themselves provoked into committing whatever offence they liked, overlooking the basic humanity that their victims shared with the well-clad white ladies. A day's hunting in the forest was not, of course, what the Whites told their wives it was. The results of such unions were naturally looked upon with abhorrence by the aborigines and destroyed at birth. But there was another aspect of this, more serious for the survival of the more primitive race. While the females were used by the European males for their own amusement, they had less chance of producing children of their own kind from their own husbands.

The Europeans could not, for the most part, plead tenderness and concern for the objects of their passions—sadism would be the more appropriate term. If a woman was decoyed to a stockman's hut she was not kept by gentleness, but by threats, the lash and the chain, if she did not at once obey the wishes of the stockman. In a community acutely short of women, most were kept entirely to satisfy the stockmen's passions and so were kept on a chain, until rejected in favour of another girl.

A Dr. Ross, describing his journey up to the Shannon in 1823, relates an incident of this nature:

"We met one of Mr. Lord's men sitting on the stump of a tree, nearly starved to death. He told us that three days before, a black woman whom he had caught in the Bush, and had chained to a log with a bullock chain, and whom he had covered with his shirt, the only one he had, in hopes, as he said, to tame her, had contrived somehow to slip the chain from her leg, and run away, shirt and all."

The doctor adds, "I fear his object in chaining the poor creature was not exactly disinterested," a truly Victorian understatement of a sexual motive, and was not surprised to hear that, not long after, this gentle lover was hanged for exercising his benevolence upon some of his own countrymen.

Another of his kind who caught an unhappy girl sought to relieve her fears, or subdue her sulks, before the "marriage bed", as it was termed, by spending the morning flogging her with a bullock whip and then fastening her to a tree near his hut, and thus found her ready to do what he wished in the evening. This same convict stockman was later found speared to death at a waterhole, and no witnesses came forward.

A settler who lived on the Esk River (thirty miles from Launceston) tells how his neighbour, wanting a gin (aborigine girl), asked him to accompany him on his Sabine expedition. He had heard that a suitable young female had been seen with a small party on an island in the river, and was on his way thither to seize her. He pointed exultantly to the bullock chain that he would use for her. Needless to say, he also had a musket, for one of the male members of the party who tried to oppose him. These incidents, a few among many, too often had only one outcome, further embittering and antagonizing the natives towards the white population.

A convict, Tom Ward, who was transported in 1818, recounts how, in up-country Tasmania in 1820, the stock-keepers at Mr. Stocker's of Salt Pan Plains were guilty of abominable treatment towards two females that they had caught. The women afterwards told their coolies (husbands), and the tribe surrounded the hut, and killed two of the three men who were there. Many instances are recorded of murders committed solely to seize the females of a mob (tribe). There are frequent recorded incidents of brutal stock-keepers and shepherds hunting down the males, torturing and castrating them, before taking the females. Horror-stricken by such tales, the benevolent Quaker, James Backhouse, exclaimed:

"They were of such a character, as to remove any wonder at the determination of those so injured to try to drive away from their land a race of men, among whom were persons guilty of such deeds. This must have been particularly horrifying to the males who no doubt had much ignorance in regard to the results of these crude operations, when they beheld the results of the tortures, on their bodies. But realization came when not only the pain of the moment, but the terrible lasting effects were realized."

The bushrangers of Tasmania were terrible foes of the aborigines of that island, both from natural cruelty and from a fancied fear of their divulging the sites of hide-outs. A bushranger called Lemon, and others, when in a merry mood, thought nothing of tying the male aborigines to trees and using them for target practice. An ex-bushranger confessed that he would "as leave shoot them as so many sparrows. At the same time, I obtain much amusement from this form of sport." Another of these worthies, a deportee of some fifty years' standing, declared that he had heard from Michael Howe, before mentioned, that that notorious ruffian would lay down his musket to induce the blacks to come towards him, but on their approach would fire at them, pulling the trigger with his toes.

The bushranger, Dunn, carried off the gins to his lair and there abused them cruelly. Being well armed it was very difficult for the aborigines to lure him from his lair. So exasperated were they against the Whites, on account of the cruelty of the wretched outlaw, that they murdered several inoffensive neighbouring settlers. A Mr. Mellville, long connected with the press in Tasmania of that time, says the following about another one:

"The Bushranger Carrots killed a blackfellow, and seized his gin; then cutting off the man's head, the brute fastened it round the gin's neck, then he drove the weeping victim to his den."

A letter, written in 1815, blames the bushrangers for being the cause of the aborigines not mixing with the settlers, and for creating their attitude and the animosity it so constantly expressed.

A colonist who had retired to Melbourne about 1865, named many instances of cruelty to the aborigines. He stated that he knew of two men who had boasted of killing thirty in one incident. A Mr. Backhouse relates that one party, out after the blacks, killed thirty in capturing eleven during the official efforts to bring them to the "Reserve" of Flinders Island. Quamby's Bluff, an eastern spur of the Great Central Highlands of the island, was named after a poor hunted creature who fell on his knees there crying out "Quamby, Quamby", or "Mercy, Mercy!" A retired magistrate, from the same region, tells how soldiers had been called in to investigate the death of a shepherd near the Macquarie River. Going in pursuit of the supposed murderers, they fell in with a tribe, camped for the night in one of the numerous gullies near the river. They shot indiscriminately at the group of men, women and children. Many were slain or maimed, but no government enquiry was ever made into the well-known happening.

An eye-witness of a similar night attack has this to say:

"It was interesting to see how they fell after they were shot. One man, being shot while bending over the fire, sprang up, turned round and round and round like a whipping top, before he fell dead."

The shooting party then went up to the fires, found there a great number of waddies and spears, and an infant spread out on the ground, which one of the party pitched into the fire.

No more vivid proof of the white man's manners towards the aborigines of that dark era can be presented, than is recorded by Jorgenson* in his account of his travels in the bush in 1826. It also shows that the Whites were not always the aggressors. "Two days after I saw Scott," he said, "a large tribe came down from Dr. Thomson's hut, which was occupied by three assigned convict servants. These men struck a bargain with some of the Blacks, for some of the women that they had brought down with them, and in return to give them some blankets and sugar. However, afterwards when the females were going back to rejoin their tribe, the convict servants sallied out, and deprived the women of the blankets and the sugar. The tribe, nearly one hundred in number, now became exceedingly exasperated at the perfidy of the servants, surrounded the hut, and would have certainly effected their revenge by burning down the hut, had not the Bushranger Dunn come timely to their assistance. Being disappointed, the Blacks, in the heat of resentment, fell in with poor aged Scott and murdered him in a most barbarous manner."

This Scott had previously been on most friendly terms with the aborigines, and his dreadful end furnishes the key to many apparently inexplicable murders of innocent people, men, women and children, by the aborigines, when the two races were afterwards in frequent collision, though the aborigines at no time raped white women.

A similar incident occurred in July, 1827. A man was killed by the Blacks up in the country, near the Western Tiers. He had been long

* A Danish adventurer sent out as a convict by the British. He became immensely popular by virtue of his strong character, and finally regained his freedom.

familiar with the tribe, having lived for some years previously with the aborigines of Australia, but had, somehow, incurred the displeasure of the Tasmanians. The neighbouring settlers gathered together for a chase after the criminals, and took revenge indeed for the death of one man; the *Colonial Times* declares: "For in the resulting engagement there must have been about sixty killed and maimed."

A party of police from Richmond were passing through bush country in 1827, when a tribe, seeing them, climbed to a hill-top and threw stones at them. The police fired in return and charged them repeatedly with bayonets. There is also the report of another incident by Mr. G. A. Robinson:

> "A party of military and constables got a number of natives cornered between two perpendicular rocks, on a sort of shelf, and in the end killed seventy of them. The women and children had pressed themselves into the crevices of the rocks, but were dragged out and their brains dashed out on the convenient rocks."

White barbarity seems unending. One wretched man, Ibbens, was accustomed to go persistently after the Eastern Tribe, with a double-barrelled gun, creeping among them at dusk, until in a few months he had killed off half the tribe. Some of these convicts would get a determined black "down" on some object, person, or tribe, rarely seen in any other group of people artificially brought together or even a natural group.

One man even boasted that he had thrown an old woman on a fire, and watched her roast to death. The *Colonial Times* speaks about one occasion when a party of "soldiers and other helpers approached to within thirty yards of their night fires, thus being able to kill an immense quantity of Blacks".

Well might Dr. Marshall of Hobart Town tell Lord Glenelg (head of the Colonial Office in London at that time):

> "The murders which, at almost every page, have blotted with blood the history of the British Colonies, cry out against us, unto the Most High God, with a voice that has not always been unanswered, for national calamity to succeed national wickedness."

"Many years ago," writes James Bonwick in 1870, "I fell in with one of the lowest order of convicts, who told me that he liked to kill a black fellow better than smoke his pipe; adding 'I'm a rare one at it too.' "

This convict related the following adventure:

"When out one evening with some armed stock-keeping mates, he climbed Maloney's Sugar Loaf, and from there saw a tribe lighting their fires for the night. He returned with the news, and bent on some good sport, they abstained from all noise, and from supper, or supper fires, for themselves. They waited till just before dawn, advanced toward their unsuspicious victims in a crescent line, so as to cut off all retreat, and fired close. 'We had some good sport afterwards too, there wasn't many of them got off.' "

Dr. Nixon, the first Bishop of Tasmania, was forced to say of such occurrences:

"There are many such on record, which make us blush for humanity when we read about them, and forbid us to wonder that the maddened savage's indiscriminate fury should not only have refused to recognise the distinction between friend or foe, but have taught him to regard each white man as an intruding enemy, who must be got rid of at any cost."

Mr. Shoolbridge, a much respected Tasmanian colonist of the 1820s, is the authority for the story of a particularly brutal incident. Two men went out shooting birds. Some aborigines, seeing them approach, hastily fled. A woman far advanced in pregnancy, unable to run and keep up with the rest, climbed up a tree, breaking down the branches for concealment, but the sportsmen observed her. One of these proposed to shoot her, but the other objected. The first, however, dropped behind, and fired at the unfortunate creature. A fearful scream was heard, and a premature birth took place. The new mother dragged her shattered body and trailing guts away to bury her head in the mud of a nearby creek, to the amusement of the sportsmen. The story goes on to say, that on that very day the wife and child of the killer were crossing the Derwent, when a sudden squall upset the boat, and both were drowned.

The same informant also told of a young fellow, who gave him an account of some "capital fun", as it was called. He and some others took advantage of a robbery at Hamilton and charged it upon an inoffensive tribe in the neighbourhood. Without warning, an expedition was fitted out in the night, and a terrible slaughter took place. The miserable remnant were infuriated at the treachery and cruelty, and revenged themselves by years of outrage and murder. The strangely vicious approach to life that eats into some people when civilization

3

becomes decadent, is responsible for far more troubles than the atrocities that any barbarian race ever committed in cold blood. And its repercussions have a nasty habit of smouldering on, an ever-present threat of conflagration. It is remarkable that these poor savages were so tenacious and lasted so long. There is something so terrible about sophisticated cruelty, for the doers know more acutely what they are doing and it should therefore be classed as the most refined of evils.

Mr. Shoolbridge's father was dining with a country settler, when one of the convict stockmen came in, shouting, "Well, Master! I've shot three more crows [Blacks] today."

The historian of Tasmania, the Rev. Mr. West, did not exaggerate when he wrote:

> "The wounded were brained; the infants cast into the flames; the musket was driven into the quivering flesh; and the social fire, around which the Natives gathered to slumber, became, before morning, their funeral pyre."

Brough Smith quotes the following from Hull, whose word can be relied upon:

> "A friend once described to me a fearful scene at which he was present. A number of blacks with women and children were congregated in a gully near Hobart and the men had formed themselves into a ring round a large fire, while the women were cooking the evening meal of opposums and bandicoots. They were thus surprised by a party of soldiers, who without warning fired into them as they sat, and then rushing up to the panic stricken natives started to go in at them with rifle butts. A little child being near its dying mother, the soldier drove his bayonet through the body of the child and pitchforked it into the flames."

Mr. Hull also adds that it was a favourite amusement to hunt the aborigines. A day would be selected, and all the neighbouring settlers would be invited, with their families, to a picnic. After their repast, all would be gaiety and merriment, while the gentlemen of the party would take their guns and dogs and, accompanied by a few convict servants, would wander through the bush in search of blackfellows. Sometimes they would return without finding any sport, at others they would succeed in hunting down a woman and collect together to kill her using the convicts as the go-betweens. Often they would mangle a man or two with the dogs after an exciting chase. But the women were considered the best sport as they did not get away so easily, especially if they were with child. In many cases no doubt the Blacks were sacrificed to momentary caprice or at least suffered much worrying. Hull also states, that one settler had a pickle tub, in which he put all the ears of the Blacks that he had shot.

The *Courier* of June 11th, 1836, admits that thousands were hunted down and destroyed like wild beasts. Dr. Broca, a distinguished French ethnologist, asserted when the last Tasmanians could be counted on the fingers of one hand, that the English

"have committed upon the Tasmanian Race (and that in the nineteenth century), execrable atrocities a hundred times less excusable than the hitherto unrivalled crimes of which the Spaniards were guilty in the sixteenth century in the Antilles. Then they become pious and pretend to act as saviours."

The public mind grows callous from continual confrontations of blood and violence, as the war in Vietnam and tragedies of earthquake and typhoon testify. For the character that formulated our colonies, it is now a futile wish that the following paragraph, written in the *Courier* in 1826, had never been, and surely it is the echo of the modern hawks:

"Let them have enough of Redcoats and bullet fire. For every man they murder, hunt them down, and drop ten of them. This is our specific—try it."

The feeling is truly exhibited in the statement of the paper of December 1st, 1826, "that the settlers with their stock-keepers are determined to annihilate every black who may act hostilely".

The cruelty took a sadistic turn with some of the out-station people. As we have already noted, Captain Holman tells of a fellow taking a pair of pistols, only one of which was loaded with live ammunition, and sought out a native. He fired the harmless one at his own ear and then presented the other weapon to the aborigine, inviting him to try the same funny performance. With grim delight he witnessed the blackfellow blow his brains out.

Occasionally, however, the picture lightens and there are records of a happier and more positive relationship between the white man and the aborigines of Tasmania. In 1822, a tribe had lit their evening fire in the bush, not very far from a field of corn that was ready for harvesting. A high wind was driving the flames towards the fields and the farmhouse that lay just beyond. The farmer wrote afterwards:

"We were doing our best to extinguish the Bush that had caught fire, with green boughs, but our efforts would have been in vain had not the whole tribe of blacks, all at once, come forward to assist me. Even some hours afterwards, when the flames again broke out in two or three places, they were on the alert in a moment to put them out. I mention this incident, as it was an act of friendship on their part, and shows that when they have not been insulted, or had cause for revenge, they are able to discriminate their friends from their foes, they are not in wanting to reciprocate offices of friendship and humanity."

From the many reports it appears that the tribes in Tasmania varied a great deal in physique. This could possibly have extended to their mentality also. The conflicting reports of the tribes' treatment of their womenfolk suggest this. It has been shown that the more primitive a people the lower their regard for their womenfolk: among the Tasmanians some tribes treated their women like dogs, but others tried desperately to protect them from the ravages of the Whites.*

The Reverend Dr. Lang, in his indignant letter to the Earl of Durham, narrates a terrible story.

"A spot," said he, "was pointed out to me a few years ago in the interior of the island, where seventeen aborigines had been shot in cold blood. They had been bathing in the heat of a summer's day, in a deep pool of a river, in a sequested and most romantic glen, when they were suddenly surprised by a party of armed colonists, who had already secured the passes out of the glen, and none of them was left to tell their side of the story. A convict Bushranger in Van Diemen's Land, who was hanged a few years ago for serious crimes committed against the European sections of the community, confessed that, when under sentence of death, he had actually been in the habit of shooting the black Natives in order to feed his dogs, when hiding in the interior."

A Mrs. Guy of New Norfolk gave James Bonwick more proof of the attempted ruffianism of the period (1828). Once when standing by her

---

* Extremes of treatment are also found in New Guinea. Where one tribe will cherish its old women, another will destroy them out of hand.

door she saw a native woman pursued by three Europeans. The female ran to the high bank, and leapt into the Derwent, and swam across the broad flowing stream. The kind lady hastened down to the poor creature, and found her much agitated with fear, and trembling violently. Taking her home she gave her some warm tea, and bound a blanket round her. The husband came later to thank the lady, and did so by cutting a lot of firewood, in her yard, in return for her kindness.

Captain Stokes's *Australian Discovery* is a useful contemporary work. This is what one of the convict servants did to his captured gin:

> "He kept the poor creature chained up with a bullock chain, like a wild beast, and, when he needed her, he applied a burning stick from the fire, and pressed it into her skin, until she screamed she was ready."

It is hardly surprising that many acts of violence by the natives were retaliation for the bloody acts of the settlers upon them and their women.

It is very small satisfaction to be told that other nations have been as bad as ourselves in these matters: that a million of the Caribs in the Caribbean Islands were reduced by the Spaniards to sixty thousand in fifteen years; that, according to Las Casas (the first Spanish missionary bishop to the New World who pleaded in vain for more humanity to be shown to the Indians), fifteen million Indians perished at their hands. Again, as Cotton Mather reports of the English settlers in the American colonies: "Among the early settlers, it was considered a religious act to kill Indians."

Some Spaniards made a vow to God to burn or hang every morning, for a certain time, thirteen Indians; one was to be a compliment to the Saviour, and the others to the twelve apostles. A Spanish priest as Vigo relates, on seeing some Peruvian Indians destroying themselves rather than work in the mines, thus addressed the remainder:

> "You wish to hang yourselves, my friends, rather than do labour; seeing this, I shall hang myself first; but I must warn you of one thing, which is this, that there are mines in the other world as well as in this; and I will give you my word that I will make you work throughout eternity."

Upon hearing this the poor Indians threw themselves at his feet, and begged him not to kill himself.

The Spanish were not the only ones who preyed upon their colonial subjects. The following quotation comes from the diary of one of the early Dutch governors of the Cape Colony:

> "December 3, 1652. Today, the Hottentots came with thousands of cattle and sheep close to our fort. We feel vexed to see so many fine herd of cattle, and not be able to buy to any considerable extent. On the other hand, if we had 150 men, 10,000 of black 'cattle' could be obtained without any danger of losing one man, and many savages might be taken without resistance, in order to be sent as slaves to India, as they still always come to us unarmed."

Commando raids by Dutch Boers against the native races were common enough. As recently as 1832, Lord Somerset had great difficulty in arresting the march of a party that had started for the destruction of a settlement of 5,000 Christian Hottentots, on the Kat River. This is the background of the present-day South Africans, so we must wonder that the relationship between black and white is not even worse than it is there at the present time.

It is painful to add to this small dossier of the sorrows of the races, that while the English Government in Van Diemen's Land issued paternal proclamations, and uttered sentiments of profound compassion for the aborigines, little energy was exerted to repress or punish those who committed crimes against them. If anything was ever done it was confined to the vicinity of Hobart Town. The *Hobart Town Times* of April, 1836, is harsh, but not unjust, in the following sentences:

> "They have been murdered in cold blood. They have been shot in the woods, and hunted down as beasts of prey. Their women have been contaminated, and then had their throats cut, or been shot, by the British Residents, who would fain call themselves civilized people. The Government, too, by the common hangman, sacrificed the lives of such of the aborigines as in retaliation destroyed their wholesale murderers, and the Government, to its shame be recorded, in no one instance, on no single occasion, ever punished, or threatened to punish, the acknowledged murderers of the aboriginal inhabitants."

chapter 4

The Black War

The "Black War of Van Diemen's Land" was a natural sequel to the events just related. The Tasmanians were very independent and bold when outraged by an injury, though very feebly supplied with the means for avenging it. Their weapons were only wooden stakes whose points had been hardened in the fire, and waddies that were merely crude wooden clubs. With these they had to contend with men armed with guns and steel. Like all weak people, however brave, they relied more upon taking their foes at a disadvantage than on meeting them in the open field. They could come upon the lone hut in the wilds, could waylay the solitary bushman, and could set fire to the badly protected dwelling.

Yet, to the great honour of the Tasmanians, they were content to fight with men. Not one single instance has been recorded, right from the early days, of the rape of a white woman, and women and children were rarely killed. When the white man bombs, even today (e.g., in Vietnam), this is rarely taken into consideration. And, unlike the people of the neighbouring islands of New Zealand, although these had a higher culture, the Tasmanian aboriginals were never cannibals.

It was frequently laid against them by the settlers in Tasmania during those times, that the aborigines attacked the wrong party. But were we any better? When British frigates went out to avenge a murder by natives anywhere in the Empire, without enquiry as to the individual criminal or the cause of the outrage, shots were directed against a village and the whole tribe. If civilized and Christian warriors act so, is it to be wondered at that "heathen savages", personally injured, and not paid to slaughter, should fail to discriminate, and confound all who belonged to the hated race.

Mr. Clark, a catechist to the remnant of the once proud race, in a letter remarks:

> "They did much mischief prior to their removal from Van Diemen's Land, but it was from a feeling of retaliation, and their also imagining the Whites to be a distinct race of beings, against which they were bound to make war after the first trouble in 1804."

This indicates that there was communication between tribes and the doings of the white people must have been much discussed. The Aborigines' Protection Committee of Hobart Town reported that:

> "the injuries and insults which the aborigines had received from dissolute characters let loose among them had led to a certain extent to an aggravation of their troubles, in addition to their savage spirit, to wreak indiscriminate vengeance."

The Aborigines' Committee that sat in 1830 also said that the dogs trained to hunt kangaroos were at first serviceable to the natives, one family having sometimes up to a hundred and fifty dogs, but that they often increased the destruction by hunting on their own, in the same way as dogs worry sheep. It was observed by a writer in 1827 that forty or fifty dead kangaroos could be found within a short distance, run down by dogs and left to rot. Thus food on which the aborigines depended for subsistence was diminished, and hence there was the added temptation to rob the settlers.

Colonel Arthur was a strong Governor but was handicapped as he lived on the borders of two ages. There was the past, of convict discipline, and there was the future, of free settlement. The rougher element had to be curbed by strong laws. The rising tide of education and freedom was preparing the way for the removal of despotic obstructiveness. Bushranging violence was his trial on the one side, and the impatient cries of a chained press was his trouble on the other. His cup of bitterness was filled to the brim by the Native difficulty. One of his Proclamations, that of June 1824, rebuked "the settlers and others", who destroyed the tribesmen, then under British Protection. An injury to them said he, "shall be visited with the same punishment as though committed on the person or property of any other".

But these were words, mere words, and nothing more than empty air. The aborigines could not rely upon them even if they understood them, and the Whites laughed at them—in fact they were a challenge to the type of immature people that seemed to possess the land. What effect could they have when it was well known that an aboriginal witness would not be heard?

Another of these Government notices appeared on November 29th, 1826. His Excellency regretted the failure of his efforts at conciliation, but the attacks of the wild men must be repressed. If they showed themselves in numbers, if they seemed as though bent on some mischief, "Any person may arm" to drive them away. Warrants could be issued against known offenders. Force was to be used in the capture.

Several of the prominent citizens of Tasmania came forward with the idea that the aborigines should be given grants of land before it was too late, but a Mr. Wilmot Horton, then Under Secretary, objected that there were millions of British subjects whose claims were of the same kind, and that the precedent would be inconvenient. It so happened, also, that the government were seriously considering the establishment of the Van Diemen's Land Co., and, as will be seen, big business prevailed.

But the British Government of the time not only left undefined the obligations it seemed to confess: it did more; it let loose on the shores of Tasmania its outcasts, its robbers and its murderers; it released them from their bonds and sent them forth to contest with the native for the animals of the chase, and allowed them to destroy him for sport. When a felon shot down a native he frequently acquired distinction for his butchery. The laws became silent, religion and humanity fell silent, and the fallen Black, like the uprooted forest, was considered merely an encumbrance, and removed.

So the law was vigorously enforced—but against the Blacks. While these were being shot down, or hanged, the Governor was protesting that he would "protect the aborigines of the colony from injury or annoyance", even to the "severest penalties which the law may prescribe". It seems that he was giving out one code for the White settlers and their convict servants, and another for the benefit of those that were watching him in England. This latter code certainly made pleasanter and more creditable reading in the newspapers in England, giving a favourable picture of the colony.

What colour were they? The legal fiction supposed them white; holding that they were His Majesty's subjects, amenable to law, having common right with the Europeans to all the protection that the law could afford. But, in reality, they found themselves anything but white. As nominal subjects, they could be treated as others if transgressing the statutes. It is true, they had never been consulted as to the adoption of British rule, had never been told that they were subjects of King George, and had never been taught the duties of such a position, nor warned of what they should not do. But they did understand the loss of freedom. They understood that the fairest parts of their country, abounding in game and wild fruits, were now in the possession of strangers, who drove them off as trespassers. They understood that they might take up their quarters in the stormy West, in the cloudland of rocks, in the silence of dense scrub, in any barren or inclement region, useless to the Whites. When thus robbed of natural supplies of food, they were free to pine in famine; but to touch an animal, feeding on pastures once the haunt of kangaroos, was a crime, and the only answer to crime was a hail of bullets. Except they dwelt with eagles on the very mountain tops, that are derilect even today, they were liable to come into contact and conflict with the white man.

On the outskirts of civilization are often found the rougher elements of our race. At a distance from authority, license prevails. Removed from moral agencies, because they want to be, the tendency in any case is downward, and the passions have a freer course. Borderers are seldom saints. The very absence of women, however coarse these may be, removes the last barrier to propriety among the so-called civilized. The prevalence of crime, in this outer fringe of society, is well recognized the world over.

Now this fringe was largely made up of convict servants, ex-convict hunters, and a floating population of cattle-settlers, bushrangers from Australia and run-away prisoners. It was only this flotsam and jetsam, forced from the centre of European society, with which the poor aborigines would have had direct contact; and then only if at any time compelled to retreat from the inhospitable hills and forest of the bleaker parts of the island. Could that association have ever been happy? All the Whites with whom they had contact had good weapons for the chase, and their own protection, and these could be turned against them. At best they were like so many pirates. The Government's real crime was allowing these conditions to continue.

Having, therefore, nothing to restrict them, the criminal fringe sought gratification in the native women, nearly always accompanying it with cruelty: in fact, they vied with each other to see who could be the most cruel. Mere love of sport, after they had finished with her, made them chase after their victim, enjoying the sight of the young naked females running in fear before a few shots dispatched them. They had never had such free license for their evil tendencies, and no Government put a stop to this. If this fringe of roughnecks were satisfied by their excesses on the native population then there was, of course, far less fear of their creating havoc among the civilized elements of society. If the stealing of a lubra (woman) brought her husband, father or brother on to the scene, it meant further possibilities for sport, torture and murder. Future revenge most likely fell not on the culprits but on some innocent explorer of the bush. Even today, the bush country of the whole of Australia and New Guinea can be dangerous for tribal groups still seek revenge for the past wrongs to their people. Whatever good there might have been in the aborigines was checked at the outset, owing to such ill circumstances; while all the evil was allowed full play.

Did the Tasmanians ever find that much vaunted protection, or even experience fair play from the law? With the worst class there was open war and with that went no quarter. But if incidents occurred near settlements and wrongs were done by either side, was justice meted out in due proportion? When flour was stolen by one of a tribe, was the offender treated as a subject? When a settler's convict servant was speared, was the captured murderer allowed the trial and the privileges of a subject? When witnesses were called was the evidence of the aborigines taken into account? When the dark deed was done by a white, was the evidence of the subject, if black, ever accepted? No! And is it any wonder that the creatures felt that, with such anomalies in the British law as practised in the Colonies, they were neither white nor black. In fact, as nothing seemed consistent, they did not know what to expect.

The whole of these times were, unhappily, far from merciful. Men in authority were easily annoyed and impatient with the complaints of settlers, even though the latter were exposed to the attacks of bush-rangers. They were being blamed by the Colonial Office also, for lack of discipline. Executions were common among the rather limited white population of the island. At one sitting of the judges, thirty-seven people were sentenced to the scaffold. If so little was then thought of the hanging of the Whites, would the shooting of the Blacks and the circumstances thereto, be much considered?

The white-skinned British Islander seems to have had, at least at that time, a revulsion of feeling against any coloured people. In India, any young and petty English official would speak of an educated and refined Hindu, with at least forty centuries of civilized ancestors, as a

"Nigger". When the Maoris, after they had become christianized, went to war against us, this was the report of a New Zealand newspaper:

"What are we to do with these bloodthirsty rebels? These people must be shown no mercy. They should be treated as wild beasts and hunted down, and slain. It does not matter what means are employed, so long as the work is done effectively. Head-money, blood-money, killing by contract; any of these means may be adopted."

Anyone might think, when reading this, that they were referring to a plague of rats, not other human beings. Such was the feeling of Christian Englishmen, in the early and mid-nineteenth century, towards the brown man. Well might a secretary for the Colonies exclaim in a despatch, when talking about the aborigines of Tasmania:

"With a view to the protection of the Natives, the most essential step is to correct the temper and the tone adopted towards them by the settlers."

The little mini wars continued. The right-minded citizens were shocked over these matters. But one remedy did remain for trial. The tribes, now scattered over the island, were all to be driven away from the settled districts, and forced back to the more isolated regions. A "Line of Demarcation" was decided upon. Across that they were not to come. They must remain in that cheerless western clime of everlasting drizzling rain, fog or frost; a region of vast and rugged mountains, dreary morasses, and almost lifeless solitudes; a locality impossible to develop due to the scrub growing almost horizontally, and, to the present day, avoided and hardly even explored on foot. Deserted by native fowl and quadruped, there the dark-skinned race was to dwell, banished from their summer home, their richer hunting grounds, and far from the graves of their fathers. It was indeed a "native quarter". Today it is the most desolate spot in the whole of Australasia.

All primitive nations and peoples have their boundaries. Trespassing upon a neighbouring tribe's domain, unless permitted, is an occasion for war, and always has been: this is the reason why we get distinction between tribes wherever they are. This territorialism is not entirely exclusive to mankind either, it is one of the natural laws. Even such humble creatures as the song-thrush and the robin have it too.

But the new law, the Demarcation Act, thrust all the tribes pell-mell upon each other. No distinction was made—such was the ignorance of the men in authority at the time. The preamble of the Proclamation of April 15th, 1828, indicates clearly the occasion of all the mischief:

"Whereas, and since the primary Settlement of the country, various acts of aggression and violence, and cruelty have been, from different causes, committed on the Aboriginal Inhabitants of this Island, by Subjects of His Majesty."

These wrongs are described, as well as the predatory incursions of the settlers. The Governor declares his intentions for the safety of both parties, and with the hope of inducing the aborigines to adopt habits of labour, "to regulate and restrain the intercourse between the white and the Coloured Inhabitants of this Colony". The latter were to be "expelled by force from all the therein districts", if not persuaded to retire. Military posts were to be established all along the "Line of Demarcation". However, once a year, for a brief season, the poor creatures might be allowed to procure official passports to enable them to gather shellfish (which was originally their principal food) on the eastern coast.

Trespass by the tribes was a declaration of war to the white man, yet, having no villages, the aborigines wandered about from place to place, and thus required more land.

A cause of exasperation among the aborigines was the destruction of game by the Whites. The extent to which this was carried out was enormous. The skin of a kangaroo sold for a few pence, was the perquisite of the stock-keepers, and long the chief objective of their enterprise. Their rugs and their clothing were composed of these spoils, and the pursuit did not slacken until the creatures began to get scarce. Jeffery, one of the early inhabitants of Tasmania (1810), tells us of the flocks of emu and kangaroo that were found at short intervals, and that a cart might be loaded with their flesh by the sport of a morning.

Posters were duly stuck on gum trees in the forest, giving these particulars. Yet what did these simple aborigines know of passports, of reading for that matter? Would they be ready to come and ask for it? Were they sure that the "gentle" shepherd of the plains would respect the Proclamation or the passport? How hypocritical! The British ministry urged the Governor to use no unnecessary harshness in driving back the people.

A considerable amount of the deterioration of relations between the colonists and the aborigines was due to the island becoming independent under the governorship of Governor Arthur, and, therefore, such a close watch could no longer be kept on native affairs. Further irritation was caused by the development of sheep farming in 1828 by the Van Diemen's Land Company, who required every spare acre for their sheep.

"Blacks" were forbidden to enter the sheltered districts of the colony in April 1828. Eventually they were forbidden to enter the areas under the jurisdiction of the Van Diemen's Land Company at all. Australian aborigines were obtained to assist in the capture of the Tasmanians; and one of these was Pigeon. He happened to be reclining in a tree one day, not far from the search party to which he belonged, when he was spotted by a European who shot at him, fortunately missing. Pigeon escaped to rejoin his party before the European had a chance to fire again. This story demonstrates the fate of most natives of the island that were seen at this time.

Occasionally Batman found natives in the vicinity of Ben Lomond, and the report books were full of entries like the following: "ten fell— two were taken in, another forty received the fire, left behind trails of blood but no captives". On another occasion fifteen or sixteen were seen to fall out of a party of seventy, three hundred rounds of buckshot having been poured into an encampment at night at a distance of twenty yards. It would be endless to recite conflicts of this kind, but they could be summed up as "five shot and one taken". The smoke of a fire was the signal for a black-hunt; there was little other amusement for the stockmen. Bushrangers would ask the women to climb trees and then shoot them down again.

Murders and outrages continued, for the natives were still at large. What could be done? A fresh Proclamation was issued. On November 1st, 1828, men read on the official poster that "It seems at present impossible to conciliate the several tribes of that people." Even the order for them to retire to the gameless solitudes, which had already been tried once, did not conciliate them. Therefore "martial law" was resorted to, and proclaimed against all Blacks anywhere but in those localities, namely, the scrub to the south-west, Bruni Island, Tasman's peninsula, the rocky north-west corner, and westward of the Huon River and the Western Bluff.

As Tasmania had had no proper survey in those days, it would have been impossible for the colonists to note some of these boundaries, much less the dark kangaroo hunter. The absurdity of it all was shown in a Hobart paper of the times, in the form of an imaginary dialogue between the Governor and "Tom", brought up among the Whites from childhood:

Tom: "A'nt your stock-keeper bein' a kill plenty black fellow?"

Governor: "But your countrymen kill those that never did them any harm—they even kill women and children."

Tom: "Well, a'nt that all same's white un? A'nt he kill plenty black un, a woman, and little piccaninny too?"

Governor: "But you know, Tom, I want to be friendly and kind to them, yet they would spear me if they met me."

Tom (laughing): "How he tell you make a friend along him? A'nt he all same a white un? 'Pose black un kill white fellow, a'nt you send along all your soldier, all your constable after him? You say, that black a devil kill a nurra white man; go-catch it—kill it—an't he then kill all black fellow he see, all piccaninny too? A'nt dat all same black fellow—a'nt you been a take him own kangaroo ground? How den he like?"

Tom laughed most immoderately on hearing the proclamation read, particularly at the idea of the tribes applying for passports to travel through the settled districts.

Tom: "You been a make a confragation—ha! ha! I never see dat foolish [meaning, I never saw anything so foolish]. When he see dat? He can't read; who tell him?"

Governor: "Can't you tell him, Tom?"

Tom: "No! Me like see you tell him yourself; he very soon spear me!"

Therefore it had to be admitted at last by the obtuse official mind that as Blacks could not read the posters, and no white fellow, or clothed aborigine, would risk his life in explaining the contents to the spearmen, that the demarcation was, therefore, useless.

A grand new expedient was, therefore, to be tried. All agreed that the aborigine had excellent eyes, that were quick to discern, and were also possessed of some imaginative powers. As we Europeans are so impressed by pictures, how much more would these children of the dark forest be? As it appeared that the printer failed to register, then see what sort of an impression the painter would make. What would the posters show? Somehow they needed to get across how the Governor loved his black subjects, as well as his white ones; that he longed for the Blacks and the Whites to love each other; that he would hang the murderers of the natives, as he did the slaughterers of the Europeans. Deal boards were procured, and after undergoing the operation of being coloured red, white and black—were hung in the bush at the most suitable places for the edification of the wanderers. These showed four pictures: (1) a white man shooting a black man; (2) the white man being hanged; (3) the black man spearing a white; (4) the black then being hanged also.

Copies of this "Pictorial Proclamation" were found under the floor of the old Government House in Macquaries Street, Hobart, when the building was being pulled down to make way for more modern ones.

This was not the only time that this primitive mode of communication was practised. The Surveyor-General, in 1830, sent, by the hand of a half-civilized aborigine, a sketch to show his countrymen in the bush. This poster sketch had, in one part, redcoats who were firing at the naked aborigines; in another, well clothed aborigines were receiving food from white friends. The moral is obvious, put on your clothes— you know they grow on the bushes—and all will be well. Very simple really!

A new departure next took place. All Blacks who would not keep to the bounds were to be caught and brought in, by persons who were duly authorized for that task and paid according to results. This order was issued towards the close of 1828, and it was in force for several years. A reward of five pounds was offered for the capture of an adult and two pounds for that of a child. "Capture parties", as they were called, were thus started. There were promises, also, of grants of land to successful capturers. The Governor thought by this means to put an end to the evil, and with the least cost of life.

For a time the plan seemed to work well, as the country settlers seemed to enjoy a sense of security, unknown for years. His Excellency was delighted at the agreeable prospect of peace. But all at once war broke out, more fiercely than ever. The aborigines resented the way that they were treated and, although there were now not many of them, there were enough for the slumbering anger of the tribes to awake into a series of attacks upon out-stations and solitary individuals, attacks which excited the utmost alarm throughout the country.

Colonel Arthur promptly answered the appeals for succour from his white subjects, and yet another Proclamation came forth, this time breathing fire and death, and intended for the Whites to read. The natives would not accept the conditions through which he had already bent over backwards to help them (in other words, they were not content to quietly die of cold and hunger in the sterile wilderness). Now they were using their sanctioned retreats as fortresses from which sorties were made against their inveterate foes, and retreating to them on completion of a crime. As it was so difficult to find those guilty, martial law was, therefore, decreed in every part of the island. This was aimed directly at the aborigines, except for those few known to be dwelling with Europeans. The state of martial law existed until October 24th, 1833.

So they did not take their extermination lying down: instead they fought on and tackled the Whites until very few of their numbers were left. From about 1828 onwards, very few children of pure blood were born, due chiefly to the fact that the family groups were being forced to wander more than their wont and children were simply an encumbrance at such a time.

To whatever extent provoked by past wrongs, it must be allowed that these children of the forest were no contemptible enemies: considering their scant numbers they made much impression, especially when it is remembered that their best weapons were only stakes hardened in the fire. They could muster only a few hundreds of tribesmen at the most, as against thousands of Whites who were well armed with much more efficient weapons. An example of how they would attack in the open is given by Mr. Franks, a contemporary settler. He was on horseback, driving cattle homeward: he saw eight Blacks forming a line behind him, to prevent his retreat, each with an uplifted spear and a bundle in the left hand. They then together, as if drilled, dropped on one knee, still holding the weapon in a menacing position; they rose exactly together and ran towards him in perfect order: while they distracted his attention in so doing, other Blacks gathered from all quarters. The rider was now in despair. Within thirty yards of him a savage stood: his spear seemed to only quiver momentarily in the air. This weapon, all of ten feet long, penetrated the flap of the saddle and the flesh of the horse for four inches, dropping it on its hind quarters. Luckily the spear fell, and the animal (plus rider) recovered its feet and fled. Then we hear, in the style true to the times, that there was a servant along with the master. He was less fortunate, and was found some days later just like a pincushion—dead.

I suppose that one could put in a word here for guerilla warfare as opposed to conventional warfare, for the aborigines knew their country like the backs of their hands. They made a bold stand, exchanging blows for blows. Had they been called highlanders of a European region, then their heroism would have been lauded to the skies, and in their final fall they would have received honour even from their victors. But they just happened to be naked aborigines of distant Van Diemen's Land. Their attacks were termed "outrages"; the lives taken were styled murders. The British attacks on them were called police measures, and the deaths doled out by this army were known as justifiable homicides. Infamy is, after all, attached more to the names of deeds than to the deeds themselves.

Yet the aborigines were most timid before a courageous front. A shepherd, Old Kemp, related how in 1821 he saw about three hundred of them, "poking", as he called it, after bandicoots. Alarmed at the number (by now they were going about in mobs as their hunting grounds for the kangaroo were receding), he set his dogs at them; and, upon the flight of the hunters, he cleared off hastily himself.

One of the first colonists, who later moved to Australia and who was a respectable attender of the Wesleyan Church, was convinced that the "natives" were not the aggressors. He had lived under the Western Tier (tier means a ridge) for three or four years, without molestation, though he was constantly moving about in the bush after stray stock. Frequently he had come across their recent tracks, and must have been the object of their observation, without catching sight of any, nor receiving harm from them. At last, aroused to fury, the tribe, which had probably sought as did the majority to avoid giving offence, then embarked on a rampage of atrocious and indiscriminate slaughter. The same man, missing his shepherd one day, started a search and came across his body pierced right through with several spears. His fears were also aroused for a sick shepherd, who lay in an isolated hut belonging to a Mr. Bryant. Collecting a party of neighbours, he made for the hut. When about three hundred yards away they met Mr. Bryant, running rapidly towards them with his clothes all torn. From him they learnt that the Blacks had arrived after he had come to visit his sick servant. He barricaded himself in the hut with the sick shepherd, and broke off the ends of the spears that were poked through the thin lattice work of the hut and those that were thrust at him through the window. He then made a desperate rush through the mob of warriors and had thus escaped. The rescuers went on to the hut. Not a Black was to be seen. They entered and found the shepherd in his last agonies, with wood burning under his bed, which the men had fired, along with the bark of the roof.

The way that the aborigines moved about during the war was amazing. Fifty miles a day must often have been travelled by them in the height of the war. It was during this war that the settlers noticed the lack of babies and children among the aborigines. This arose from the policy of the tribes, who, finding themselves hampered by the young on their marches, and fearing betrayal of their haunts by children's cries, had resolved upon the destruction of their families.

Mothers were even known to murder their own babies, rather than have them fall into the hands of their mortal enemies.

Mrs. Meredith records a few sad tales about the Tasmanians. In the year 1826, a man was noticed staggering about in the bush. As investigators neared the terrible object, they were shocked to perceive his battered head and speared body, his wounds swarming with maggots, though he was still able to cry. One of his eyes was knocked out and the other was knocked in from a blow. In a few words the unhappy man moaned his story. He had received a spear in his chest, while trying to get away from a mob. After some difficulty he managed to get rid of this, as the aborigines' spears were rather crude and often barbless, and he ran on again. But the mob followed and another spear pierced his back, this time breaking off short in the wound. Sickened with pain, he slowed up and the savages reached him. Several spears were thrust into him, and waddies beat heavily about his head. Blinded, he was left for dead. Reviving, he made an effort to reach some settlement, and so fell in with the party. Upon further conversation, the rescuers were horrified to hear that the attack had taken place several days before—hence the maggots. He was taken to hospital but they could do little for him, and he died soon afterwards.

A settler, Josiah Gough, lived with his wife and two daughters in a remote part of the interior. One or two things caused him to fear for the safety of his family out there, and he went off to town to get assistance in order to remove them to a safer place. He locked up well, but the aborigines came down the chimney into the hut, speared and then brained the poor woman and set to work on the children with their waddies. Taking what they desired, the murderers withdrew. The father arrived soon after, and heard the sad tale from the lips of his dying girl. We cannot be surprised that incidents like this brought fearful retaliation by the neighbours.

A farmhouse was attacked under similar circumstances in 1827, when the master had gone to a military party. The wife, daughter, two sons, a servant, and a traveller, were in the hut when the natives surrounded it. The armed inmates defended themselves with much courage and coolness. The contest continued for some time until the enraged aborigines set fire to the thatch of the roof to drive out the family, that they might be more readily and certainly destroyed. Just as this was happening, a dozen soldiers appeared through the forest and soon put the tribe to flight.

So intense was the hatred of the aborigines for the Whites that every expedient was adopted to carry out their malevolent purpose, and torments were used with an almost Indian refinement. In the early days, as the men wore only a moccasin of kangaroo skin, sharp stones and pointed burnt sticks were put by the aborigines on those paths used by the white men, so as to pierce the feet. The most abominable atrocities were carried out upon those that they killed: in particular, cutting off the testicles and placing these in the mouths of the victims. This type of treatment seems to have increased with the molesting of the aborigine females, and was also a form of retaliation for similar cruelties practised upon the males by the Whites. The few white men that were caught were usually emasculated and handed round the camp fire for each member to use his or her particular kind of torture refinement. Eventually, when the White was dying, he was handed over exclusively to the gins, who, with sharp stones and torturing hands, would work on what was left of the genitals, to add poignancy to his last agonies. Several bush hands have recorded such stories—most would be impossible to publish in any detail—but all this certainly does indicate the revulsion of feeling that the Blacks had for the Whites, and how deep-rooted was their revenge syndrome. The object of some of these outrages was clearly personal, for the victims were often known to the tribes that carried out the "operations".

A leading settler of Swanport had his home beset by the Wild East Mob. The party within the house was well armed and maintained the siege with high spirits, the house itself being also well built to resist attack. One of the besieged managed to slip away, and set off to the nearest military post, at Pitwater, fifty-four miles off. He made it, breaking records in doing so (and so great was the strain that when he had reached the town of Sorell, about half-way there, his hair had turned completely grey). Help was sent rapidly and the siege was lifted, though murders in the neighbourhood continued for a considerable time after. There was much discussion about this siege and the trouble, for people could not make out the reason for the attack. The settler was one of the few who had always been on the most friendly of terms with the aborigines. In fact, he had often employed them, and they were always well satisfied. As usual, this was set down to the "Natural Devilment of the Blacks", and from then on no means were spared to exterminate them in that part.

However, some twenty years afterwards, someone well acquainted with the facts stopped for the night at a roadside inn. He was seated in the bar, and one of the callers, under the excitement of the drink, was talking about his early days in the colony, and especially those with the black crows—as he called the aborigines. The first man took no particular interest in the narratives told, until he heard particulars of the outrage mentioned above, as well as the explanation of what had, at the time, appeared to be so unwarranted an attack.

According to the testimony of this story-teller, he had been out shooting with his father and, seeing a black fellow hiding behind a tree, he cried out to his father that he had got a capital mark for a shot. The settler reproved the wanton cruelty of his son, and told him to come along home with him. The other resolved not to be cheated out of his sport; so, watching until his parent had gone on down the trail, he took aim at the inoffensive aborigine, and dropped him dead. Of course, he never told the house the deed that he had done, and it was only two or three days after that that the attack on the premises took place. Thus it appears that the wicked action of the lad had nearly caused the destruction of all his family.

Of course, the casualness of life in those pioneering days was also a lot to blame. Most parents now would have waited until their son had got over the urge to see the "nigger" fall or run, and not gone on without him. One notices quite a lot of this casualness among the stories told in the early relationships between the Whites and the aborigines.

Many narrow escapes are recorded. A stock-rider suddenly found himself beset by a mob in the Abyssinian Marshes. Rising in his stirrups, and setting spurs to his horse, he charged among them, wielding his stock whip vigorously, and the field very soon became his.

But occasionally the aborigines found the white women too much for them. Between Banks and Spring Hill, about forty miles north of Hobart Town, was a beautifully wooded region, and living there was a settler with a moderate sized farm. When he was absent with his two farm hands the ever watchful natives descended from the nearby ridge to the farm, where the mother was alone with her two children, a boy and a girl. Being washing day, a large pot of water was hanging from the chimney hook over the fire. Immediately, on hearing the cry of "The Blacks", they all rushed into the house, but not before the little boy had received a severe spear wound in the leg. Nothing daunted, the family prepared for resistance, knowing that if they could hold out for an hour or two the father and the hands would return. The poor mother, almost nine months pregnant, seized a gun from over the mantel-piece, and fired at the attackers. Keeping a watch at the opening in the wall, she waited until her still suffering boy had charged the weapon, then again sent its contents among their attackers. This was repeated time after time, the brave little boy helping his mother regardless of the wound. Thus unexpectedly repulsed, the enemy prepared another, and more dreadful, mode of attack. Darts of lighted bark were hurled against the bark roof of the hut. This created a diversion and the attackers made a new rush at the door. But here they were met with the heroic actions of the little girl, who, bidding her mother keep to her firing, calmly and resolutely took up her own station at the fireplace, and with her pannikin steadily threw water from the pot on the blazing bark roof that the aborigines had ignited with their "wing-wangs".

Her mother, in the meantime, continued firing at the aborigines. This contest had been continuing for some hours when distant guns were heard. The enemy at once disappeared, and the family were reunited. Governor Arthur was so pleased when he heard of this heroism that he presented the woman with a grant of three hundred acres of land, and undertook for the future of the boy and girl.

Mr. Robinson, a former bricklayer and later the "Apostle of the Blacks", spoke of a party who were out kangarooing one day, and came upon a "mob" of aborigines rather suddenly. The members of the party admired the fine, tall naked chieftain who led the band, and then shot him. At this the other aborigines ran shrieking over "The Fourteen Tree Plains". In their anxiety not to be part of the sport, they dropped several children, and these were picked up by the hunters and were taken to be brought up at the Orphan School at New Town. They probably belonged to the dead chieftain.

An old carter recounted to Mr. Bonwick an incident when he was at Flat Top Tier, some twenty miles from Hobart Town. One morning the cook of the station had gone down to the nearby creek for some water, before preparing a meal for the shepherds who were expected to return soon. Aborigines who were watching speared him there. When the shepherds returned, they found their meal unprepared and the hut vacant. A short search soon found the body of the cook. Seizing their guns they set off hot-foot after the tribe that had done the deed. After a long and vain search they returned to the station to find it burnt to the ground. The aborigines could be extremely elusive when they wanted to be: there were many places difficult to search thoroughly, and European knowledge of trail-following was inadequate against the natives' bushcraft.

A party of the "Ouse Mob" burnt down the hut of a shepherd and murdered the owner. However, when they came at his little daughter, who he also had with him in his hut, she went down on her knees and sought their mercy. Their savage hearts were softened, and they left her alone.

Captain Gray of Avoca was often seen standing on the threshold of his house with a loaded musket. Men regularly took out their muskets when they worked in the fields, keeping it well within reach.

In the early days of Tasmania, it was the settlers' common custom to keep the flour in an uncovered cask in the hut. As it was a most popular commodity with the aborigines, robberies were frequent. A shirted aborigine would approach, full of smiles and friendliness, and enter "upon a jabber" with the inmate, all the time seemingly just fingering the flour, while in reality he was quietly conveying it by rapid movements up his sleeve. The trick was often detected before the flour had gone very far, if only because it was such a well-worked ploy. The popular story told over the bush fires by the shepherds concerned a certain chief who was apt to help himself indiscriminately to the flour from a barrel, when he suddenly gave a yell, and withdrew his arm minus his hand. The shrewd farmer had planted a strong steel trap, used for catching the Tasmanian Devils, in the flour, and though the flour was spoilt he had made his point to the aborigine. Years afterwards, this same chief was one of the last few of the Tasmanians who were taken to Flinders Island, and was one of the showpieces for visitors. The government officers would always ask why he kept one arm secreted under a blanket or rug, and he looked uncommonly sulky when they asked him. He never liked any allusion to the accident of former years.

Some of the incidents recorded between settlers and natives remind one much of the constant confrontations that the American colonists had with the Indians. The dense pine forests were cleared with the axe, and the gun was always there slung over the shoulder. The colonists had a village fort called a blockhouse, to which, in times of emergency, the inhabitants retreated for protection from the Indians. Every river, hill and township had its traditional tales of horrors. For a while, so close were the constant dangers, that the hope of a permanent settlement being made in some areas of the country were well nigh abandoned. There, too, as in Tasmania, the outrages of the Indians could be traced in most instances to the frauds and the cruelties practised upon members of their tribes by the unprincipled among the Whites. There too, as in Tasmania, indiscriminate attack and slaughter followed the perpetration of crime by the individual. In many of the cases a girl would be raped and killed and the distraught lover would kill the person whom he thought responsible. Then the white man's response was swift, the village would be sought out, the people found there killed and their stores destroyed. Deprived of stores, the Indians would again seek the Europeans, who could despatch the men at leisure and rape the women at their convenience before despatching them also. The children suffered longest. We know too, by the constant sight of the Indian-Negro mixture that is found in America today, how often the once proud Indians and the poor negro slaves must have been lumped together.

It was a custom of the civilized colonists to deal wide blows in return for the fault of a few. This method was used also among the rude and cannibal Fiji Islanders: the crime of one man was revenged upon the whole tribe. It was so among the New Zealanders. The same law existed among the ancient Israelites, and the English, Scots, Welsh and Irish people. Even today, in far too many instances, such as in Vietnam, the community is called upon to suffer for the misdemeanour of the few.

While the woods echoed with the discharge of musketry against the aborigines, many a cry arose from terror-sticken hut-keepers. For example, on March 13th, 1829, a Mr. Miller was returning to his homestead, which was on the east bank of the River North Esk, when he saw aborigines on his farm. He could not reach it so ran to neighbours for help, and there beheld a scene of horror. One man lay dead, twenty yards from the house, while another was found with a dislocated neck and with eleven spears in his body. Now filled with indescribable anxiety, he ran to his own dwelling, which was silent, but with the door ajar. On entering he saw his wife upon the bed, her head bashed in and her brains scattered around by waddy blows. Sugar, flour, powder and clothes had been taken away.

Two prisoner stockmen were attacked by a large mob on the York Plains, which are on the northern side of the island. For five hours, by shots and putting on a bold front, they kept the foes at bay. But when the long grass around their defensive position was fired by the aborigines, and the wind drove the smoke and the flames over them, the convicts ran for their lives, and did not obtain assistance for half an hour. These, and other convict servants, thought it a hard case that they should be exposed to continual terrors while protecting the property of their masters, to whom they were assigned at a standard only a little above the slaves. Moreover, the slightest neglect of duty meant flogging by the military who were brought in in small numbers to "look after" them, and who also played their share in "the end of the Tasmanians".

Within six years, 121 outrages by the Blacks were recorded in the central Oatlands district alone. Mr. Anstey, a provincial magistrate for the district of Oatlands in the county of Monmouth, about fifty miles from Hobart, held twenty-one inquests upon murdered people between 1827 and 1830, and in the public office for the district there were one thousand pages of manuscripts solely concerned with these inquests and the outrages committed.

Some children of the white settlers suffered also. In a valley among the ridge regions of the central interior and far from the town of Jericho, lived a farmer named Hooper, with a wife and seven children. The aborigines, for reasons not explained, lay in wait for three days near the homestead to catch the opportunity of finding Hooper away from home without his gun. They caught up with him when helpless, and he was surrounded and speared to death. The others of the tribe then proceeded to the hut and destroyed all the inmates. Another farmer, residing in "The Den", one of the most isolated parts of the island, had gone hoeing in his fields, leaving behind his wife, who had recently borne twins. Looking back he fancied that he saw the door of the house open, and then shut, too quickly. Fearing the worst he ran, but arrived too late. His family lay speared and beaten to death, killed by some half a dozen braves.

A Tasmanian woman named Walloa, a gin to a chief in the north-western part of the island, became a terrible foe of the Whites, although she had at one time been a servant to a settler in Hobart Town. Later, she was stolen by a sealer, and, while in his care on an island in the Bass Straits, had learned the use of firearms. In the end she escaped and returned to her hard-pressed tribe. Naturally a strong character, her misfortunes had made her a domineering and querulous person. She caused such unrest and discontent among her people with her frequent quarrels that they sold her to another sealer. Again escaping, she raised a band of malcontents, an easy task in those unsettled times. She led them in every kind of outrage, particularly against the solitary hut dwellers, boasting much of her "bloody work" among the "black snakes", as she termed the Whites.

A characteristic tale of this time is told by Dr. G. F. Story, of Swanport, a member of the Society of Friends in Tasmania.

"Having seen today," he writes, "one of Thomas Buxton's daughters, she has given me rather a different account of the attack by the Natives of Mayfield. The Natives encamped in the morning, on the other side of the river, and opposite to Thomas Buxton's hut, which was built of sod. Some of them came across to the hut and said that all their party were tame blacks, not wild ones, meaning that they were all peaceable. At this time the Natives had learnt to speak English (therefore they were neither tame nor wild thus having lost their fear of the paleface, yet still having their savage ways, and, as often the English had been picked up from the lowest dregs of the town society, they were to be far more feared than the children of the dark forest).

"They asked the Buxtons to come over to their camp and have a 'yarn'. After dinner two of the Buxton daughters took the cows to a marsh about a quarter of a mile distant and from there they observed that the natives were showing signs of warfare, by painting themselves. Balawinna, the head of the tribe, a tall, strong man, nearly six feet in height, was marked all over with red ochre. They ran to tell their mother, who immediately called her husband and three other men, who had gone to cut some thatch for a small stack of wheat they had just got together (their only stack, for they had been in the field only a short time). In the meantime, the natives had crawled up to the hut, and almost stripped it, taking two guns, the only ones that they thought the Buxtons possessed. The last native was leaving the hut with a loaf of bread, as Thomas Buxton entered, caught him round the neck and made him drop the loaf. The other men were speared before they could reach the hut. The natives, having taken the plunder to their camp, and thinking that there were no more guns, came up boldly again, and one of them was just about to light a branch in the fire that was just outside, probably to fire the hut. But it happened that a pistol had been put away by one of the daughters, and this having been loaded, T.B. fired at the Black who was at the fire. Then the others took their wounded man away, and tried quickly to fire the hut from a distance. But T.B., having cut 'port holes' in the walls of the hut, stationed the children and the men at the holes to watch: and when any approached, the pistol was poked out at that hole.

"When night came, the Blacks retired up the creek, and made a fire there for the night. T.B. despatched a man to Waterloo Point for help, and George Meredith, and some men came before the morning. In the morning the natives came once again; and one with a fire-stick fixed to his spear, came to the hut, and threw it on the stack of wheat. When those in the hut saw what the Blacks were doing, they rushed out with their guns. The natives, seeing the men with their guns, made off at once, and the rick was saved. At night the fire of the natives was seen up the creek, and the party going to it, killed several of the Blacks, and recovered some of the plunder."

Dr. Story relates one of his own experiences:

"We settled at Kelvedon in 1829; Francis Cotton, his family and myself, living at Waterloo Point, the military station, until a hut should be built and some land cleared. Three convicts were employed in clearing a piece of land, for the garden and the homestead, to be placed on the side of the creek. While at breakfast one morning, they observed the bullocks come running and looking fearful to the hut, as if something had frightened them; but, not thinking that it was the aborigines, took no further notice of it. [Domestic animals were generally terrified of them.] The men went as usual to their work, taking with them their guns, and placing them at the butt of a fallen tree, and began to lop off the branches as a prelude to burning the trunk. While thus engaged one of them happened to look up, and to his horror, saw the aborigines, one of them even handling the guns, approaching him, and fled. As it happened, the piece of land that they were working upon, was thickly wooded. There was a lagoon between it and the sea-beach, and a creek on the other side. On the north side the men's hut stood. Jones, in running away, received some spears in his body, which he managed to extract as he was going, and crossed the lagoon; as did also, Rogers who was accompanying him. The other man, Flack, jumped over the north creek, and escaped unhurt, though very frightened. The aborigines, not liking to cross the lagoon, had to go round it. Jones (who was the first to see them) got away by this means, but Rogers was followed by one more per-severing than the rest on the sea-beach, Rogers was keeping close to the surf, while the Black ran along the side, every now and then throwing his waddy at him. But Rogers, coming originally from London, dodged with his head the well aimed blows, and the waddy went beyond him into deep water, which had to then be retrieved by the Black, thus they went on until they reached the end of the beach, where the Black became exhausted and gave up the chase.

"Jones by this time had got some distance on the road to Waterloo Point, when he met his master coming along as usual to see how his workmen were doing; and called out to him 'Oh, Master! Make haste and get back! The Blacks are after us, and they have killed Rogers.' Francis Cotton turned around immediately, and reported it to the Commandant, and the military and the constables were immediately sent to the spot. But when they arrived at the hut, there was no trace of the Blacks to be seen. But they had stripped the hut of everything and had also taken away two Kangaroo Dogs. Incidentally one of these dogs returned after two or three days, and it had been badly wounded with spears. The other had probably been kept, as it was of a milder disposition."

It seems that all the settlers kept dogs to chase the kangaroos. This must have been very annoying to the aborigines as the kangaroo was their staple food. The two men who had been wounded were ill for some time.

> "The inhabitants were kept in constant alarm by the repeated attacks of the aborigines, which called forth the sympathies of the Lieutenant-Governor, Colonel Arthur, yet no means could be devised to rid the country of so fearful scourge."

The aborigines hated the red-coated soldiers; and no soldier when sent on escort or other duty was allowed to go alone, and never less than two were sent anywhere. For the protection of the inhabitants, several stations were formed, where two or more soldiers were placed. A soldier at one of these stations called Boomer Creek, was sitting among some young wattles peeling the twigs for a bird's cage, when the Tasmanians stole up upon him and beat him to death with their waddies.

Two sawyers were at work at their pit near Mayfield House, when the Tasmanians came upon them. However, they escaped to the house; but one was so terrified that he fell into a fever and died.* So it was not only the animals that they left terror struck, but people as well. Often, in spite of having both a physical and a mechanical superiority, the Whites were in so much fear that they could not defend themselves. The rather ferocious Tasmanian creatures, the Tasmanian "tiger", and the Tasmanian Devil, though so small, also helped instil a dread of the forests and remote places in the settlers.

A most beautiful part of Tasmania is on the banks of the Clyde. During the Black War and the 'twenties and the 'thirties of the last century a Mr. Sherwin made his home there. This was attacked by the Tasmanians, who fired the outbuildings and even the house itself. While the farm servants were busy moving the flour from the burning store, the shrewd Tasmanians set fire to a neighbouring fence. This distracted the attention of the servants, and gave the Tasmanians

---

* The reasons for the attack on the two sawyers were as follows: a group of two hundred aborigines visited Launceston and, when they were crossing Petterson's Plains, were fired on indiscriminately. They continued on their way, dragging their terribly wounded companions with them, and the first Whites that they happened to come across were the two sawyers.

easier access to the greatest object of the attack, the flour bins. But, as usual, they did not stay to really fight. They usually fired a place in order to distract the attention of the owners, often knowing beforehand the site of the flour bag.

This bold outrage upon an established household in a settled district of Tasmania excited the fears of the colonists very much, and increased the sense of insecurity which troubled every bush household. The Governor, who was more of a writer than an activist, instantly put into motion a formidable order, which appeared in *The Gazette* on February 25th, 1830. After the details of the Clyde "Outrage" had been made known, His Excellency assured his people that such outrages:

"Demand simultaneous and energetic proceeding on the part of the settlers, who, it is to be regretted, have hitherto been too indifferent to the adoption of those obvious measures of protection, which are more or less within the means of almost every individual."

The murder of Captain Thomas and his convict overseer, Mr. Parker, excited much interest in 1831. Captain Thomas was agent for the Van Diemen's Land Company's Establishment and was well known to the Port Sorell tribe of his neighbourhood.

However, they may gradually have realized what the Establishment would really mean to their way of life when they saw more and more settlers arriving, with their kangaroo-chasing dogs. As before noted, the kangaroos were to the Tasmanians what sheep were to the settlers and, in another context, what the buffalo were to the Plains Indians.*

---

* The rise of the Van Diemen's Land Company coincided with the fall in number of the aborigines. Some of the constitution of the company was remarkably insidious: for instance, it stipulated that if the people in the field employed convict labour (which was either cheap or free) there would be reductions in rent and loan interest. The company also had rights to the seashore, and for the minerals in places where no stock could be kept, and thus there were no hiding places for the aborigine to seek refuge or be at peace. The Governor of the Van Diemen's Land Company was the Lieutenant-Governor of the island, so it was in his own interest that the land be exploited to the full.

The land for the company was bought in huge blocks, and altogether they owned half a million acres (the fact that one of the blocks constituted a quarter of a million acres will give some idea of the size of the project). Kangaroos were treated as vermin, and sheep were put in their place. These the aborigines could not kill without falling foul of the stockmen, which of course they inevitably did. Large areas of land, which had contained much of the food of the aborigines (for example, ferns), were burned and cleared for sheep.

The policy of the Establishment was to open up more and more land for the settlers and their sheep, which, of course, encroached on the tribal hunting grounds of the Tasmanians.

The bodies of Captain Thomas and Mr. Parker were found about a fortnight after they had been speared to death. The jury at the inquest returned this verdict:

> "We find that Bartholomew Thomas and James Parker have been treacherously murdered by the three black natives now in custody, aided and assisted by the residue of a tribe to which they belonged, who were known by the name of the Big River Tribe, during a most friendly negotiation, while endeavouring to carry into effect the conciliatory measures recommended by the Government."

The only evidence procured was that of a native woman, who professed to have been present at the murder. It must be noted that if the Whites had murdered some of the Blacks, then the natives were never brought forward as witnesses. (A fact also unfortunately true until very recently in New Guinea, and which, perhaps, still is the case in the remoter parts of the island.)

One of the most stirring incidents in the history of the Black War is given in an official communication to the Colonial Secretary, dated August 25th, 1831, by Captain Moriarty, so well known and respected afterwards in the port of Hobart Town. It tells the circumstances of an attack on an isolated homestead, and the heroism of a half-caste woman, Dalrymple Briggs. She was so named from being born at the port of Dalrymple, and was the first of her race on the northern side of the bay, a most exclusive area. She had married a settler in the interior, and, in her contention with the Tasmanians, the blood of her own race was subordinate to her feelings as a wife and a mother. For six hours she held up a siege, and defended her position. Her castle was

---

First of all Bengal cattle were imported, then the best of the English breeds, the climate and the land being so suitable for cattle and merino sheep.

Tickets of occupation were granted to the settlers, who were able to establish large flocks and herds on the lands of the crown. In 1816, 10,000 pounds of salt meat were exported, and this figure had risen by 1820 to 386,000, as well as 47,131 bushels of corn. Both these products, and the increase in their exportation, necessitated the use of more land.

The company was formed by subscription in England and, since it was thought that there was more land than in fact existed, it was oversubscribed; and this led to overexploitation of the land that there was. The wildlife and the aborigines and the land itself suffered in consequence.

a simple slab hut; though the bark roof, fortunately for her, had been recently covered with a coat of river mud and lime to keep out the rain. The captain tells this about her siege:

"The only person in the hut when the natives arrived on the scene was this woman Dalrymple Briggs, with her two female children, who, hearing an unusual noise outside, sent the elder child to see what was the matter, and hearing her shriek went out with a musket. On reaching the door, she found that the poor child had been speared. The spear entered close up in the inner part of the thigh, and had been driven so far through as to prevent her passing back into the hut. However, her mother moved the spear so that her child could enter. She then barricaded the doors and the windows, and availed herself of every opportunity to fire at the assailants, while she drew out the spear from her child's leg. But the Tasmanians kept very close to the chimney, or to the stumps close to the hut, so it was very difficult for her to be effective, especially as she only had duck-shot. After a time though she managed to hit one of them. Their plan was evidently to pull down the chimney, and effect an entrance in this way, but they were intimidated by her stand. Finding that their first attack had failed they went off and returned in about an hour. The intervals on their part had been employed for obtaining sticks and wood, which, on their return, they kept lighting and throwing on the roof, on the windward side, with a view to burning her out. She, however, shook them off as fast as they threw them on, and maintained her position with admirable composure, till the return of Thomas Johnson, the stock-keeper, and then the Blacks retreated."

Such a sturdy defence caused much public congratulation, and this extended to the Governor.*

* In a different context there is a story told, in connection with the early American settlements, of a man whose house was attacked by Indians during his absence, and who returned only to find the ghastly remains of his wife and children amidst the smouldering embers of his hut. This more or less drove him to madness, and he vowed that he would devote the rest of his life to seeking out the tribe who had done the dastardly deed. Alone he followed the trails of the Indians. In silence he pursued the murderers of his family. Feverish with the excitement of the chase and worn out with fatigue, and often ill through exposure, he still went on and on, year after year, dealing sure but stealthy blows at any of the tribes. All attempts to divert him from his purpose were unavailing. It is true that he visited some of the settlements but this was only to obtain fresh supplies of ammunition. He said nothing of his exploits,

Though they were very primitive the Tasmanians had quite a sense of humour, and it was lucky for some of the Whites that they had. A shepherd of Jerusalem—which lies in a carboniferous region of the island—oppressed with the boredom of his occupation and the heat of the day, placed his gun against a tree and fell asleep. Some Blacks came softly round, took away his weapon, and, with a loud simultaneous shout, startled the bushman from his dreams. He jumped up in a great fright, saw the Tasmanians gathered all round, missed his gun, and leapt about in such indescribable confusion that the humorous faculties of the robbers were much excited; and so, after a hearty laugh at their intended victim, they let him leave in safety—minus his gun.

At Bagdad, another very beautiful and fertile spot, especially well known for its unusual geological features, was a farm that belonged to a Mr. Espie. One day the tribe attacked the overseer, who happened to be a man of energy and tact. Quickly closing the door, shouting loudly and firing through the window, he brought down one marauder with a shot. Then, through holes in the slab sides of the hut he continued to fire, calling out in many different voices (he was an excellent mimic) and, at the same time, letting part of his body be seen with more than one change of a coat and cap, to impress the enemy with the strength and the support to be found in the hut. This ruse succeeded and the deceived warriors departed.

One old bushman who had retired to Casterton, in Victoria, relates the following story: In 1821 the aborigines in his neighbourhood, who lived in and around the Norfolk Plains of the expatriate Norfolk Islanders, were very quiet and harmless. But, when the new overseer arrived at the station, a pretty gin was demanded. The chief, her husband, tried to stop the arrangement with the Englishman, but was brutally knocked down with the butt end of a musket, and the tribe minus the gin were driven off. "From that time," said Old George the bushman, "they became regular tigers, and speared right and left."

---

though the Border lands rang with his deeds; and the Indians whispered low, as they huddled around their fires, and the children were told of the bogey man of the White Hairs, who was sheltered by the evil spirits.

Something similar to this could be told of some in Van Diemen's Land, for so many vicious deeds were perpetuated on either side. Indeed, with the odds weighted against them, it is really a wonder that the Tasmanians lasted so long. Probably it was only the numerous forest fastnesses which enabled them to survive as long as they did. Many there were who lost relatives in native attacks, and who were less silent than the American in their search for revenge, vowing vengeance against the whole race of natives. They were unsatisfied by the slaughter once they had started and therefore continued, unrelenting, until they died.

above Alphonse, the Tasmanian, from a portrait by T. Napier; *below* two of Péron's sketches, Paraber and Ouriaga

An engraving from Péron's
Voyage of a Tasmanian mother
with her child

Young New Guinea women.
Notice the strong similarity
in appearance with the
Tasmanian mother and child
shown above

Three more early engravings of Tasmanians: *above* a typical Tasmanian man and woman; *below* the Tasmanian that Péron refers to as Bara-Ourou

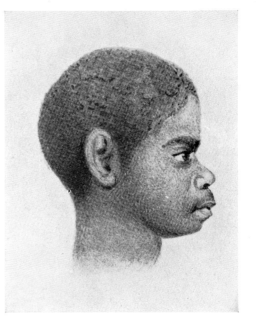

A water-colour by T. Bock of
the profile of a typical young
Tasmanian man

A water-colour by T.
Bock showing the way
in which the Tasmanian
males would coat their
long hair in ochre

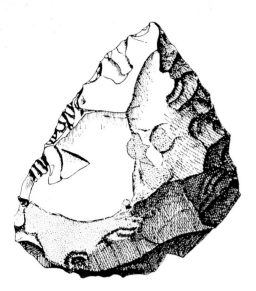

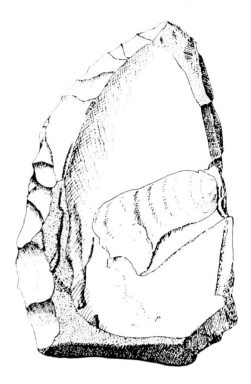

Tasmanian tools of chipped stone: *above left* one of the most primitive forms of tool, preceding the development of the handaxe; *above right* a slightly more advanced form of tool, the side scraper

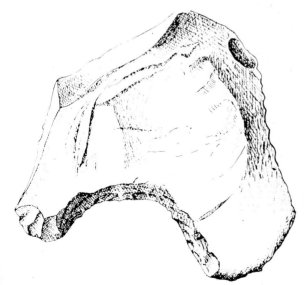

left and above two fairly simple end scrapers

Plates 11, 12, 13, 14

Captain Matthew Flinders,
R.N., the explorer after whom
Flinders Island was named

Abel Tasman, the Dutch
navigator and explorer

Portrait of Captain James Cook
holding a copy of the French edition
of *Voyage Round the World*

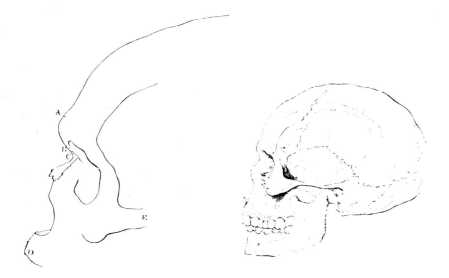

above left the profile of a Tasmanian skull. Some difference can be seen in the skull of the Tasmanian Aborigine when compared with the average Caucasian skull: *A* The Glabella is more pronounced; *B* The superior region of the orbit curves more forward; *C* The Nasion is very depressed, there being no bridge to the nose; *D* The Upper Alveolar bone in most skulls is concave but in the Tasmanian it is convex and shorter; *E* The Zygomatic arch is narrower than is found in most races. This is considered a primitive trait. *above right* a typical Tasmanian skull; *below* the skull of a female Tasmanian from the front and from the side

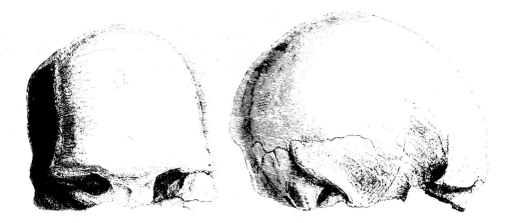

A sketch by Péron of
Tasmanian graves

left a bag for carrying water,
and *right* a basket

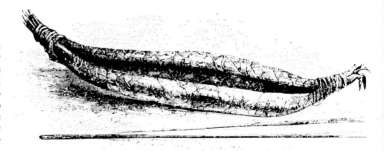

Péron's sketch of a
Tasmanian boat, used for
travelling short distances
only; the Tasmanians had
a great fear of water so
that their boats needed to
be suitable for no more
than crossing rivers or
small stretches of water

A Tasmanian crouching
behind his crudely
constructed windbreak

Plates 22, 23, 24, 25

A contemporary illustration of Robinson surrounded by Tasmanians with their dogs. Notice the long fire-hardened wooden spears, which were the most effective weapons the aborigines had

Plate 26

A portrait of Manalagana after the original by M. Duterreau

Wooreddy, who was the husband of Truganina, the last Tasmanian

Plate 27, 28

One of the last Tasmanians, Patty, here shown as she dressed in Oyster Cove for holidays

Walter George Arthur with his wife, the half-caste Mary Ann

Plunder was usually the primary object of an attack by aborigines, but many a hut was stripped by convict servants and others, and the offence blamed on the natives. Mr. John Batman related several instances of such unfounded accusations. A letter from Ben Lomond, also, said:

"The report to the *Colonial Times* respecting the natives plundering Mr. Bostock's shepherd is entirely false; and I am sorry to say, similar falsehoods are daily spread, which oftentimes leads parties astray who are in pursuit of the Blacks. Not a Black has been seen in these parts for the two months past."

It appears quite clearly that there were a fair number of people bent on making mischief: it is hardly surprising, considering that they were probably sent to Tasmania in the first place for doing just that.

An old settler in the interior told Bonwick, the contemporary writer, that once, when he was confined to his bed with a splinter in his foot, he heard the natives coo-ee, and he sent a lad to reconnoitre with the instruction to return quickly and not to call out if he caught sight of any Blacks. The lad was so terrified by what he saw that he hid himself. Johnstone, the old settler, got up, and looked out at the advancing party. Forgetting his injury under the stress of the moment, he rushed out and ran four miles to Salt Pan Plains, where a shepherd kept a flock: without his realizing, the splinter came up through his foot with the violence of his running. Another man informed Bonwick that he had only escaped through wearing an old shirt. His hut had been fired by the Tasmanians and, as he tried to escape, he was seized by the shirt sleeve. The piece gave way, and he managed to get clear.

There is a fine hill that rises from the plain at the junction of the Blackman and Macquarie rivers. It gets its name, Don's Battery, from a man called Don, who, being chased by some aborigines, reached this rampart just in time, and from its top defended himself for hours with such courage and success that he wearied the attacking mob, who left him the victor.

One of the most remarkable circumstances connected with the Black War is that, although the Tasmanian women had been so cruelly abused by the Whites, the male aborigines, though ready to inflict death by the spear, abstained from raping or inflicting other sexual excesses upon the white women. This, as we have seen, did not extend to the men, for on quite a few occasions they were emasculated.

West, a good authority, distinctly stated in his *History of Tasmania*,

4

"In all the incursions made by the Blacks into the settlements, it has never been known for a single white woman to be violated by them." The only approach to this crime was made by half-civilized natives, who were the greatest ruffians in the war. It would seem that not until they became acquainted with the practices in warfare of Western civilization, could they be guilty of the atrocities that have stained the armies of Europe. (The horrors of the Peninsular War and the Thirty Years' War were heightened by the new dimensions of the sufferings of the women, on a scale not hitherto practised.)

Spear wounds, inflicted by sharpened points of wood, were far from being so severe as wounds that could be inflicted by other kinds of weapons. Again, the spears of the Tasmanian aborigines were barbless, for they were simply stakes of hard wood whose points had been further hardened in the fire. Very rarely were these spear wounds mortal, as they seldom went in very far if thrown, rather than thrust. The "stick" could often be withdrawn without any serious consequences. Several stories are told of men left for dead, when transfixed by several spears, and then making marvellous recoveries.

Near the banks of the Isis (Tasmanian style) and within view of the snow-clad Ben Lomond, stood Ellenthorpe Hall, the ladies' boarding school of the period. It was conducted in those days by Mr. and Mrs. G. Clark. Being situated in a lonely place, about half-way between Hobart and Launceston, some alarm was expressed by the parents who lived at a distance, lest their daughters should be carried off by the wild savages. To allay their fears, a military station was set up in the neighbourhood, although there had never been an attack upon women and none had been abducted. In fact, it was a case of people only believing what they wanted to believe. Very few of these dogmatic attitudes do change with time: many men who survived forced labour on the "Burma Road", chiefly having to work in southern Thailand, have told the writer that if it had not been for the Chinese women, who every morning braved the rifle butts of the Japanese army to bring the prisoners food, they are convinced they could not have survived "The Road". Yet many of these same people still refer to "The Yellow Menace", and there has never been any form of public acclaim for the Chinese women who helped the allied soldiers so well. The insincerity of humankind towards one another is amazing.

Mr. Salmon of Jordan, near Jericho, had a series of bloody tales to tell, as that place was particularly infested in the 1820s and 1830s with thieves from a probation party several hundred strong. It was there, near Lemon's Lagoon, named after a celebrated bushranger of whom we shall hear more later, that Mrs. Gough, her child and Ann Geary were killed. The Quoin and the Lofty Table Mountain there were the favourite haunts of the Tasmanians, from which they would make their descents upon stray colonists.

A Jewish lad had formed some liaison with a gin there, and was found by the Tasmanian men and killed. When his corpse was eventually recovered, it was found to have been horribly mutilated by the jealous members of the tribe. The genitals had been thrust into the mouth of the corpse and the jaws tightly shut upon them.

It was in this neighbourhood that Mr. A. Jones became the subject of an attack, which is thus described by himself at the inquest before Mr. Anstey, P.M. (Provincial Magistrate) of Oatlands:

"In November, 1826, I was attacked by a numerous tribe of aborigines at my residence at Pleasant Place, in the parish of Rutland, in the county of Monmouth. On Thursday evening I left my wife and family at home, proceeding myself in search of some sheep, and returned about ten o'clock of the forenoon. I had scarcely entered my dwelling when my little boy came in crying that the Blacks were about; I seized my musket and went out and saw two. I pursued them; when having got halfway to the tier [ridge], I saw about twenty natives in ambush among some wattle trees. My wife was at the time standing at my door, with a loaded pistol in her hand, and called me to come down, which I did. The natives followed, even swearing at me in good English. They now extended themselves, and as the trees were at that time standing close to the house, they singly skulked behind them. I was on the alert, for I observed one man on one side, and another one on the other side, with lighted bark in their hands; the women and the children were up on the tier. I was much perplexed at this, for I was obliged constantly to run forwards and backwards. The centre of them worked down when they saw the opportunity.

"It had been a high flood the day before, and the water had scarcely left the marshes, so we were hemmed in on all sides, the river behind and the Blacks before us. Mrs. Jones had several times prevented the men from coming in the house by presenting her pistol at them, which so exasperated them, that he who was taller than the rest, and seemed to be their chief, exclaimed in a great passion, and in English, 'As for you, ma-am, as for you, ma-am, I will put you in the river, ma-am' and then he cut a number of capers. We had then with us a very courageous and faithful girl, who proposed to go up a scrubby little hill, about a mile distant, to tell the sawyers who were at work there, the dangers to which we were exposed; but we could not allow it, fearing that she would be speared; it appeared afterwards, however, that she had crawled along the fences and succeeded in getting up to the sawyers. Guessing that she had proceeded thither, in about half an hour we had coo-ed, and been speedily answered by the men. The native women on the tier gave out a signal, and the Blacks all fled. We pursued them, and I got very close to one as he stooped under the boughs of a fallen tree, and I could see no more of him. We eventually came up to a spot where there had been a fire and the remains of a kangaroo, in fact there was half a kangaroo there, it having been half-roasted. We then observed the Blacks ascending a second tier, and then we quitted a further pursuit, as it would not have been safe to have left the house and the family unprotected for such a long time. This engagement with the natives lasted four hours."

It seems that guerilla warfare, which was considered dignified in Spain, heroic against the Persians in Greece, and to be expected in the Vietnamese War, was regarded by the British in Tasmania as the blind fury of a herd of savages. Sometimes the convict servants would speak up for the natives, as in the following instance, when talking about the bold deeds of the Big River tribe:

"They fought well, I admire their pluck. They knew they were the weaker, but they felt they were the injured, and they sought revenge against many odds. They were brave fellows. I'd have done the same."

They fought so hard that one tribe, known to have possessed three hundred fighting men at the arrival of the English, was, within ten years, reduced to twenty-two.

To turn away a little from Tasmania and to make a comparison, a Dutch observer in New Amsterdam (later New York) tries to explain a colonial native difficulty thus: "In 1642, some Dutch traders, having sagaciously contrived to get an Indian drunk, robbed him of his valuable dress of beaver skins. In vengeance for this injury, the warrior's friends killed two white men." A barbarous war was the result. But some hundreds of the Red men fled to a tribe near the settlement of New Amsterdam. The Governor, Kieft, would not rest. "A band of soldiers and colonists were despatched on a horrid errand: the unsuspecting savages were surprised in their sleep, and were lined up for the slaughter one by one. The Indians living on the Huron rose to revenge this cruel treachery, and were also joined by the tribes of Long Island. A confederacy of eleven clans, numbering more than fifteen hundred warriors, was formed, and a furious war was to be found in progress wherever a Dutch settlement happened to be." A little substitution in the names could make this a record of the "Black War" of Van Diemen's Land.

The year 1831 presented appalling scenes in the colony. Outrages were still increasing. The exasperated aborigines saw no hope for their future, and seemed also resolved to die as warriors, defending their native land and at the same time doing the enemy as much harm as possible. They stopped at nothing and seemed very difficult to contain, due mainly to the rapidity of their marches. The sky was illuminated by their fires and the fires that they lit on the properties of the colonists. Spears were thrown here and there with such terrible energy as apparently to multiply their numbers very greatly, and to keep the country settlers in an ever fearful state of harassment and watchfulness. It was only about one hundred and fifty warriors that managed to keep the whole colony pinned down with fear and apprehension, a colony that otherwise would have been prospering.

This terror was well described by a colonist of the time.

"Thus they continued to menace the settlers," he wrote, "and murdering those that were found alone and unprotected so that it was altogether unsafe for a person to travel alone and without a gun, and the mind had to be made up beforehand, as to which would be the nearest house to run to in case he was beset by the Blacks. He must not fire his gun, but to keep them at bay was the best answer while the retreat was in progress. For by this time they had learnt a little about firearms and some of them had learnt to use some of the captured specimens of course. They knew that the machine they thought would go 'pop, pop, pop', would only go 'pop' once after all, and then this being over they were in a position to rush upon some unfortunate, and soon despatch him with their spears and their waddies."

Relationships between the two races had now deteriorated to the extent that every White was a guerilla warrior and every Black an assassin.

chapter 5

The Mosquito Bites

Mosquito, the desperate leader of many an outrage by the aborigines, played a prominent part in the "Black War". He was really a "foreigner", a New Hollander (Australian aborigine) rather than a Tasmanian. Although endowed with great physical prowess as well as a vigorous intellect and indomitable will, which helped him to achieve his position of power over the other aborigines, he was indebted to his acquirements in civilization for his extra ability in working mischief. He belonged to "The Broken Bay Tribe", whose territories were located north of Sydney, and while there was thrown into association with the lowest members of the convict population that surrounded his neighbourhood. From them he learnt many tricks of the trade, which were to stand him in good stead in Tasmania. The crime that brought him to the notice of the Australian Government was committed in association with another man, commonly known to the settlers as "Bulldog". These two Australian blacks waylaid a pregnant female English convict, raped and ill-used her, and finally murdered her. After the murder, they ripped open the woman's body to destroy her child. Despite the lack of European evidence, the authorities sent them to the penal settlement on Norfolk Island, where "Bulldog" subsequently died.

After Bulldog's death, Mosquito was sent to the convict island of Tasmania in 1813, where he was, according to custom, assigned as a servant to a Mr. Kimberly of Antill Ponds. Even while there, and as a convict servant, it seems he must have carried on with some of his trickery: however, he must have behaved tolerably well, or so carefully guarded his acts as to keep out of the hands of the constable. An old man named Elliot, who came to the colony from Australia in 1815, could fill in something about his previous life around Sydney. He had known Mosquito when he was in service there to a Mr. Lord. While there he had formed a liaison with Black Hannah, whom he subsequently murdered in a fit of passion.

Mr. Melville mentioned that Mosquito was employed in Tasmania to track bushrangers who were wanted by the police. He was particularly well suited for this: very tall and slim, with a wiry frame, he had exceptional acuteness of sense, even for an aborigine. These attributes, combined with a profound love of excitement and mischief, brought considerable success to his tracking activities. But as the constables with whom he associated were also men of the prisoner class, some even being ex-bushrangers, and all with a powerful sympathy for the hunted men, except in cases where capture meant a cash reward, the zeal of Mosquito soon excited their ill will, and plots were laid to get him into trouble.

He was sent down to Hobart Town in 1818, ostensibly to keep him from mischief in the up-country regions, as he was a recognized troublemaker. In the town he formally linked himself to some half-civilized, drunken aborigines who lurked around the town, and, with his superior mental ability and mischief-making skills, he soon established his authority over them. The Rev. Mr. Horton, on his visit to the colony, fell in with this so-called "tame mob", and wrote the following account for a London magazine in 1822:

"It consisted of persons (twenty or thirty of both sexes) who had absconded from their proper tribes, when the tribal system was near to breaking in the interior, and is governed by a native of Port Jackson, named Muskitoo. This man was transported from Sydney to Van Diemen's Land, some years ago, for the murder of a woman, and was for some time after his arrival employed as a stock-keeper. How he was raised to his present position, as a leader of this tribe, I know not, unless it was in consideration of his superior skill and muscular strength. This party, like the rest of their race, never work, nor have they any settled place of abode, but wander about from one part to the other, subsisting on what is given them by the benevolent, and upon kangaroos, opossums, oysters, etc., which they procure for themselves."

This man was acknowledged by the dissidents as their chief in a way not usually found among the equality-loving Tasmanians. Many of them had transgressed tribal laws in their own districts, and been obliged to live without their tribes for a while. The attractions of town life may have seduced some others from the forests.* Others, again, came from a distance to place themselves under the wily New Hollander.

It was easy for him to play the part of a ruler, dominating the others: he chose the best of the women for his wives, keeping others whose favours he used for bartering with other tribes or the Europeans. One woman, the really fine looking "Gooseberry", originally from the Oyster Bay Tribe, he kept for his exclusive use and service, but he eventually became so jealous of her that he murdered her in the Government Domain, just outside Hobart Town. Other cruelties allegedly committed by Mosquito against his women included cutting the breasts off one of his gins, because she would persist, against his orders, in keeping and suckling her child.

He hung about the neighbourhood of Hobart Town for some time, asking for bread for his people, although he often exchanged this for tobacco or rum. Receivers and exchangers were readily found at the huts of the convict servants. His manner of life is referred to by Thomas M'minn, a witness in a murder case, giving evidence before Mr. Anstey, the police magistrate for Oatlands township:

"I arrived at the colony in 1820, and was placed in the service of Captain Blythe, near Oatlands, with whom I remained until his death which was in 1823. The Blacks were very quiet when I first arrived here. Mosquito and his mob came to Mr. Blythe's hut very often. Mosquito had three wives or gins at that time. He would not allow any man to have intercourse with them. However the other gins that he had control over were allowed to prostitute themselves to white men for bread and other things. Mosquito would order a gin to retire with a white man and she obeyed his orders. This happened, I am told, very often."

According to the account of a Mr. Ward, Mosquito also kept other wives.

Often he sent the Blacks to rob and slaughter the settlers. He would lurk to gain information, lay his plans in a skilful manner and then, from his retreat, despatch his band to carry on the warfare. He knew that there was trouble between the Tasmanians and the Whites and he cashed in on it.

* Most of the attacks on settlements were by aborigines led by those who had lost fear of the white man. We find the same with the highlanders of New Guinea: it is the ex-cook boys of Mission and Government stations that often lead the cannibals.

It was among the Oyster Bay mob, of the East Coast, that Mosquito worked, and for a long period with a considerable measure of success. He and his people kept the land in a state of terror. An old settler gave many vivid impressions of his activities, one being the horrible death of a woman and her daughter at the Ouse River, and declared that the "darkies were as quiet as dogs before Mosquito came". In the words of Mr. Meredith, a settler living in the district at that time, "They spared neither age nor sex; the old woman and the helpless child alike fell victims to their ferocity." He adds: "Owing to their extremely cunning activities, and their cat-like nature, retaliation was all but impossible."

It does not appear, however, that Mosquito was a favourite with all the members of the tribe; for a number of them set on him once and nearly beat him to death with their waddies. Doubtless this arose from a little political feeling, some of the old chiefs who generally paid tribute to him resenting the assumption of his premiership as he was a foreigner,* though a good white-man hater. But he was generally considered a strong man, and this type of man is much admired by primitive people.

Mosquito was joined by Tom Birch in 1822. Tom was a young Tasmanian aborigine who had been brought up from boyhood by a Mr. Birch of Hobart Town. From the aged wife of Mr. Birch, the following information was gained. He was a good and useful lad, so obliging, gentle, honest and careful, and thoroughly devoted to his master. He spoke English correctly and could also read and write. By his attendance at church, and general behaviour, he gave promise of developing into a truly civilized person. But unfortunately he met Mosquito, who poisoned his mind against Europeans, representing them as the enemies of his race, and showed the boy the hopelessness and the aimlessness of his future. What could he ever be but a slave to the Whites? Could he ever hope to get a wife among them? Would they ever admit him to an equality with themselves? Would they not always look upon him as a "black dog", and would they not treat him accordingly? Tom was introduced to drink and the sexual excesses and orgies of the roaming tribe. His white master and mistress saw the change coming over him, and strove to counteract it, but in vain, although his regard for them was too strong to let them suffer at the hands of his vicious friends. But he could not stay in town, and so fled to the bush where he became an active accomplice of Mosquito's.

Although his chief managed to keep himself out of the law's reach by

* The Australian aborigines despised the Tasmanians as a race because of their ignorance of the womera (throwing stick).

his duplicity and unscrupulous sacrifice of his colleagues, Tom Birch
was soon captured. His old employer wielded enough influence to
preserve his life from the demands of the law and, instead, he was
sentenced to go to the dreadful convict settlement at Macquarie
Harbour. He was not long there before escaping, and he joined up with
the Abyssinian mob, beyond the Ouse River. This gang was engaged
in the "Black War", and it was while he was with them that Tom
Birch was involved in several robberies and murders committed near
the Shannon.

His European friends in Hobart Town heard of his whereabouts, and
determined, if possible, to find him and bring him back to civilization.
They sent a representation to the Governor, pointing out the desira-
bility of obtaining the help of so intelligent a native for his plan of
conciliation, and overtures were made to the outlaw. Tom Birch
accepted the terms, and from then on was attached to one or other of
the roving parties, proving himself a valuable friend to both the
contending races. But a life of exposure in the bush proved fatal to him
at last, and he died of dysentery at Emu Bay, in 1832.

Another henchman of Mosquito's was Black Jack, who subsequently
came to trial with him. He was very different to Tom Birch, although
also able to read and write a little. Before taking to the bush, he was
often heard to exclaim, "I'll kill all the White Bastards." Another
favourite expression, while torturing some white victim was, "Jack's
going to touch him there again, as he don't like it", and that "touch"
was the torture that eventually killed.

A rough justice finally caught up with Mosquito's mob as a result of
a murder committed near the East Coast on November 15th, 1823.
Mr. Meredith, who was living near the scene of the crime, recorded the
event. It appears that Mosquito came to Grindstone Bay with some of
the Oyster Bay tribe. They were seen on the ranch belonging to Mr.
Silas Gatehouse, but when questioned by Radford, a stock-keeper,
they said that they were there to hunt kangaroo. The stock-keeper,
however, saw Mosquito about to seize some fine kangaroo dogs and
called out, "Don't take our dogs away." The response was a spear from
Black Jack that wounded him in the side. The mob rushed to the hut
killing Mammoa, a Tahitan native, and William Holyoake, a convict
stock-keeper, who were inside. Radford ran wounded, in bare feet,
chased for three miles by members of the mob.

Another version of this story was told by an "Old Hand" at
Warrnambool, who claimed to have been with Radford on that
occasion. He was an old man when he recorded the story, and had left

Tasmania with the Batman family in 1835, but for several years before leaving had been one of the "hands" at the Ben Lomond home, and had a good reputation. There were probably many good reasons why some of the things he spoke of were not mentioned earlier.

The beginning of his story is much the same as the others. Radford and he happened to leave the hut one morning without their guns, contrary to their usual custom, as it was raining. When the Blacks appeared the two men could not get back to the hut, and so had to make a run for it. During his flight he received two spear wounds, one being in his thigh. He informed his master, who is said to have sworn not to rest two nights in his bed until he had taken revenge upon the attackers. Collecting a party of thirty, including constables, soldiers and neighbours, he set off to execute his threat. One, Douglas Evans, a Sydney aborigine, was met along the road and from his information they learned that a large body of aborigines had camped for the night in the gully by Sally Peak, six miles from Bushy Plains, on the borders of Prosser's Plains.

They proceeded stealthily as they neared the spot; and, agreeing upon a signal, moved quietly in pairs until they had surrounded the sleepers. Hearing the whistle of their leader, volley after volley was poured in upon the dark huddles of the sleepers around their little camp fires. (This method of attack was almost always perfectly safe for the well-armed Whites.) Few of the Blacks escaped, and many of the children were left crawling about wounded. Typical of this and similar incidents, a sergeant seized hold of a small boy, who, though wounded, was attempting to rush by him in the darkness; the man exclaimed, showing the others what he had caught, "You little bastard, if you ain't mischievous now, you will be," and proceeded to swing him round and dash his brains out against a convenient tree. Women were also lying about gasping in their death agonies with their babies still trying to suckle. Such was the story given by the old man.

The extraordinary cunning of Mosquito enabled him to elude several snares for his capture, but he met his match eventually, through the courage of Tegg (another half-civilized native). Tegg was a young lad, and although he had been brought up by Europeans he was known to have communications with Mosquito. His help was sought in an attempt to catch the cause of so much terror. He agreed to attempt the capture, if provided with the company of constables, and was promised a boat if he should succeed in the venture. (His ambition was to own a boat and trade between Bruni Island and Hobart Town.) Day by day he sought the retreat of Mosquito, who had now separated from his gang because of the hot pursuit, and was in hiding with two of his gins near Oyster Bay. Two constables, Godfrey and Marshall, were with Tegg when they came upon his lair. Sending the Europeans to secure the women, this youth of only seventeen ran towards Mosquito and shot him in the thigh. Amazingly enough, Mosquito was not armed at this time—generally he had at least two spears with him—and had to run as best he could for his life, pursued by the young aborigine, who fired the second barrel at him. Brought to bay by loss of blood, Mosquito leaned against a tree and, filled with impotent rage, kept roaring and throwing sticks at the advancing youth. The others came up, and he was taken down to Hobart Town, where, for a while, it was touch and go whether he would survive. The problems faced by the settled inhabitants of Tasmania in administering justice and trying to keep law and order were immense and must be borne in mind. They had to put up with the excesses of not only the convicts that had been sent there from England, but also the black ones sent from Australia and the South Pacific. Then there were the escaped convicts who lived in the bush while on the run, besides the native mobs. Under such circumstances it would be very hard to pin down a murder or outrage unless there were actual eye-witnesses of the event, which was otherwise attributed to whatever group bias and prejudice dictated.

Mosquito and Black Jack were tried for the murder on November 15th, 1823, of William Holyoake at Grindstone Bay, and were committed in December, 1824. Mosquito was found guilty of the charge but Black Jack was acquitted. Although Black Jack was found innocent of this crime he was convicted of the murder of Patrick Macarthy, a hutkeeper on Sorell Plains. He implored the judge to send him to the penal hell of Macquarie Harbour, instead of hanging him (discreetly saying to a friend, "Then I'll soon run away and be back with you"). His Honour apparently shared this private view and declined to grant the favour.

The inhabitants of Hobart Town had the satisfaction of seeing Mosquito and his lieutenant, Black Jack, "tucked up comfortably" as they termed it. They were hanged in company with five bushrangers at what was then called Mr. Mustermaster Mason's Place, on February 25th, 1825.

The execution was, of course, public. Before it the chaplain, the Reverend W. Bedford, forcefully addressed the multitudes of curious spectators forgathered there:

"These poor unhappy fellow worms, whose lives have become

forfeited to the laws of violated justice and humanity, implore you to shun the path that leads to death."

All the officers who were there thought that they had to show some form of expression, even if there was, as appears to us now, a colouring of hypocrisy about it. Several of the condemned men joined in the singing of their own funeral dirge, but Mosquito preserved a sullen silence, despite all the exhortations of the clergyman.

Black Jack, however, was more aware and much alarmed. He seemed to realize that his life was soon to be forcibly taken from him by fellow human beings. The "Old Hands" who saw it all were fond of telling the story that, upon the clergyman exhorting Jack to pray, he exclaimed, "You pray yourself; I too frightened to pray, I know what going to happen." Upon this, to quote from a newspaper's report of the proceedings, "the hapless offenders, after a short interval, were launched into eternity".

Without a doubt the execution of Mosquito, who exerted such an influence upon the simple tribes, had important results. Many aborigines came into town to implore the pardon of this man; and, upon the failure of their efforts, and seeing the procedure of justice, returned to the bush with much more bitter feelings against the dominant white race than ever before.

Mr. Gilbert Robertson observed in 1831:

"Although Mosquito has been removed, yet the lesson he afforded the aborigines of this island has not been forgotten by them; experience has taught them craft, cunning, activity and watchfulness, and at this moment they have found the means to spread terror among the Colonists residing in the interior."

The "Black War" is, indeed, dated by some people from the death of Mosquito.

The captor of Mosquito, Tegg, did not get his longed-for boat. In sullen anger he took off to the bush but before going he is quoted as saying: "They promised me a boat, but they no give it; me go with 'Wild Mob' and kill all white men come near me", and, in fact, many murders were attributed to him. He was, for instance, concerned in the murder of two convict stockmen belonging to Messrs. Cox and Barclay. It has also been recorded that an aborigine woman, brought up from infancy by the Whites, and far advanced in pregnancy, was speared to death by this revengeful fellow. Strange to say, he eventually returned to Hobart Town, and received his boat, which was, said a newspaper "to placate the youth's unfortunately aggravated feelings"!

There seems to be a kind of casualness in dealings with some of the criminals which is hard to understand these days. Again, it seems we have another instance of unnatural crimes being committed by the half-civilized, or the half-tamed, so similar to what also occurs with half-tamed animals. Finally it is worth noting that, although a chosen few of the Tasmanian aborigines were taught proper English and mastered the language, most were taught pidgin and otherwise patronized or ignored.

chapter 6

The Line

The Line, the most formidable part of the "Black War", was formed towards the close of 1830. It was not like the Thin Red Line of the Crimean War, but a cordon of a more unequal character, intended to drive the aborigines into the inhospitable region of Tasmania already mentioned.

History is not without the parallels of a line operation. A Line of similar purpose was made during Macquarie's governorship of Australia. The natives of New South Wales had been very troublesome, interfering with the development of sheep farming and the necessary extermination of kangaroos from certain areas and it had to be stopped. In 1816 General Macquarie summoned the colonists together and, with the help of all available soldiers and constables, rode again against the common enemy, driving them even beyond the Blue Mountains. It goes without saying that many were killed. This great "victory" may have commended a similar operation to the authorities of Van Diemen's Land, and the method eventually was adopted there, though naturally on a smaller scale. A remarkably hopeful government paper had appeared in August, 1830, urging the colonists not to hurt those of the natives who were well disposed, but rather to give them a dinner, with smiles, and then to let them depart with a blessing. Loud complaints from his people induced Colonel Arthur to qualify this statement.

While probably not intending to ape the policies towards the Blacks of General Macquarie, he had to consider the development of the country. The result was Government Order 166, issued on August 27th, 1830, which stated that while no measure of conciliation was to be spared, it was not intended that the people should "relax the most strenuous exertions to repel and drive from the settled country those Natives, who seize every occasion to perpetrate murders, and to plunder and destroy the property of the inhabitants".

But the colonists' unrest continued and Colonel Arthur was forced to take more positive action. After much discussion it was decided that the roving parties were insufficient to protect the settlers and must be replaced: these roving parties, commonly known as "five pound catchers", received, as their nickname suggests, a five-pound reward for every native they caught.* As the natives were by now keeping fairly clear of the colonized areas, the ill-organized raiding parties had little effect. So it was decided that a more thorough and better organized drive against them must be made. Never, in these discussions, was mention made of the inevitable and intended destruction of native lives.

It was proposed to station the military in certain centres of the settled districts, and to call upon the people who lived there to volunteer their help, placing themselves under the commander of whichever military party they preferred. A charge was to be made simultaneously from these various centres, upon October 7th: "one great and engrossing pursuit", it was termed. No special rewards were offered, though there was the thrill of the chase, and the Government did hint at special land grants for zealous participants.

Although not intended as a Line proceeding, this act was the forerunner of that military movement. It also has an all too familiar ring about it—rewards of land being given to those who are successful in the eradication of families ("nests of pests") from an area it was theirs to colonize. William the Conqueror had a similar policy against the Welsh.

Not much care was bestowed, therefore, on the natives that were encountered on these expeditions, few were captured because there was little that could be done with them and, according to the general consensus of opinion, they were both idle and ugly.

The Government Order calling for volunteers was issued from the Colonial Secretary's Office, September 9th, 1830. This, like other

---

* Five pounds was paid for every adult aborigine and two pounds for every child brought in alive. The Lieutenant-Governor asked in a letter to London (on April 15th, 1830) for all transports of English convicts (2,000 being the figure mentioned) to be of useful classes (not Irish) in order to distribute them among the settlers of the interior for protection. He mentioned that there were now only about four hundred natives left.

orders of the period, gives the several stations to be occupied by these volunteers. The colonists were immensely pleased with the Order. The *Hobart Town Courier* of September 11th already saw, "by anticipation, crowds of these poor benighted creatures marched into town". The editor sagely recommends the volunteers and the military to seize upon the women and the children first, as the men would then surrender themselves.

However, it was at the same time admitted that at least thirty aborigines who had been previously caught by the five-pound catchers, and even initiated into English customs, had returned to the bush and their own countrymen, becoming ringleaders in the attacks on the settlers, so giving a new twist to the old adage that a little knowledge is a dangerous thing.

Before the invitations to volunteers could be issued by Colonel Arthur, the Governor, a change in the arrangements occurred. There was considerable criticism due to the number of meetings and conferences taking place up and down the country. It was contended that it would be comparatively useless to have the war made at so many points, affording opportunities for the natives with their superior bushcraft to pass between the forces when and where they wished. It would appear from this that the Whites had not very much confidence, fearing the natives would continue to keep the colony in constant terror. However, the inhabitants were anxious to co-operate with their rulers in any project offering relief, for they saw that they would have really valuable holdings were it not for the "scourge" of the natives.

A public meeting took place on September 22nd in the Court of the Request's Room, ostensibly to make arrangements for the formation of a Town Guard. The chairman of the court was Joseph Hone. Anthony Fenn Kemp, one of the earliest officers in the colony, gave the audience some particulars of the first attack, at Risdon in 1804. Mr. Gellibrand, the attorney, admonished the colonists not to shoot any fleeing aborigines. A Mr. Hackett doubted the ability of the dark race to know the wishes of the Government, as not five people could speak their language, and it would be very difficult to have a peaceful agreement with them.

However, in spite of the preambles, it passed some resolutions. The first of these declared it to be the duty of every man cheerfully to contribute to the common cause every assistance in his power. The second suggested the means; that of personal service in the field, or performing the duties of the military during the absence of the latter from the town. The third pledged the meeting to five weeks' service in the capital, dated from October 2nd. The fourth urged the council of the inhabitants to select their own particular scene of duty, and the election of their officers. The last of the resolutions concerned the nomination of fifteen people to form a committee, six of whom were to wait on the Governor. Two dozen gentlemen also volunteered to take the battery guard, if independent of this general committee.

Opinion was not entirely united. Mr. Gregson, a barrister and an orator, had been opposed to the Government on political grounds, and took legal exception to their mode of procedure, contending that such a warlike demonstration was entirely uncalled for, and that the natives, who were after all the original Tasmanians, ought not to be forced from the territory bequeathed to them by their forefathers and now usurped by the British Crown. He would not, therefore, go himself or even permit any one of his servants, "To follow to the field some war-like Lord." His opponents professed to be surprised that a gentleman owning such dignified, moral and correct sentiments, should continue to hold an estate as fine as his, upon a title granted by public robbers of a nation, and urged him to leave a land desecrated by such violation of the rights of man and the honour of civilization.

Even at this time, 1830, there were not many of the Tasmanian aborigines left, according to government reports, and they were it seemed already doomed. Perpetually on the move, they had few children, fearing that these would hamper them in their long, cross-country treks, or fall into the hands of the colonists. The few pure-bred children born were certainly insufficient to keep the population steady, let alone increase it, a fact of which the Whites seemed quite unaware.

The Governor felt himself strengthened by the moral support of his subjects and, therefore, modified and expanded his original views. Instead of a number of separate and unsupported, though simultaneous, operations over the whole of the island it was resolved to make one grand, united effort to capture the Oyster Bay and Big River tribes, by drawing a line from Waterloo Point on the east to Lake Echo on the west, thus driving the Blacks into Tasman's Peninsula, at the south-east corner of the island.

The Survey Department was sorely tried on this occasion, as everything depended upon knowledge of the country, which the department simply did not have, and there lay the weakness of the scheme. It was years before a trigonometrical survey of the country was carried out. Men took up land before it had been surveyed, and adjustment of acreage between neighbours was an established source of contention. Even prominent points or physical features were incorrectly laid down.

So the leaders of the parties were each provided with a copy of the little map published by a Dr. Ross, who was editor of the *Courier*. With this they were expected to guide their march. The Government Order then described the routes as well as they could be indicated. The objective was to drive the natives from other parts into the area that made up the county of Buckingham, then forming the settled southern side of the island, and through that to the East Bay neck of Forestier's Peninsula, a narrow neck of land, rather flat and only a few hundred yards in width. It united the mainland with the Peninsula of Forestier, so called by Commodore Baudin after the French Minister of Marine, and connected with Tasman's Peninsula by Eagle-Hawk Neck, a smaller isthmus than the other. At this time (1830) Tasman's Peninsula was occupied by convict penal stations. To prevent runaways getting to Forestier's Peninsula, and so on to the mainland, fierce dogs were chained across Eagle-Hawk Neck, in addition to the guard of soldiers. Though the top is flat, the immediate neighbourhood of East Bay Neck is high land and scrubby miserable country at that.

The Government Order expressed a desire for the magistrates to organize the force in parties of ten, with a leader and a guide. The military commanders were to be accompanied by some of the roving parties who had already had a few years' experience hunting the Blacks, and who were, therefore, judged valuable auxiliaries to the movement. The ticket-of-leave men, as occupying the first of the social steps towards freedom, were to be treated with more distinction than the ordinary convicts, who would be in the field as assigned servants of patriotic settlers; magistrates were to give each prisoner a written pass with his division described, and exercise discretion about entrusting some with firearms. Fires were to be kept burning on certain hills as marks to steer by.

The change of policy, which astonished many, was approved by most. The idea of the Line was a source of merriment to those who were political enemies of the Government. The *Launceston Advertiser* was delighted to have the opportunity of attacking the authorities by a hit at the editor of the semi-official newspaper, the *Hobart Town Courier*, that had just then, by arrangement, announced the plan that should be adopted, and which was put into practice a day or two afterwards by the Government.

The *Advertiser* of September 27th said:

"While we give to the kind hearted, and worthy, but invisible editor of the *Courier* every credit for his advice of a cordon to catch the Blacks, and then to place them on Tasman's Peninsula, we must just say that it is one of those visionary schemes, to be wished for, but not practicable. It reads thus: 'Let a cordon be drawn across the island early in the morning, and before nightfall, drive all the Blacks in that division up in one corner; and mind, men, do not shoot or hurt one, but catch them all alive! And be very careful you don't hurt them, and if they should attempt to run away from you, tell them to stop, or you will certainly shoot!,' and the bare words will arrest them in flight, only you must first learn them the language in which it is spoken. It is little better than idiocy to talk of surrounding and catching a group of active, nimble-minded, naked men and women, divested of all burdens of all sorts . . .''

The *Sydney Australian* of October had the following article upon that month's intended movements in the southern isle:

"We call the present warfare against a handful of poor, naked despicable savages, a humbug in every sense of the word. Every man in the isle is in motion, from the Governor down to the meanest convict. The mercer dons his helmet, and deserts his counter, to measure the dimensions of the butcher's beef. . . . The farmer's scythe and reaping hook are transmuted to the coat of mail and bayonet! The blacksmith, from forging shoes for the settler's nag, now forges the chains to enslave, and whets the instruments of death. These are against savages whose territory in point of fact this very armed host has usurped. Savages who have been straitened in their means of subsistence by that very usurpation. Savages who knew not language, nor the mediations of their foes, save from the indiscriminate slaughter of their own people."

The important public announcement of proceedings connected with the Line operations was issued on September 25th, 1830. The text ran thus:

"The community being called to act en masse on October 7th next, for the purpose of capturing those hostile tribes of natives, which are daily committing renewed atrocities upon the settlers, and the Whites generally wherever found."

The Oyster Bay and the Big River tribes at least were to be captured. Major Douglas was to have his chain of posts from the East Coast by

St. Patrick's Head, across to Campbell Town, and thence to the Lake River, aided by Major Grey, Mr. Batman and others. Each party of ten was to have a leader. Parts of the 63rd, 57th and 17th Regiments, besides a host of constables, were to be reinforced by the whole body of male settlers. Particular directions were given to the several parties as to their duties, and the localities they should occupy on specified days.

Mr. Austen, the very active magistrate of Oatlands, had a powerful force of volunteers and their assigned servants. Captain Donaldson was to hasten from the Norfolk Plains towards Lake Arthur and Great Lake, nearly four thousand feet above sea level, to arrest any escape of aborigines to the western mountains. Captain Wentworth must take the Shannon, Ouse and Clyde country, west central. All were to march onward in successive stages. The daily ration to each person, given in weekly amounts, was 3 oz. of sugar, ½ oz. of tea, 2 lb. of flour, and 1½ lb. of meat.

The object of these exercises as stated in the proclamation was

"to capture and raise them [the aborigines] in the scale of civilization, by placing them under the immediate control of a competent establishment, from whence they will not have it in their power to escape and therefore to molest the white inhabitants of the country".

There were 119 leaders of parties, with a guide to each. In addition to the array of soldiers called in to do the work, there were hundreds of constabulary, and 738 convicts assigned as servants to the Line. In addition, a considerable number of free labouring men ranged themselves in the parties. There were ticket-of-leave convicts also. All these, together, made up an army of about three thousand men on the Line operation. Also in the parties were a number of Tasmanian-born white youths, who took an active part in the skirmishes.

The commissariat were efficiently managed by General Browne. Drays and pack-horses were used for the carrying of provisions, and firm orders were issued that none were to leave the Line for rations. Boots were in great demand: although due notice had been given for each man to bring a couple of pairs with him, the sharp rocks played havoc with the leather. Thus Captain Mahon wrote to Major Douglas who was back at the base:

"I have worn out two new pairs of strong boots since I left Oatlands, and in a few more days I fear, I shall be as naked as the Blacks."

Trousers and jackets were also in heavy demand. A note from the Governor to the Colonial Secretary states:

"The men employed in the roving parties I find almost destitute of clothing, from their having been employed almost incessantly in scouring the scrub, which is full of sharp thorned bushes."

The thorn bushes were also often covered with ants. This note accompanied a request for 140 pairs of trousers, 50 jackets and 90 pairs of boots. There was much complaint in the ranks and, in order to keep the men contented, an allowance of a quarter pound of tobacco a week and half an ounce of soap a day was issued. The diet was not exactly a healthy one, and it indicates the dearth of knowledge there was then of the way that diet affected the well-being of people. Little green food and fruit appears to have been consumed.

Due provision was made, of course, for war materials. In addition to the weapons that every man carried, a central depot was set up at Oatlands, containing a thousand muskets and thirty thousand rounds of cartridge, and three hundred pairs of handcuffs, the last more than enough for every aboriginal man, woman, child and baby. This is surely a suitable instance of a sledge hammer being used on the mosquito. These supplies give us every indication that the mission was not intended to "bring them back alive".

It was a very anxious time for the Governor. He had only just succeeded, after years of trouble, in putting down the numerous white "gentlemen of the road", that had freely roamed wherever they liked throughout the island. These used to wander across the country in bands somewhat similar to the Viking raids of old. Now, in calling out so large a number of the able-bodied men of the colony, he could not but feel concerned for life and property in the colony; for, in reality, the island was one large penal settlement. Many of those in custody had had a double conviction and were real died-in-the-wool criminals, requiring close supervision. These and others would be only too ready to begin again their predatory and criminal activities in the general confusion of the times. Yet another anxiety for him was the arming of the assigned servants, who would be permitted to roam the bush, without adequate overseers or guards. Many believed that such men would see this as a favourable opportunity, when the people concerned with law and order in the land had their hands full, to rise in rebellion and then establish, as had more than once been threatened, an island home for the prisoner class where, emancipating themselves and ejecting the free, they would make all haste to set up an independent government of their own. A more probable difficulty lay in the engagement of convicts, who were in those days "dead" in the sight of the law, as guardians of the public peace, for nearly all the constabulary belonged to this class of society.

One who was a bondman thus referred to the condition of such parties:

"The Government had placed them in a situation different from that which the law had directed; they had acted as free men; and when once permitted to do so, could the law, or for that matter any known power, compel them to return to their former servitude?"

But the newspaper the *Tasmanian Review* was delighted to acknowledge that

"fifteen hundred men of THAT class are now with arms in their hands, anxiously desirous of showing, that they are trustworthy on all occasions".*

When all was in the process of being prepared, the Governor, Colonel Arthur, thought it good and proper that the blessing of Heaven should be poured upon the expedition. Prayers were ordered in all the churches for the success of the hunters on the Sunday before they started out. While entreating the Divine favour on behalf of an enterprise which would, if successful, be attended with the bloodshed of the aborigines, an urgent request was offered for their speedy conversion to Christianity. This was held to be slightly inconsistent with the principles of the New Testament, though admitted to be agreeable to the practices of numerous Christian governments. It thus was not so unlike the conduct of the warlike Bishop of Norwich, who, after making Wat Tyler's rebels kneel and confess their sins, very episcopally gave them absolution and afterwards, very baronially, ordered their throats to be cut.

Several parties were at length got under way. That which gained the most applause was the Launceston Corps under the command of Captain Donaldson. Nearly three hundred and fifty men were led forward in a good fighting condition and fully supplied with guns and

* Many of these men were the offscourings of Cockatoo Island, the worst penal settlement in Australia. When the authorities couldn't do any more with them they were sent to Tasmania.

ammunition. A public notice praised Captain Donaldson's party, which had indeed faced awful conditions, although little different to those that the aborigines endured nearly every night. Donaldson's party of eighteen went from near Deloraine to the top of a bluff some four thousand feet high. Torn by the scrub, hungry and wet, they had to pass a night without tents, exposed to rain, wind and cold on that bleak mountain, huddled around the fire, or stowed away in the hollows of trees. Several of the party wanted to go home, their sense of discomfort overcoming their love of adventure and their devotion to duty.

Every care was taken by Colonel Arthur to keep his forces in order. Minute regulations were issued nearly every day. Copies of the General Orders were sent to the different commanders, who had to put their signatures to the official document as evidence that they had seen it. So active was the pen of the Governor that some amusement was occasioned by the frequency of the missives, and their occasional contradictions.

It seems incredible that such a force could have ever been formed, let alone put into the field, particularly when bearing in mind that Tasmania was only a remote colony and rather a small island at that. Yet, somehow, it had managed to get into the field a force that was larger than some that had conquered vast territories. One cannot help but be reminded of the grand old Duke of York marching all his forces up the hill and then down again.

All this effort was expended on a handful of poor miserable naked and nomadic aborigines. These, if the settlers had allowed themselves the slightest pause for observation, would have been seen to be decreasing rather than increasing in number, due to the dangerously low birth-rate caused by the constant harassment by the Whites. (In the end, 1869, of the seven surviving representatives of the Tasmanian race, the six old women had been born before the colonization of the island began in earnest and the seventh, a young man, had been brought up by a white family. The old women, too, had been protected by the Whites as they had either lived near the centre of the town or been brought up by Europeans. The truly wild forest aborigines were gone.) Future settlers would be untroubled by any descendants of the fifteen thousand men and women who formed the population when the first colonists arrived at Van Diemen's Land.

The array of most of the able-bodied male Whites in Tasmania was now ready to meet the foe, come what may. But where was the foe? With a few thousand men beating the bush and scouring the tiers, to what possible retreat could they fly? To use a common Australian expression, "they had them sewn up". A tribe of forty, seen westward of the Norfolk Plains, were chased by one of the Line parties, until they crossed the Shannon and were lost in the labyrinths of the scrub. The baffled Whites left a notice of the incident on a piece of bark, nailed to a tree, which was found years later. Among the spoils collected from the fugitives were a chemise and a little child's frock. For all the understanding that the aborigines had of the affair, they may have thought that these were the very things the Whites were after!

Jorgen Jorgensen saw some of them, however, when he was travelling alone in the bush, as he records in the following letter:

> "As I went this morning over the Brown Mountain, on rising a steep hill from a very deep gully, my horse began to rear and snort. Everything was thrown off, saddle and all. My trousers were literally torn to pieces; and, just as I had got the horse quieted, there stood over me three Blacks."

Some men might have been frightened at this, even if they were not alone. But the Dane goes on to inform us that he had but to draw his cutlass and the warriors of the woods melted back into the surrounding woods. It is interesting that his horse was disturbed, because there are frequent mentions of horses and cattle becoming very nervous when aborigines were in the vicinity.

Rumours about the aborigines were circulated with celerity. The natives were, according to the stories, invested with every facility and cunning. The great eagerness of the Governor for new plans and ideas, and the desire of the commanders to humour him, were very much played upon, and therein lay the origin of some remarkable and not always reliable stories.

The following is a typical example: One dark night, some sentries heard the rush of many footsteps in the scrub, but were unable to see any human figures. The noise was repeated several times, and the fire-sticks of the warriors were seen in the gloom. As a man lay down his musket, the easier to pick up firewood, he received a spear in his leg. He seized a fire-stick and threw it at the enemy. As he did so, another spear pierced his shoulder and, forgetting his musket, he shouted lustily for help. The approach of the other sentries scattered the half-dozen aborigines.

A small force of Europeans could easily have penetrated the ill-regulated Line, let alone the forest braves. Two or three instances of the aborigines having got by the sentries came out after the completion of the Line movement, and there were probably more unknown instances. The men could not possibly keep to their posts along the Line all the time, day and night. Many were too frightened to do so, especially in the dark and stormy nights. Company and a smoke with a companion made the arduous call of duty so very much more bearable, with the result that distances between men were not always observed, even when practicable, and large gaps were left.

The Government Orders became more and more precise about preserving the correct distance between each man. On October 17th, the colonel again urged attention to this regulation. He then contradicted everything by requesting them to camp in parties of three at night, with a fire between the separate gatherings. When the contradiction was pointed out, the sentries were ordered to walk to and fro from the fire, but to make sure they did not meet each other. In some of the better regulated parties, after they had proceeded through the bush and were getting ready to camp for the night, they would halt for all to come up, and cry one, two, three, four, etc., to see if any were adrift.

So little faith had a Mr. Broadribb in the security of the Line that he offered to convey a letter for Colonel Arthur through any part of the Line, without meeting an individual; and, to the Governor's vexation, he accomplished the feat. A settler chased one aborigine by moonlight, but missed him through tripping over some dead timber. Despairing of seeing him again, he carelessly turned to go back, when one of the supposed charred branches was slowly lowered before his astonished eyes, and a black body rapidly rolled off into the thicket. However, the Line must have made many difficulties for such nomadic people as the Tasmanian aborigines, who had to look for food some time.

The best story of the Line concerns a Mr. Walpole, who had the merit of being the only person of the three thousand wanting to make a capture rather than a killing, but it was attempted at the cost of ruining the whole affair, at least as it seemed in the eyes of the Governor. Mr. Walpole himself gives the account of what he did in a letter dated October 29th, 1830.

"I heard the Aborigines hunting, and, on going closer, saw their dogs hard at work. I watched them for four hours or so, and, on convincing myself that they were settled for the night, I returned for the rest of my party, and in the evening placed them within three hundred yards of the Natives, where we waited until dawn of day (26th), and crept to one of the Natives, without being perceived by any of the others in the windbreak and there I caught him by the leg. There were five men in the windbreak, and the other four rushed away, while others of the party were stooping to catch them. One, however, was caught, after he had fallen into the creek, and the other two were shot. There were five other windbreaks across the creek, and in the centre of very thick scrub."

Instead of merely catching a man and a boy, the whole tribe might have been secured if he had given notice to his superior officer. The eventual fate of that tribe of forty is thus recorded by Mr. Surveyor Wedge, one of the supporters of the Line:

"I am inclined to think that it warned them of their danger and put them on the alert to escape from it; and this they accomplished, a day or two afterwards, at or near Cherry-Tree Hill, unknown to any at the time, except to the party upon whose encampment they sneaked up to unobserved, and rushed past in a body, and speared, it was said, one of our men slightly in the leg. Why their escape was kept a secret, I am at a loss to imagine, unless, as it was suggested to me by my informant, the party in question thought that the discredit would attach to them, if the fact was officially made known. The lieutenant-Governor being in ignorance that the Natives had escaped, the force was kept in its position a fortnight or more longer. At length an advance was ordered to East Bay Neck."

The results of the meetings between aborigines and Whites were now getting monotonous. The aborigines were killed and maimed and left to die in the bush. No group could afford to stay long enough to help a wounded member, whose fly-infested wounds would cause a death more horrible and protracted than any outright bullet shot: in the heat of the excitement the majority of the men used their guns.

Though the objectives of the Line, as set down on paper, had the interests of the aborigines at heart, the real motive in the hearts of most of the participants was nothing more than the destruction of vermin, backed by the fear not only of what the native might do to their persons, but also the menace he presented to their crops and their flocks. His presence upset the White settler, in a deep way, which we should now term psychological, for the Tasmanians were very primitive people and appeared to the white man as sinister beings with whom he did not know how to cope, except violently. Their very helplessness in the face of gunfire may have acted almost as a goad to the settlers, for there was something primeval about their feelings, with their strong element of "the survival of the fittest".

Whenever there was evidence of aborigines being within the Line, every place on the route that might possibly afford extra concealment was well searched. The aborigines of Tasmania, like the highlanders of New Guinea, whom they resemble in many ways, hate to travel or move about at night, due to their superstitious fears of ghosts. However, now that they were being hard pressed they did not hesitate to travel in the darkness. In fact, a night of storm and an intensely black sky was selected for a rush at the Prosser's River crossing, a few miles from the coast, and thus not far from the East Bay Neck. Several were seen to pass by Lieutenant Owne's Division, though a vigilant lookout was maintained. Perhaps the aborigines realized what their fate would be if they were seen about in the daytime. The country around that region was described in the letters sent back to the lieutenant's family as being unexplored as well as most difficult of access, due to the rocks and the dense scrub. Five roving parties of ten men each were detached to search the locality believed to contain the aborigines, under leaders well versed in bush duty.

A rush was made by six men in that portion of the Line occupied by the Richmond force, on October 27th, but they were driven back again. One Englishman was prevented from bringing a native down only because he tripped against a dead tree while cocking his firearm. Of the six Tasmanians seen, two were observed with blankets round their shoulders and were probably women, while another carried a bundle of spears. An opossum hunting party might also have been taken, had not an officious constable given an untimely coo-ey for support.

However, great hopes were still maintained for the final success of the enterprise. The *Courier* announced jubilantly, that "no doubt but several hostile tribes were now enclosed". The Governor, in messages to the settlers who dwelt in the vicinity of the East Bay Neck, asked them to refrain "from everything that might create alarm, or interrupt the passage of the fugitive Natives". They were, furthermore

"to keep themselves within their homesteads, and to avoid collecting their cattle, lighting fires, hallooing, shouting, or otherwise making a noise in the Bush, in order that nothing may present itself to deter the aborigines from entering the peninsula".

A letter was brought to the Governor that still further raised the hopes of that optimistic man. It came from Mr. Robinson, who worked at the prison depot of Swan Island. The letter announced that he had had some success in contacts with some of the aborigines who had dwelt in a district that was circumscribed by the Line, and who were not in that particular operation to be trapped by the colonial forces. (Their turn would come in a later expedition that would be going to the north-east of the island, following the success of the first Line.) The letter began:

> "I beg to acquaint your Excellency that a successful intercourse has been effected among those sanguinary tribes of Natives who have for so great a period infested the settled districts and known as Little Swanport, Ben Lomond, Cape Portland and Piper's River aborigines."

He goes on to give some more wishful thinking of the kind that so pleased the Governor: "the whole Aboriginal population could be brought together by the same means that has hitherto been adopted".

Yet quite a number of members of the Line did not share the enthusiasm for the success of the scheme. At first the novelty of the occasion was fun, the excitement of camping out, the freedom of the life, supported them in their march. But when the heavy rains set in, and continued almost without ceasing for some weeks, they dampened faltering enthusiasm.

It was no surprise, therefore, that there were so many desertions from duty, as a letter from Macquarie River mentions, in which the writer, obviously of the patriotic breed, indignantly exclaims:

> "I blush to the bone when I tell you that certain volunteers from this neighbourhood have crawled home from the Line within the last fortnight."

To complete the success in repelling any possible advance of the encircled tribes, Colonel Arthur, on October 25th, recommended the formation of a barrier of tree trunks at the rear of the Line to halt the fugitives, so that they could be captured even more easily. The forces were told to take advantage of the long trunks of trees lying parallel almost along the position of the Line: at the back of these they were to raise a palisade of sharpened sticks cut from the bush. These, it explained in some detail, should be two or three inches thick, and driven into the ground, so that a native would be unable to clamber over them. Extra trees were also to be felled to make the abatis and to mark out, as it were, the actual physical presence of the Line, thus making it more of a reality. Moreover, a pictorial illustration was made which was sent to each commander, so that there could be no possibility of a mistake!

On October 30th, yet another Government Order was issued. It congratulated the officers for their zeal in constructing these barricades and for carrying out the additional chore of cutting down the scrub that was in front of them. There was now a Line to see.

The "Three Thumbs" are often mentioned in records of the Line proceedings. It was a region of distinct advantage to a besieged party. The "Three Thumbs" were three hills placed about two hundred yards apart and covered to the summit with huge gum trees. Beneath these trees was undergrowth, so dense that it was impossible for anyone other than the aborigines to travel in the area. This region of dense scrub was some seven miles long and between two and four miles broad; and, being situated half a dozen miles to the south-west of Prosser's Bay, was therefore not far from the peninsula. It was decided to storm this citadel of the aborigines. According to the *Courier*'s special correspondent, "into this ambush the great body of the Blacks have embowered themselves", and to quote from Dr. Russell: "The difficulties in accomplishing this are of course immense, but we trust not insurmountable, and the thing must be done."

Accordingly the siege was laid. Three hundred of the very best of the corps entered inside the Lines in order to seek out the aborigines, themselves like a wall around the particularly dense growth of bush. The enemy were known to be there, for the invading and advancing force came now and then upon the remains of the Tasmanians' fires, often still smouldering: they saw, too, the chips from the newly made spears and waddies; but the nomads themselves were never seen. Nevertheless, they must have been hard pressed, as they had to keep moving all the time and their necessary supply of beach shellfish had now been cut off. We hear later of the hardships that they suffered and how they even had to put to death their children, in case their cries gave away the whereabouts of the rest of the party, because their youth slowed down the march. So the Line, from this aspect alone, caused great hardship to the aborigines, and reduced their ranks and potential enormously.

The Europeans, when unable to force a way through the scrub, either in desperation or futile effort would send a heavy fire of musketry into the leafy thickness. They also kept up a continual discharge, like beaters trying to drive out game, for once a native was forced out into the open his capture would be easy, or so it was maintained. The anxious Governor directed the assault here and there, with encouraging reinforcements and the hopeful expectation of a triumphant return with handcuffed captives. In the end, when they had combed the area through and through, they found that it was completely deserted of men, and even the opossum, the kangaroo and the birds had departed. The crackling of flames was the only sound to be heard. The enemy had yielded that leafy fortress and gone to another.

This severe disappointment was not the only trial. As the first few, big drops pattering on the large leaves gave warning of an impending storm, so rumours of movements in the rear of the Line indicated the outbreak of new and even more appalling outrages. Word arrived that defenceless homes had been attacked by the now enraged and hunted aborigines. A hut near to Jerusalem had been robbed, and the woman there speared to death, one of the few cases of a woman being fatally attacked. Fires began to redden the sky to the rear of the Line and shrieks of terror also began to tell their tale of woe. A letter from Perth (Tasmania) said that one hundred and fifty aborigines had burst through the Line, and were plundering to the rear of Major Gray's force, at Avoca. Thirty were seen and chased by the energetic John Batman, who succeeded in capturing a large number of the party with very little bloodshed.

The mood of the Launceston papers was now one of annoyance at letting the northern part of the island remain defenceless. They demanded that all the effort of the colony should now be directed to the capture of the two tribes of the Oyster Bay and Big River. It seems obvious that nowhere on the island was there any kind of a rapport between the aborigines and the white men. There was no one who had sufficient knowledge of them, or the friendship of their chiefs, to parley for a truce, as was constantly happening in the United States at about this time. But, more important even than the lack of knowledge, was the lack of care for the native peoples that it implied.

A northern magistrate wrote of four men speared near Launceston, saying:

"I have no person I can send after these Blacks. I have no one that I can spare, nearly all the constables being out of the country, catching the Blacks in Buckingham."

Such stories increased the anxiety of the Governor to hurry on the operations at the East Bay Neck. At that time every officer was sure

that, though a handful had escaped, the majority were "in the bag".
Forty parties, each with seven men, and taking four days' provisions,
were now sent forward. One of the leaders reported that he saw, in
the peninsula itself, evidences of the aborigines having been there,
though he was unable to say how long before his reconnoitring this
might have been. He also saw in the forest sticks stuck into the soil, to
mark a way forward for those following behind.

The colonel in command now believed that the final stage had come
in the campaign, and that it was an opportune moment for the final
charge to rout them out. This stage of the war was reached on the last
day of October, and he issued this address to all the commanders:

"A few days must now terminate the great work in the most
satisfactory manner, and His Excellency earnestly hopes that the
leaders will, for the remaining short period, continue to show the
excellent spirit which has all along been so conspicuous in their
parties, for they will perceive that the advance of the scouring
parties will render redoubled vigilance necessary on the part of those
who guard the Line, as the Natives, when disturbed in the interior,
will undoubtedly increase their efforts to break through the position."

This was followed by another Government Notice, relative to the final
operations, and dated the same day, and the order closed thus:

"By this movement, which should, if possible, be effected by
twelve o'clock on Monday, the Line will remain of its original
strength, and the scouring parties will be in readiness to advance,
which they will do as soon as the vacancies have been closed. These
parties will then advance towards the south-east, driving the
Natives in that direction, or capturing them, and on the fourth day,
will reach East Bay Neck, where they will receive further orders.

"The Investing Line which will remain in position, must, during
these four decisive days, put forth every effort to prevent the
possibility of the Natives passing through them, as the tribes will
naturally redouble their attempts to pass when they are disturbed
in the interior."

It reads very much like a handbook on the work of beaters at some
country shoot.

When the force was thus extended from Sorell to the sea, the "Long
Black Line" extended thirty miles with a space of forty-five yards

between each man. The right wing was at Sorell and the left at Spur Bay, the centre at the White Marsh. The Neck was gained at last, all was excitement and expectation. Every possible precaution was taken to prevent escape, even the shore was watched. The capturing parties were told off. Then the Neck was crossed, the peninsula entered, the search made, but nothing found.

Not an aborigine was there.

Thus the Line had so far proved a failure, though its indirect advantages were great, as the aborigines now knew how formidable the forces of the Government really were, and how keen the Government was on absolute submission to their authority. The work of the Line was over for the time being and its members could return to their homesteads and farms. The Reverend West in his *History of Tasmania* wrote of this homecoming:

"The settler-soldiers returned to their homes, their shoes worn out, their garments tattered, their hair long and shaggy, with beards unshaven, their arms tarnished, but neither blood-stained, nor disgraced."

The cost to the Government of this expedition was £30,000, but to the colonists, all in all, it was much more, for they had to bear the brunt of it, and Mr. G. A. Robinson, of whom we will hear more later, sums up the expenditure thus:

"The entire cost to the Colony was upwards of seventy thousand pounds, and the result was the capture of one Black and even this led to much controversy."

An English newspaper had a little more to say on the subject:

"That a soldier had killed a Native, and, if punished for the fault, all would have been well; but as this was not done, the Blacks rose in wrath; and, lastly, that it had taken 6,000 Europeans to quell their revolt!"

But the Governor was game to the last and, conscious of having done his best, professed to be satisfied. He dismissed his army with dignity, acknowledged their service with gratitude, and promised their speedy deliverance and that of the whole island from the "Native Troubles".

His parting order, November 26th, 1830, held forth the belief that future good would follow the efforts thus made, that the poor native creatures, now seeing the hopelessness of the struggle, might now be induced to surrender. He could not contemplate their possible extermination but as "an event fearfully to be apprehended", but somehow believed that his own policies could not have this result. He was happy to announce the capture of a tribe in the north, without bloodshed. However, he confessed to a conviction that "it would be in vain to expect any sort of a reformation in these savages while allowed to remain in their native state". But those natives already secured, about thirty in number, would form the nucleus of an asylum on some neighbouring island.

At a self-congratulatory meeting of the Liners, held at Hobart Town, on December 22nd, 1830, resolutions were passed condemning and denouncing the Blacks, while at the same time praising the plans and the deeds of the Government. Public dinners were the order of the day throughout the colony; should not the colonists rejoice, when the Government had spent among them thirty thousand pounds of British money? They had now also conquered the Blacks—all two hundred or so of them.

However, while the loud hurrahs at the exulting meeting were ringing out, there boomed in the distance the sound of conflict. From the depths of the forest to the expanses of the plains, a cry of horror was heard. Men returned to their homes to find, instead of the wife and the little ones they had left behind, a heap of smouldering ruins, and a pile of ghastly corpses. Wives awaiting the return of their husbands were transfixed with spears, children brained by waddies. For the wrath of an infuriated race had been vented in the only way it could. It had turned on its oppressors, and the country that had been scoured high and low for their presence now echoed with the cries of their victims. Still, it is worth noting, no women were raped.

What measures were to be taken against them now? Were fresh cohorts going to sally forth against them? Were new and more vigorous assaults going to be made upon those wretched aborigines? If, in the first case, thousands of men backed by thousands of pounds were insufficient to overcome those feeble and disorganized bands of nomads, were even more men and greater expenses about to be employed? When all the power of a strong Government, and the warlike appliances of an advanced civilization, were exhausted in one vain attempt, should there be another?

Here is an extract from a letter written by the Hon. John Wedge, about these circumstances:

"A plan of the expedition, and the carrying it out in detail, was, as might be expected from the political feeling of hostility that was entertained against the head of the Government, criticized and commented upon in no measure of terms. I thought at the time, and I still think, that the circumstances which imperatively required that an attempt should be made to put an end to the deadly warfare that was carried on between the occupiers of the out-stations and the Natives, and mostly to the advantage of the latter, were not considered with that liberty of feeling to which they were entitled. Frequent, and almost daily, representations were made to the Government about the depredations and the murders committed by the Natives. Neither sawyers, splitters, shepherds, nor herdsmen could attend to their work with safety; nor could the solitary hut-keeper show himself out of doors, without the danger of being speared, even when not the least suspicion was entertained of there being anything to apprehend. A general feeling of insecurity was felt throughout the colony; and a demand, as with one voice, was made that the Government should adopt measures for the greater security of the colonists and their property. I believe that there was scarcely any possessing knowledge of the country and experienced in traversing the forests, and who knew anything of the habits of the Natives, who anticipated any other result than a failure of the expedition, so far as their capture was concerned. And I was led to believe, being present when the Lieut.-Governor was speaking on the subject, that few were less sanguine of success than His Excellency."

He finished the letter saying:

"I could not at the time suggest, nor have I since been able to surmise, how the forces could have been otherwise employed, which would have afforded a greater chance of success—nor did I ever meet with any of the fault-finders who could do so."

A year after the episode of the Line, the aborigines held one of their greatest jamborees, the collecting of the swans' eggs, a favourite food of theirs. This jamboree was also a time of tribal reunion, the anniversary of family greetings and of festive joy, in fact, not so unlike our own Christmas in feeling. There was a wooded rocky peninsula, into the eastern waters, called the Schouten Peninsula. It was too barren and rough for any form of colonization, too distant for a visit, and thus was a secure habitat for a large breeding colony of Australian swans. The swans returned here year after year to breed, and in so doing attracted the aborigines, who, year after year, journeyed from all parts of the island to the peninsula. Advantage was now taken by the Tasmanians of the lull in the war, and they had come, stealthily in ones and twos, to the old spot. But their tracks had been sighted and their intention guessed, and the colonists resolved upon their extermination.

The alarm was sounded; nothing seemed easier now than their capture, here was the proper locality for Line operations, a cordon could be drawn across the narrow isthmus, thus cutting of the peninsula; and the Blacks could then be secured at leisure.

Troops, constables and settlers gathered in joyful confidence at the gateway to the peninsula. The year was 1831, and the October spring in Tasmania is the loveliest of all seasons in the bright little island. The Neck was only a mile across, and it was upon this that the Europeans took up their positions. Great eucalyptus trees also straddled this narrow part, sentinels to the last little group of a wasted people. The peninsula consisted of almost impenetrable scrub land and pathless woods, intersected by complicated creek systems. The enemy sought to gain this bastion by firing the vegetation. Soon the flames could be seen penetrating even the darkest gorges, and climbing the rocky steeps. The strong colonial force constructed their huts, established their sentries, and kept up the vast fires for observation and destruction. Gradually long black lanes were made through the thickets, and augmented by reinforcements from the townships the Whites seemed assured of victory.

It was the time of the full moon, and soon the roaring flames abated. Now nothing but the charred timber or smouldering ashes remained, and when the moon gradually waned evening after evening, its decreasing light brought a time of watchfulness for the encampment, alert to ensure that none escaped. Troops were gradually assembling; and while some guarded the entrance with dogs, fires and arms, others were to pass down the peninsula and seize or kill the egg-gatherers.

In fear, though with determination, the aborigines waited for a favourable moment. A night of misty blackness came. They had crept as closely as they dared to the lines, their very dogs keeping silent, and then with a bound and a cry, followed by their yelping friends, they dashed by the fires and the guards once again, and gained the dark forest and beyond to safety. The only captures made by the large array of besiegers were a few young puppies who could not keep up with the rest. But of the aborigines there was no trace.

chapter 7

Search Parties

Mention has been made already of the system whereby anyone capturing an aborigine, or "Black" as they were termed, received a prize of five pounds.*

It was the very perplexity of affairs that caused the Governor to seek the advice as well as the co-operation of the most popular and intelligent of the settlers. As a result, the leading magistrates of the country were contacted. A typical reply came from James Simpson, the J.P. for Campbelltown, on November 18th, 1828. He recommended that one particular tribe should be selected and followed, night and day, by the largest possible number of men until they were all run down and secured. We can imagine how much patience the followers would have with an aborigine, particularly after a long and difficult hunt.

Another who had many ideas and suggestions to offer the Governor was Thomas Anstey, J.P., of Oatlands. In a note sent on November 14th,

* In a letter to Viscount Goderich dated January 10th, 1828, Lieutenant-Governor Arthur expressed the wish that the natives be placed on an island. He felt that if they abandoned their nomadic ways and instead made bread they would be less of a nuisance to the colonists, thereby altering their economy from hunter/fisher to a stationary one. He implies that every stock-keeper in Tasmania was opposed to the natives. In a later letter to London, April 17th, 1828, he declares that the feelings of the settlers were running so high that retaining the aborigines on the mainland would be impossible, and repeats his plan to incarcerate the natives on an island.

The townspeople were in favour of conciliation between the two races, but those of the interior preferred harsher methods. In many cases the letters from Hobart to London admitted that the original aggressors were the settlers, and mentioned the seizure of native women as the primary bone of contention.

1829, he suggested that parties should be organized, under suitable leaders, to be sent in pursuit, and that a few active men should be selected to watch for native fires at day, lie in ambush near, and to make their capture in the cold light of the dawn. He added:

> "To rid the country of this scourge, a considerable number of troops would be required."*

It was his opinion that the employment of prisoners, or at least of men seeking an extension of freedom, would be most advantageous, as these would be trying hard to obtain a free pardon by their labours.

The Governor decided to try this scheme, and directed the magistrate to make a trial selection. By the end of November, four convicts had been chosen. Three were ticket-of-leave men, John Hopkins, Samuel May and William Wakeman, and had acquired a knowledge of the life of the aborigines in the bush. The fourth, still in the primary class of bondage, was John Danvers, a man of very great ability and energy. There were also about twenty other persons engaged in the enterprise, all of a more elevated social standing than the convicts. One, a Mr. Roberts, took four Bruni Island aborigines from a Port Davey tribe. It is not stated what he did or what was done with them. Another of the party, Mr. Tortose, was to receive a thousand acres in addition to the five pounds bounty if he caught twenty natives in twelve months.

But little was really done until the energies and the experience of Mr. Anstey were brought into play. In May, 1829, all leaders of the bounty parties were directed to make their monthly reports to him. It was at his suggestion that twelve men were placed under the authority of Mr. John Batman, six with Mr. Nicholas of Campbelltown, five with Mr. Sherwin of the Clyde, and five with Mr. Diran of New Norfolk. A man named John Small was promised a free pardon should he succeed in bringing in ten captives during the year of his engagement. While five pounds was paid for the possession of an adult, and two pounds for a child, a promise of large grants of land was held out to all the leaders of the bounty parties.

Mr. Anstey's devotion to duty reminds one of Spartan soldiers, and the parting words of a Spartan mother to her son: "Either come back on your shield or with your shield." When his son, then out with the Line and in pursuit of the aborigines, began to suffer the hardships of

---

* It was an age of slaves and blackbirding, and the black skin was at a low premium. If the Tasmanians had been found a little later on, they would have probably escaped extinction; they were the victims of the age as much as anything else.

the bush and wrote requesting to return home for a season, his father replied: "Stay till all is lawfully dismissed. If you return before, the house will be closed against you."

His children were as energetic as their father: one son became an influential legislator in South Australia; another, Chisholm Anstey, was well known as a prominent member of the English House of Commons. But it was his son George who has the doubtful fame of distinguishing himself in the Black War. On July 27th, 1830, some aborigines were heard prowling about the family farm at night. Heading a small number of servants, the boy, then only sixteen years of age, dashed after the "enemy". The ground was covered with snow, and their tracks could easily be followed in the darkness. The tribe was found and charged, four were captured and the rest fled in terror without a shot being fired. Among the spoils were fourteen dogs, fifteen blankets, and five spears. The colony rang with acclamations of the daring deed, and the courage of many a wilting bush-tracker revived. The Governor honoured the boy with a *Gazette* notice and the gift of 500 acres of land, even though three of the captives were females.

When the four were being taken to Hobart Town by the constables, the man in the party feigned illness. The constables were compelled to place the "dying" captive in a wheelbarrow and trundle him to a hut for the night. Leaving him there to groan his life away in peace, the guardians indulged in some sleep, feeling perfectly assured of the safety of the prisoner. But, in the silence of the night, the cunning captive climbed the chimney and once again walked the forest paths.

One part of Mr. Anstey's scheme, the employment of soldiers to capture the tribes, was not a success and did little to improve the fast deteriorating relationship between the Whites and the aborigines. The soldiers were slow in movement, had no bushcraft, they had little stamina due to their poor diet and always had to wear their brilliant red coats! They were also often cruel: one corporal with a party of forty earned a reputation by the atrocious massacre of a large number of men, women and children whose fires he came upon suddenly.

Yet another project was put forward in June 1829. Mr. Horace Rowcroft, seconded by Major Gray, suggested the introduction into Tasmania of Maoris to catch the aborigines. It was contended that, as they sold female slaves for a musket each in their own country, they would be quite content to catch Tasmanian "Black Fellows" for the same rate. Their greater intelligence, their crafty methods of working in the bush, their warlike bearing and their use of weapons, made the plan acceptable to many. But, Colonel Arthur feared that the Maoris, who were then cannibals, might go too far and massacre for the pot what, after all, were his own subjects.

Conditions were now terrible within the tribes, and it was from this time onwards that they began to deteriorate rapidly. One main cause was the custom that the labour of the camp fell solely to the women, who thus found the additional burden of children impossible. The aborigines themselves sold many of their female children to the settlers or anyone else who would have them. Hence female aborigines of child-bearing age were in short supply: the old women would return to their tribe to die, if of no further use to the settlers.

So the "Bounty Five" (the colloquial name for the bounty catchers) continued, and were not stopped until June 1832, when all those taking part were informed by the Governor that the reward was no longer offered, because the "present tranquil state of the colony no longer warranted such a measure". Probably even more relevant was the fact that very few aborigines were now left to cause offence.

The head hunters certainly earned their five pounds, for once caught, the aborigines were not easily retained. Their naked bodies, covered with a good smearing of opossum grease, made it exceedingly difficult to keep the captives, and handcuffs were permanently in short supply. Thus four were one day surrounded, and held for a time, at St. Paul's Plains; but three, perhaps particularly greasy, managed to free themselves and escape.

That ever watchful paper the *Courier* hastened to publish an infallible cure:

> "Some Persons," stated the paper, "adopt the plan of getting behind them, and thrusting their arms beneath the armpits of the Black, to bring the hands round behind the neck or head, and, being thus clasped, completely secure and overpower him (or her)."

A remedy with strong overtones of catching a bird by putting salt on its tail! No doubt others found it far easier to shoot them rather than trying to catch them.

Some independent aborigine-hunting parties were considered highly successful. For instance, Mr. Howell of the Shannon obtained a thousand acres for his exploits. Mr. James Parish, an Australian by birth, was said to have secured no less than twenty-two aborigines and a host of dogs close to Swan Island, where he also managed to place them. One aborigine escaped after being captured, but was wounded by a shot during his retreat. He managed to get to the seashore, and made an attempt to swim away, but was soon exhausted and retaken. His wound was dressed and he was placed in a hut for security. But again he escaped, this time for good. Two more were caught by a man placing a "sugar bag" in an exposed position in the bush, and lying in wait until the aborigines found it and started dipping in.

It is obvious that the aborigines were terribly harassed by these roving parties. Their sufferings were severe, especially as they were afraid to light fires to warm their bodies, for it was often very cold, or to cook their food. Children and the weak rapidly sank from fatigue and want, for their main supply of food was from the seashore and often they could not get there for fear of showing themselves. Maggots and gangrene each took their toll from among the many wounded. Their wounds, too, were of a far more serious nature than any they had previously experienced. The damage inflicted by a fire-hardened wooden stake was little in comparison with that inflicted by a bullet. All they could do was oppose force with craft, making use of their ancestral woods and forests, concealing themselves in the densest of the many thickets in the interior. They also learnt, at least in the hard times, to keep a vigilant lookout, and knew how at the right time to silence their faithful and obedient dogs (which were *not* some form of dingo).

In normal times, they had been accustomed to indicate to those that followed them through the pathless regions of the wilderness the way they had gone by breaking off little bits of branches, or of pointing little sticks in the ground—a practice similar to that used by the Indians of the American forests and still used by the New Guinea people today. But the Tasmanians had agreed that when they were being pursued by the Whites and their hirelings, these sticks should only occasionally be placed in the right position, elsewhere they were to be put wrongly. And, where wrong, the sticks would be placed with sharp points and sharp stones just above the ground; an effective method of wounding or laming the feet of their trackers, who, as often as not, were barefooted or wearing only home-made skin moccasins.

The guides of the parties were either white bushmen, or "tame" aborigines, often from Australia. The latter were not to be depended upon; and when captive on Flinders Island, some acknowledged having brought the leaders near the sought-for tribe, and then refused to go further, or having led the party in the wrong direction. For instance, Black Jack, who was out with Mr. Gilbert Robertson, told Mr. Jorgenson that, after he had been beaten by that gentleman for some supposed fault, he often saw the tracks of his countrymen but would not follow them up. Mungo was another and an intelligent one who did similar good service: the son of an influential chieftain, he accompanied both Mr. Robertson and Mr. Batman, but died early of disease.

As the wild people were caught, they were transferred to the nearest gaol. At first some were taken to Mr. G. A. Robinson at Bruni; or under his care, to the prison establishment at Newtown, a few miles out of Hobart. A Mr. Stirling was in charge of this "concentration camp", but it was soon found to be of little use as, although large numbers were brought in, there were also many escapes.

There was certainly success among some of the hunting parties, for 236 aborigines were taken by the end of 1832, but there was also the beginning of a feeling that great destruction of life had taken place. Mr. Carr, manager of the Van Diemen's Land Agricultural Company, calculated the effects of the raids upon the aborigine population as a whole. His findings, which became known as the "Five Pounds Proclamation", sarcastically declared:

> "The Proclamation, as usual, will enjoin the sparing of the defenceless, and that the people are not to be killed, but taken alive; and the way in which it will be acted upon will be by killing nine for every one taken."

Some such feeling was also felt by the authorities; for a Government Notice, appearing on August 20th, 1830, bears upon the subject, and again utters a warning against cruelty:

> "The Lieut-Governor has learned with much regret, that the Government Order of the 25th of February last, offering certain rewards for the capture of the aborigines, appears in some recent instances to have been misapprehended; and in order to remove the possibility of any future misunderstanding on this important subject, His Excellency has directed it to be distinctly notified, that nothing can be more opposed to the spirit of the above named order, and to all that of the different Proclamations and Orders which preceded it, than to offer any sort of violence or restraint to such of the aboriginal natives as may approach the European inhabitants with friendly views. The reward was offered for the capture of such Natives only as were committing aggressions on the inhabitants of the Settled Districts, from which it was the object of the Government to expel them with every degree of humanity that was practicable, when all efforts for their conciliation had proved abortive."

Much has been said in regard to John Batman, who was one of the chief leaders of the parties, and a very good man he seems to have been. He was an Australian, born at Parramatta in New South Wales, and subsequently became a farmer under the shadow of Ben Lomond, in Tasmania. Although considered humane he was also severe, and always carried a gun. In an official letter dated from his estate at Kingston, Ben Lomond, on June 15th, 1829, he writes:

> "I have formed the determination, provided it meets with His Excellency's approval, under certain conditions, of devoting some time, and all the exertion that I am capable, toward bringing in alive some of the much injured and unfortunate race of beings."

This gives the key to his conduct. He regarded the aborigines as injured—in fact "much injured"—and his sympathies were aroused on behalf of these unfortunate people. They were being mown down by soldiers, constables and settlers—in fact everybody seemed to have a finger on the trigger and to enjoy the fun of being able to kill legitimately. But, being civilized, the killers needed to have some cloak of respectability. The savage may do his evil deeds in the open, but civilization, in its hypocrisy, requires a cloak. The Tasmanians were termed beasts, therefore, and were hunted down ruthlessly like beasts. Man, whether civilized or savage, has like the animals a hatred, and indeed fear, of the unusual, the deformed or the different. In medieval days in Britain it was the clever woman who was thought a witch, in the Victorian era it was the naked savage, and in these modern times it is the one that does not follow the trend of the common cynicism of the day.

Although not a professional Christian, Batman's desire to help the Tasmanians was no less sincere than that of Mr. G. A. Robinson, another man deeply concerned about the plight of the Tasmanians at that time. The difference, and the striking difference, between them was that while one took weapons the other did not. Robinson always fled from any aborigines who, rejecting his overtures of friendship, pursued him. Batman, however, used to the alertness and insecurity of bandit hunting, was always resolved to fight rather than run when he failed to win the friendship, which he always tried for first, preferring to face to the death those who rejected his proposed kindliness.

The *Launceston Advertiser* of August 24th greeted his appointment as chief of the capture parties with satisfaction, saying:

"We learn from good authority that Mr. John Batman is to be employed for some time as Conductor of a party of ten Crown Prisoners, part of whom are to receive in due course emancipation, and part ticket-of-leave, if they behave well. Their task is to capture all the aborigines, or as many as they possibly can."

He seems to have gone to work at once, for a letter of his dated September 18th, gives a record of progress:

"Seeing a number of Natives approaching towards us, I ordered the men to lie down, and not to fire upon them, but, when I should whistle, to rush forward and seize them. When they approached within forty yards I gave the signal. We all ran forward, and secured three women, two young children, three boys, and two young men."

Evidently they were not greasy ones! But greasy or not, the settlers of the times considered this a wonderful feat, as the captives were said to have belonged to a particularly troublesome tribe. The capture took place between Break o' Day Plains and Oyster Bay, near the East Coast. Seventeen large dogs were obtained, and a considerable quantity of stolen goods, such as blankets, knives and clothing, were obtained from their camp nearby.

Unfortunately, in the September of the next year, a sad affair occurred. Sad, at least, for the aborigines, it was one of the few instances of real violence between Mr. Batman and the Tasmanians. He had been busy penetrating the intricate forest glens of Ben Lomond, which were the special hideout of the last of the tribes, when he suddenly found himself confronted by a well-armed mob of over seventy, belonging to the most cunning of tribes on the island. A flight of spears saluted him; and so determined an assault followed that he was constrained to order a discharge of musketry, just in case they thought they could get away with such an attack. Although fifteen of the front-line warriors were killed, their valour was so great that all the women and children of the tribe escaped except for one woman and a child taken prisoner by the Europeans. The dogs, which had nobly stood beside their dead masters, shared the same fate. Among the spoils Mr. Batman collected were thirty or forty spears, some as much as fifteen feet in length. This is one of the last times that such a large group of Tasmanians were seen together. The outcome of the encounter was considered a great victory by the Europeans.

That there was some justification for the colonial terror and some need for armed parties to restrain attack, when unable to make peaceful terms, is shown in a letter of Mr. Batman's sent from his ranch near Ben Lomond:

"I have just time to say that the Natives last Thursday week murdered two men at Oyster Bay, and the next day they beat a sawyer to death. On the Sunday after they murdered a soldier. On last Wednesday, they attacked the house of Mr. Boultby, when he was absent; and if it had not been for a soldier who happened to be there, they would have murdered Mrs. Boultby and all the children. On Friday last they murdered three men at a hut belonging to Major Gray, and left a fourth for dead."

However, in this account, no mention is made of any provocation from the other side, although the entire concept of the raiding parties might well be classified as such. What the natives did was on each occasion termed murder, but when it was a white man or men who caused the loss of life, it was, naturally, termed something else; perhaps it was called a punitive expedition, or suppression, or simply policing, but never, ever, murder. So even the illustrious and fair (in the white man's eyes) Mr. Batman, fell into the trap of the double standards prevalent at the time. If this fair-minded man who was supposed to be sympathetic to the aborigines had ordered the killing of several, little could be expected from the ordinary settlers and the convicts that made up the bulk of the population; not to mention those who were openly hostile towards them.

Mr. Batman was the first of the Europeans to employ aborigine women as spies and guides. Mr. Robertson, another European closely associated with European raiding parties, also followed this same method, again to much advantage. The women would bring in information about the wanderers on walk-about and, as they were allegedly in sympathy with the views of the two European leaders, rather than merely female Judases, they sought to induce their people to accept the proffered protection. They were made to understand the intentions of the Governor, to remove them from the bad and the cruel Whites to good hunting grounds which their enemies could never approach. But in the light of after events the "could" should be changed to would, for few people would actually want to inhabit the cold and bleak Flinders Island.

Three of Mr. Batman's females succeeded on one occasion in prevailing upon nine men to come to Kingston. It so happened that

Mr. Batman was not at home, and Mrs. Batman and her daughters were very much terrified at the visit. She, in her panic, sent for her neighbour, Mr. Simon Lord, who later gave a graphic account of the incident. He found, when he arrived, about as wild a bunch as the country could furnish. They were all armed, and were prying most curiously, but good-humouredly, about the premises. Some were enjoying the mysteries of the mirror, and one had a girl's cap perched upon his greasy locks. Yet another was sporting pieces of feminine underwear on himself. They stalked about nude, and made free with whatever pleased them, but carefully abstained from liberties with the household. As they were hungry men, they made much havoc and Mr. Batman afterwards wrote:

> "Their appetite was enormous and they devoured everything they met, they are particularly fond of half roasted eggs of every description, those of geese, ducks and hens, and of course the poultry; so much so that Mrs. Batman's poultry yard will cut but a sorry figure after their company."

The master arrived home at sundown, to the great relief of the family. He gave the bush party a mighty welcome, and took no measures to force them into any form of confinement, the result being that the tribesmen left in the night, though returning on a subsequent day. Six had been on another occasion to Launceston, and the commandant, not knowing what to do with them, would have let them go free, had not Mr. Batman convinced him that they would be shot as an affront to the white women if released.*

Mr. Batman, being originally an Australian, had had experience of the fine tracking powers of the Australian aborigines and wanted to have some of them to help in his work of catching the Tasmanians. So he wrote to the Governor of Tasmania on the subject on March 18th, 1830, describing the kind that he required:

> "They should be got from the interior, as those about the town of

---

* There are two sides to this story, that given above being the version of Bonwick. Governor Arthur, on the other hand, stated that the aborigines kept the Batman household in fear for nine days, destroyed everything they could, and carried away large quantities of loot in the dead of night before Batman returned. According to Arthur, they then went on the rampage and killed any White they came across. Arthur's story seems to be a political construction, since it is vague and, in particular, no numbers of dead are quoted.

Sydney are accustomed to the drinking of spirits, and have in a great measure lost their natural gift of tracking."

Colonel Arthur approved of this suggestion and eventually two Australian aborigines, Pigeon and Crook, were obtained, and worked for several years with Mr. Batman. According to the *Courier* of September, 1831, others were sent for by the authorities, "to be employed as instruments under the direction of properly qualified persons, to conciliate and civilize the Natives of our own Isle".

The newly arrived Pigeon and Crook were renamed John Pigeon and John Crook: these names they only suffered with the Whites, among themselves they still retained their aboriginal names, such as Bollobolong. They were employed for a dollar a day, a suit of clothes and a medal. They brought back John Waterman, William Sawyers, John Peter and John Radley.

Their conduct, real or made up, provoked much discussion at the time. It was said that they would be bloodthirsty destroyers of the "*poor* Tasmanians" and, instead of helping to improve the social condition of the latter, they would introduce fresh vices and incite them to even worse hostilities. The dreadful deeds of Mosquito, the Sydney aborigine, were always being paraded before the eyes of the populace. None more violently objected to the engagement of the Australian aborigines than Mr. G. A. Robinson. Some asserted that his opposition was due to jealousy of their success. But he was adamant in affirming that they were untrustworthy, that they corrupted the Tasmanian females and that they were drunken reprobates.

After skirmishing for some time, the two leaders in Tasmanian aboriginal affairs, Batman and Robinson, came to open rupture about the strangers. Mr. Robinson complained about them and accentuated his point by reminding the Governor that they came from Mosquito's own country. Mr. Batman supported them. He gave instances of their good deeds, and related cases in which they had stood by him in great straits, and how they had at one time helped him successfully to capture, without bloodshed, a mob of thirteen aborigines.

Favourable reports about Mr. Batman were sent by Major Gray and the magistrate at Campbelltown, Mr. James Simpson, to the Governor, and the following Government Notice was issued on September 9th, 1830:

"Mr. John Batman, having served the period of twelve months in pursuit of the aborigines, the Lieutenant-Governor, placing every confidence in the certificates of James Simpson and William Gray, Esquire, J.P., as to the seal which he has manifested, has directed a grant of two thousand acres of land to be made to him."

Even if the two thousand acres were not the best grounds of the dispossessed Tasmanians, anything would have been better than Flinders Island, the new home of the race with whom Batman was supposed to be in sympathy. Conditional pardons or tickets-of-leave were given to the prisoners who had served under Mr. Batman's orders during that period.

Mr. Batman was pleased with the work of the Sydney guides. Ten pounds was presented to each and, at the end of the following year, he recommended that Pigeon and Crook should be made bush constables, and put on the police staff. He suggested also that the same favour should be granted to Black Jack, the Tasmanian guide. He also procured better rations for those that had helped him so well. But, all the same, it was a small price to pay for gaining two thousand acres of land.

Anxious for home and rest, Batman retired for a while in October, 1830, and transferred his Australian aborigine trackers to his friend Mr. Cottrell. The Governor, in his despatch of November 20th, referred to his labours for Tasmania in the following manner:

"Mr. Batman treated the savages with the utmost kindness, distributing to them clothing and food. They were placed under no restraint, but all the indulgence that had been pledged was manifest toward them. Mr. Batman, who has taken the most lively interest in conciliating these wretched people, and has been one of the few who supposed that they might be influenced by kindness, was, with his family, most assiduous in cultivating the best of understandings."

From all accounts, Mr. Batman tended to show the aborigines kindness at times, but there is little evidence to show that his family did likewise, unless a radical reform set in after the visitation of the nine braves to the Batman homestead when Mrs. Batman had sought help from Mr. Lord, a neighbour.

Batman himself never seemed to lose interest in the work concerned with helping the aborigines. His year of success was that in which Mr. Robinson, his rival for acclaim as aborigine protector-in-chief, had been able to accomplish little. After the "retirement of Mr. Batman" from being official protector, all operations were left in the hands of Mr. Robinson. Although the Ben Lomond farmer actively laboured for the good, as he thought, of the unhappy race, he objected to the system of clearing the island of all of them without exception, and pleaded hard for the retention of children and adolescents educated by settlers and devoted to their service. This policy brought him into collision with Mr. Robinson, who was always jealous of his friendship with Colonel Arthur and the higher officials who had thought so well of his work. He formally complained of the presence of two Tasmanian boys on Batman's farm at Ben Lomond.

Over this matter, a dispute with far-reaching effects occurred. Mr. Robinson was backed by the Aborigine Committee of Hobart Town, while his rival had the support of officialdom. Mr. Batman declared that he did not wish to be an exception, but that he was acting as guardian to the two boys because their mothers, on being sent to Flinders Island, refused to take them away from his care. The committee wrote to Mr. Batman at Ben Lomond, urging the removal of the boys, as there were to be no exceptions: if he, a respected member of the community set a precedent, others might try the same thing and then where would they be? etc. They also stated that there had been a clamour on Flinders Island among the aborigine outcasts there for the boys. Lieutenant Darling, the beloved commandant at Flinders Island, espoused the side of Batman in the matter, and wrote to him on March 24th, 1834, telling him what the mother of one of the boys had said in answer to his question: "No–No–No! Let him stay at Mr. Batman's till he gets a long fellow." Mr. Darling then continues:

"I have seen Jackey (then ten years old) driving the plough at your farm and have expressed to you my admiration of his shrewdness and intelligence and my hope that under the care and kindness, with which he and little Benny are evidently treated by your family, they would one day become useful members of society."

He expressed a wish that all the children in Flinders could be so suitably placed. Ultimately, however, Mr. Robinson gained his end, and the partly civilized pair were placed with their wild cousins. If the two had been able to remain with Mr. Batman the whole course of the Tasmanian's plight might have been changed. Even if only one or two had been able to read and write, they could probably have done so much to help their race, at the same time pleading their cause with the Whites, who in a spirit of colonial paternalism might well have responded, if only to try and "civilize savages" into a shadow of English Victorianism. It was not to be so and forever the gulf remained.

One thing natives and settlers did have in common was the primitiveness of the way they lived, though admittedly one race chose such conditions while the other had no such choice. The following is a description of what hut life among the Whites could be like in early Tasmanian days (and dates from about seven years after the incidents recorded above):

> "I started from Kingston, under the guidance of a convict shepherd, who carried the swag, and led the way. He entertained me with narratives of bushranging and native hunting, to lighten my toilsome march. After travelling for about ten hours over very rough ground, the sun was setting before the welcome sound of a dog broke the silence of the mountain solitude, and guided us to the lonely hut of old Boco, the one-eyed tenant of Ben Lomond. He was lord of the wastes, the supposed shepherd of a flock feeding on the sparse vegetation of the rocky slopes.
>
> "He received me heartily, and proclaimed his ample store of mutton, damper and tea, for my entertainment, objecting to the opening of the haversack which my companion carried. The hut was of slabs of unhewn timber, rudely plastered with clay. The floor was of mother earth. The huge fireplace opened into the hut; and, being unprovided with a chimney, furnished the inmates with a sight of the stars, or a sensation of rain, according to the weather."

The billy was swung and the tea made, the chops were fried, the damper was brought, and the weary wanderers were soon at ease. Old Boco had led a chequered life and acquired a reputation to go with it. His hut was, perhaps slanderously, supposed to be the receptacle of curiosities and belongings surreptitiously conveyed there from more populous places. He was of the most forbidding aspect, torn and rent by years of usage, like the mountain under which he lived. Also in his hut when the two travellers arrived were a number of friends: two shepherds were seeking lost animals; three men out on a kangaroo hunt; three were servants sent to cut posts and rails for fencing; two others were constables on the tramp. All were of the convict class, but apparently out on their own. Each man seemed to have a dog; and the noise that these creatures made through the night would have disturbed the rest of any but a bushman.

"Supper over, the chat commenced vigorously. Old Boco apologised to the company for the absence of grog, it had all been drunk and he had nothing to offer but Good Ben Lomond Ale [water]. A very dirty pack of cards gave amusement to one party, some indulged in a song, while others smoked before the blazing logs. Being all early risers, there were in any case speedy arrangements for bed. My guide had an opossum rug for me, which he disposed on one of the three side bunks of rough slabs. As soon as I settle myself, a peculiarly odorous splitter enveloped himself in a filthy blanket, retaining his boots, and occupied the spare place beside me. The rest folded their rugs or blankets around them, and coiled about on the mud and the moistened floor.

"Some were not ready for sleep and called upon a scholarly mate to give them some literature. He produced a disreputable looking book, and brought the light near him, as he lay upon the floor. The candlestick was a disabled tin pannikin. The tallow was the fat of the chops poured off from the hissing pan. The wick was a piece of Old Boco's well worn shirt, and gave forth a flickering and smoky flame. Jack read a very characteristic work, considering the company —'The Wonderful Escapes of Jack Sheppard'."

Batman had several long and futile journeys, without capturing any Tasmanians, and often he had to make the entry in his log: "No sign of Natives". He was even obliged to build a substantial hut as a depot for provisions for the man trappers. He tried sending the men out by themselves but they brought in no one. Then he tried sending them out with Tasmanian women to entice in the males of their tribe: but the women would go on strike. He therefore struck a happy medium: the men assisted the Tasmanian women with their chattels, dogs, knives, pipes, etc., to a certain spot, and then the rest was left to the women. It was they who went into the deepest parts of the forest after the tribesmen working there. Often there was success and the women brought them in in ones and twos. Mr. Batman trusted them in these matters and they rarely let him down. He even wrote: "I have every hope of the women bringing in their tribe." He alone carried firearms, not one of his men being permitted this indulgence.

Sometimes he would participate in the pursuit of some particularly mischievous gang, though he came too late to catch the murderers of the three men at Major Gray's, as already mentioned. But hearing of a mob attacking Mr. Hooper's place, he rode hastily there. His record for that day says:

"The house surrounded by Natives, I galloped down, and the whole of them fled. The first thing that we saw was the dead body of Mr. Hooper, and then a great number of goods lying outside of the house."

He was quite ready to acknowledge something to the credit of the settlers' foes. When ordered off to another reported scene of outrage, where it was alleged that a Mr. Newland's man had been killed, he arrived to find the whole thing to be false. "The man who had originated the story was a cripple, or I should have taken him before the magistrate."

Another notice indicates his kinder feelings:

"They went also into a house where a woman was, took one blanket, and did not hurt her. This shows that they do not commit murders as often as they might."

After another expedition he wrote,

"I returned without seeing the least trace of any Natives, and think the whole of the report to be false."

When the parties went out in search of the aborigines they walked anything up to twenty-five miles a day (this was not bad going as often the terrain was very rough: evidence of this is shown in the numerous diary entries concerning foot trouble). It was often very wet and cold, particularly on the higher ground where there was often snow up to three or four feet in depth, which might lie for a week at a time.

Batman seems to have had regard for the aborigine women and children as the following extract suggests:

"The women here all day. This evening the young child, belonging to one of the women, that sucked at the breast, died. I put it in a box, and buried it at the top of the garden. She seemed much affected at the loss of the child and she cried much."

The next day's entry begins:

"This morning I found the woman that had lost her child, over the grave, and crying much."

As he was never very generous with the written word, it shows all the more his concern. Some other of this entries read as follows: "The Black women could not walk well"; "Caught a kangaroo for the women"; "The women much tired: and gave them bread and mutton"; "The black women arrived here about twelve o'clock, made them tea and gave them some bread, etc." He was evidently very uneasy about any long absence of his women. For a whole fortnight there is in his diary, "No sign of the women." When he heard that the reason for their absence was that they had been snowed up, he was much concerned about sending them relief. Then, upon their final return, he would not allow them to leave their hut for several days because of the snow.

Meanwhile, Mr. Robertson had not been successful to any great degree, his only, rather doubtful, success being the "capture" of the bold chief Eumarra and four others in October, 1829. Eumarra became his friend and helper. When Mr. Robertson retired from service in 1830, he was given a grant of a thousand acres of land. This Mr. Robertson must not be confused with Mr. Robinson the conciliator, of whom we shall hear much more later.

In December, 1831, Mr. Anthony Cottrell caught two men and a woman and made such good use of them that he secured the rest of their tribe, which lived in the north-east of the country. In the following November he made what was termed an excellent haul, and he was proud to say in his official report:

"There was not the least of force used toward the people that joined us on this occasion, and they were allowed to retain their spears, and to do as they pleased."

The majority of those that survived were sent to Flinders Island, and we can understand the fate that they met there. Among the least of the island's faults was that it was very exposed: however, the majority of the people who had been sent there came from sheltered, well-watered areas of the mainland—and fresh water, of course, was another problem. On Flinders Island there was very little. The only supply that the authorities could discover was one that came out of the sands when the tide was out. It is true that when they first arrived there were a few kangaroos that they could chase but evidently it was a case of "man does not live by kangaroos alone". As soon as they arrived at Flinders Island a rot, both internal and social, started to set in. They became lazy and acquired previously alien vices, the least of which was drink. Another problem was that their entire social structure had been broken down; and we know now that this is often the cause of deterioration of a people. Indeed it can be the sole cause, as in the case of some of the American Indian tribes who, when they were put on the reservations, did nothing but drink afterwards. Although the Tasmanian aborigines all looked alike to the majority of the settlers of those times and the others who came in contact with them, we have reports, from some of the earliest naturalists who visited the island at the end of the eighteenth century, that the tribes varied greatly in size and feature, and also, it was suspected, in intelligence as well. On Flinders Island all the tribes were lumped together. This was bitterly resented and led to much friction. The overseers did not, or would not, understand this, thus causing more friction and bloodshed and consequent punishments, which were also resented. So the Tasmanian race descended from hopeful to hopeless on Flinders Island.

In the course of Mr. Cottrell's hunting down of the aborigines for the reservation on Flinders Island, he went to the West Coast to follow the Arthur River tribe, or what was left of it. They had been an active tribe, having speared a Sydney aborigine sent to track them down and made Mr. G. A. Robinson run for his life. Thus it was time that they were taught a lesson, although it was obvious that, as a tribe, they were doomed.

Two of Cottrell's helpers were drowned at the mouth of the Pieman's River, before he himself, on January 30th, 1833, fell in with the remnants of the tribe. He found some twenty-six of them thirty miles from the Macquarie Harbour Heads, and might have met with a favourable response to his appeals, but for the shrewdness of the chief, Edick. They agreed to submit, and did stay one night and part of a day with him. But, passing through some dense scrub-land, Edick persuaded the tribe to leave their white "friends". Cottrell was unable to detain them for he had no trinkets and provisions with which to persuade them to stay.

However, he pressed forward in pursuit, and at last saw them on the opposite shore of the Arthur River. A raft was hurriedly constructed with the assistance of Mr. Robinson's son. They tried to cross but the frail craft struck a bar and was wrecked. One of Stewart's party made a rude form of a canoe. A few of the aborigines on the other side of the river made signs that they were willing to go with Mr. Cottrell if he could reach them. One of the party, a Black from Sydney, undertook to take the "canoe" to them and bring them back one by one. By doing this he managed to bring back five men, two women and a child. Edick observed the final crossing. Furious at the deceit of some members of his tribe, he rushed down to the shore with his spearmen. The Sydney man lightened the canoe by leaping into the water, leaving the last "rescued" man to paddle furiously for Cottrell's party, who were waiting. The storm of spears rained furiously, but the Australian aborigine, instead of swimming blindly on, dived deep whenever a spear came at him, rising to draw breath and then diving once more before the next missile could reach the spot of his last appearance. He made the shore safely though very much exhausted. Mr. Cottrell took the eight who came to him on February 5th and placed them temporarily on Grummett's Island, in Macquarie Harbour.

Another man catcher was M'Geary, who, though illiterate, had great experience in bushcraft and knew the ways of the Tasmanians well, and could speak some of their languages with fluency. He was associated for most of the time with Mr. G. A. Robinson, but once, when he was alone, he came across a tribe at Cape Portland. There he showed great diplomacy, and so convinced the aborigines of their peril if they met with the Red-Coats (soldiers) that they agreed to go with him. Accompanied by their forty-two dogs, they followed him to the Swan Island Depot.

Mr. M'Kay was also very active at bringing the aborigines in. In 1830, assisted by M'Geary, he captured thirteen at one go, and twelve on another occasion. He was also successful in catching four of the infamous Big River tribe. It was M'Kay who, on one occasion when attached to Mr. Robinson's Conciliatory Mission (as his group of catchers was termed), was severely treated by some fierce aborigines. In imminent danger of having his brains dashed out by their waddies, he produced the weapons which he had secreted, against orders, on his person. Such was their power, that four of the aborigines were dropped and the remnant departed in haste to the scrub.

Mr. Surridge, when coxwain of a boat at Waterhouse Point, to the north-east, captured several Tasmanians; and with the help of some sailors obtained others. In October, 1830, he placed three males and two females on the windswept Gun Carriage Island. In November, with the aid of aborigine gins, he obtained eight men and two women near Forster's River to the north-east. The recounting of all these captures reads very much of the last captures of the Greak Auk—the period is much the same though the clime is different, but both species were doomed.

The exploits of Mr. Jorgen Jorgenson, the Danish adventurer, are worth recording. This extraordinary man was an adventurer of no ordinary kind: he had been wanted for many years by the British police, and at one time had been uncrowned king of Iceland. His "reign" ended when the Danes came to collect him and he sought safety in London. However, the British authorities were so pleased at seeing him again that they gave him a free passage to Van Diemen's Land!

Yet, although in reality still a convict, his fertility of resources, drive and absence of shyness, brought him to the notice and forefront of the island society. A good writer, a diligent worker, an able and agreeable servant, he attracted the attention of Mr. Anstey when the roving parties were formed. Although getting on in years, the Dane made himself so useful to the police magistrate that he was eventually appointed to the command of a party himself. Typically, he proudly styled himself the only prisoner of the Crown entrusted with such a commission. He pleased Mr. Anstey and the Government at the same time with the detailed and regular reports that he produced in regard to his activities that he was allowed an extra king's shilling when out looking for aborigines.

A clever, shrewd, but calculating old man, he secured the approval of a few, the indifference of some and the dislike of many. Mr. Robinson appears to have been jealous of him as of some others, and tried in vain to dislodge him from the confidence of Mr. Anstey. In the end he was his own downfall. His old drinking habits began to tell and he retired, only to write occasionally upon the aborigine situation.

In a well written paper he unfolds the various causes of the lack of success in the existing arrangements:

"1st. Want of a plan of combined operations.

"2nd. A total absence of discipline.

"3rd. Inveterate laziness, which induces the parties to proceed over the best ground they can find from one place to another: the Natives, thus knowing their customary haunts, can therefore easily avoid them.

"4th. That the men forming the parties have been promised indulgence at the expiration of a certain time, without the additional condition that none would be granted unless the Natives were fallen in with, captured or otherwise disposed of.

"5th. The imposition and deceit practised by prisoner leaders, wishing to stand well, and be called good fellows by their fellow prisoners, and thus indulge the parties in idleness and stifle all complaints.

"6th. (But which I advance with a very great caution), Black Tom and the other Blacks accompanying the expedition not being willing to bring the parties to where the Natives would be likely to be.

"7th. The imposition practised, to screen idleness, to hold out that the aborigines are men of superior cunning, and amazingly swift runners, whereas the facts show to the contrary."

The enemies of Jorgenson, while forced to admit his facility of composition and his ability to find fault, went further and pointed out triumphantly the poor results that he had in the field. He reproved others for their absurd methods and incompetent ways, but failed in catching any Blacks himself.

The last known wild Tasmanian aborigine family consisted of an old man and an old woman, three elder children, and a little boy destined to be the last of his race.

A reward of fifty pounds had been offered for these people. The native female companion of one of the leaders of the hunting parties brought them in by pretending to the frightened creatures that she would show them the way to some very fine hunting grounds, where no Whites would harm them. Once in the boat they were powerless, as they became helplessly seasick. In that condition they were taken to a concentration camp near Cape Grim.

The Hobart Town Aboriginal Committee, now that nearly all the aborigines were in, decided against continuing the roving parties. The frequent charges brought against them of shooting the aborigines at last bore fruit, and at last steps were taken to have the roving parties withdrawn. On February 2nd, 1830, the committee wrote to the Governor saying that:

"they were of the unanimous opinion that martial law should be suspended during the period of Mr. Robinson's Peaceful Mission; and they are of further opinion that more missions of a similar nature could be employed to take charge of the parties, and see that no harm came to the Natives".

But the roving parties still continued to function for some time, however; until, by force of persuasion from the supporters of Mr. Robinson, they gradually disappeared. But the damage had been done: the family units had been broken and the tribal system was no more.

PART THREE

Conciliation

chapter 8

Mr. Robinson—The Bailiff

The man of the moment was George Agustus Robinson. He was of no high lineage and no worshipper of chivalry, nor did he inherit any special enthusiasm for the aborigines or have any direct training for a mission. He was but a plain man of very moderate education, with no elevating surroundings. He was, in fact, the Hobart Town bricklayer. This was the man who undertook to bring peace to a sorely troubled colony, and he believed that it was in his power to do so. He felt he had more ability than the thousands of soldiers and constables, and was stronger than the law (in fact, towards the end, he had more influence than the Governor). His promises were derided by the European populace of Tasmania, and his offers of service were neglected for a very considerable time. Only after official wisdom seemed to have failed and military prowess was vainly employed did the simple bricklayer manage to succeed, but his success was imperfect and in reality he hastened the end of the Tasmanians.

What was the basis of the man's confidence? He felt that he had the necessary qualifications. But what were these? Sincere conviction, hearty sympathy, active benevolence, sound common sense, a healthy body, unquailing courage in the face of danger, and resolute will. True heroes are developed only by circumstance, but they must be inspired by high purpose. G. A. Robinson had a blind faith and trust in God, and he thought that God had called him to do the work of saving the aborigines, and that God would show him the way. His attitude appealed to the sanctimonious trends of the day. The settlers, like so many Pilates, could then use him as a scapegoat if the work they had started should end in failure. But he was no mere sentimentalist nor even a religious maniac. Over the tales of the aboriginals' wrongs he did not shed the abundant tears of sentimentality for the wronged. Instead he groaned in spirit as he dwelt upon the horrors perpetrated in the bush. He was not satisfied with grieving over wrong, but was spurred to redress the evil done and to avert the still threatening foe.

If not scholarly, he had his faculties about him, ready for prompt and direct employment. His social sphere was limited but sufficient for his purpose. He did not, like many, hope for more favourable circumstances, nor pant after unattainable conditions, but in true workmanlike style he made do with the tools that were available.

His plans were well thought out and matured, yet few to whom he told them believed in their practicability. Good men and women wished they might succeed, yet shook their heads in doubt. However, one man of influence accepted the bricklayer's views. This was Lieutenant Gunn, the giant superintendent of the Hobart Town penitentiary. A man of the world, a stern military disciplinarian, a controller of the roughest elements of the convicts, a contender of armed bushrangers, one not easily swayed by smooth humanitarianism. But George Robinson had to wait until the time was ripe.

Meanwhile, he went on with his own way of tackling the aborigine problem. Any possible chance of blessing an unfortunate Tasmanian was eagerly embraced. In his leisure he visited the sick and the fallen. The caged prisoners were the object of his Christian zeal. He worked, too, with the Whites, the sailors and the whalers that he met on the shore, as secretary for the first Bethel Mission of Hobart. An ardent Wesleyan, in Sunday School or on the highway, he taught, he pleaded, he prayed, he preached his way to fame. This Robinson had nothing of the gloomy ascetic about him, though one who knew him well said that his whole bearing seemed to imply "that he would knock down St. Paul's to carry out his purpose". He was strongly built, of middle stature, and fit to encounter bush hardships.

The Tasmanians appreciated Mr. Robinson's interest in them, and hung about his workshop and home. His wife and his children shared his interest in this maligned and oppressed race, though they could give little except indications of sympathy. But all this was in the 1820s and, when the terrible times of conflict burst out, when the bitter and unrelenting war scattered the tribes, the pleasant gatherings at the bricklayer's abode ended. In the climate of European opinion there was no place for such rapport between races.

Mr. Robinson certainly had enthusiasm for his work, but it was based mainly on the ideal of the brotherhood of man. He was an idealist when what was really required at that time was a more influential and practical person to be concerned with the Tasmanians, one who could act as a supremo for their cause. Only in this way could the tribes have been saved. Also, the natives felt that there was no one to speak up for them—no chief—only a white tribesman.

In March 1829 the following notice appeared in the Hobart Town *Gazette:*

"In furtherance of the Lieutenant-Governor's anxious desire to ameliorate the condition of the aboriginal inhabitants of this territory, His Excellency will allow a salary of £50 per annum, together with rations, to a steady man of good character, that can be well recommended, who will take an interest in effecting an intercourse with this unfortunate race, to reside on Bruni Island, taking charge of the provisions supplied for the use of the Natives of that place."

Mr. Robinson felt that the appointment was aimed at him, but that:

"there are many powerful reasons against my entering upon such an enterprise, I have a wife and several children dependent upon me. But my mind was under the impression which I could not resist. I reasoned the matter over with Mrs. Robinson, and with difficulty obtained her consent."

On March 16th, 1929, he wrote the following application:

"Feeling a strong desire to devote myself to the above cause, and believing the plan which your Exellency has devised to be the only one whereby this unfortunate race can be ameliorated; that as the Hottentot has been raised in the scale of Being, and the inhabitants of the Society Islands are made an industrious and intelligent race, so likewise, by the same exertions, may the inhabitants of this territory be instructed. With these impressions, I beg to offer myself for the situation. I would beg leave to submit to your Excellency that a salary of fifty pounds per annum is not sufficient for the support of my family—would therefore request that you would be pleased to make such additions to the salary as you may think meet. Should my offer be accepted, I do not wish the superfluities, I only desire to procure the necessities, of life. I wish to devote myself to this people."

He was, due to his enthusiasm, eventually accepted at a salary of a hundred pounds per annum.

Bruni Island, which was named after Admiral D'Entrecasteaux, lies between the Channel and Storm Bay, and extends to the south-west for fifty miles. Rather a bleak spot for people who had been used to the sheltered glades of the more central parts of a large island. South Bruni, in which Cook's Adventure Bay is situated, is united to North Bruni by a low, narrow neck of land, and was uninhabited at this time. Upon the northern portion there was a salt works and mines. The rocky coast was a dangerous cauldron, shunned by mariners. In fact, the indentations of the coastline were so extreme that the enormous waves seemed at time to engulf the island. This was the place that the administrators had chosen for "these unfortunate people", as they termed them. The station for the aborigines was made in a little cove on the western, or inner side, of Bruni, called Cap de la Sortie. In fact, this was really the only possible site, as there was so little other suitable terrain, and thirty years of suffering lay before the Tasmanian race at this encampment.

Rations and bread and potatoes were served out to any of the aborigines who could be persuaded to reside at the station. These rations were poor in quality and deficient in quantity. The biscuits were the refuse of supplies, and a few potatoes each day were a miserable substitute for the plentiful and varied foodstuffs that the sea and the forest provided for the free rangers. It is no wonder, then, that the Tasmanians forced to settle on Bruni, although officially for their own protection and civilization, sickened in the prison which, in reality, it was. They were heartsick and homesick, and that is what most of them died of. If the authorities saw the crime that they were perpetrating, they did nothing about it.

The Tasmanians themselves did try to do something about it. Despite the difficulties and a large number of drownings, many of them succeeded in making their way back to the mainland, where they were, as often as not, shot or taken back to Bruni. They were treated in this respect like the worst of prisoners, and the terrible irony of it was that it was chiefly prisoners or ex-prisoners that meted out such treatment to the wild, free men.

Among those that remained behind, sickness took its toll, and Robinson vainly attempted to bring them relief. He shared his own personal rations with the poor creatures, urgently wrote for help, and asked for a small amount of tobacco for those that had acquired the habit of smoking from civilization. Some tea and sugar were also

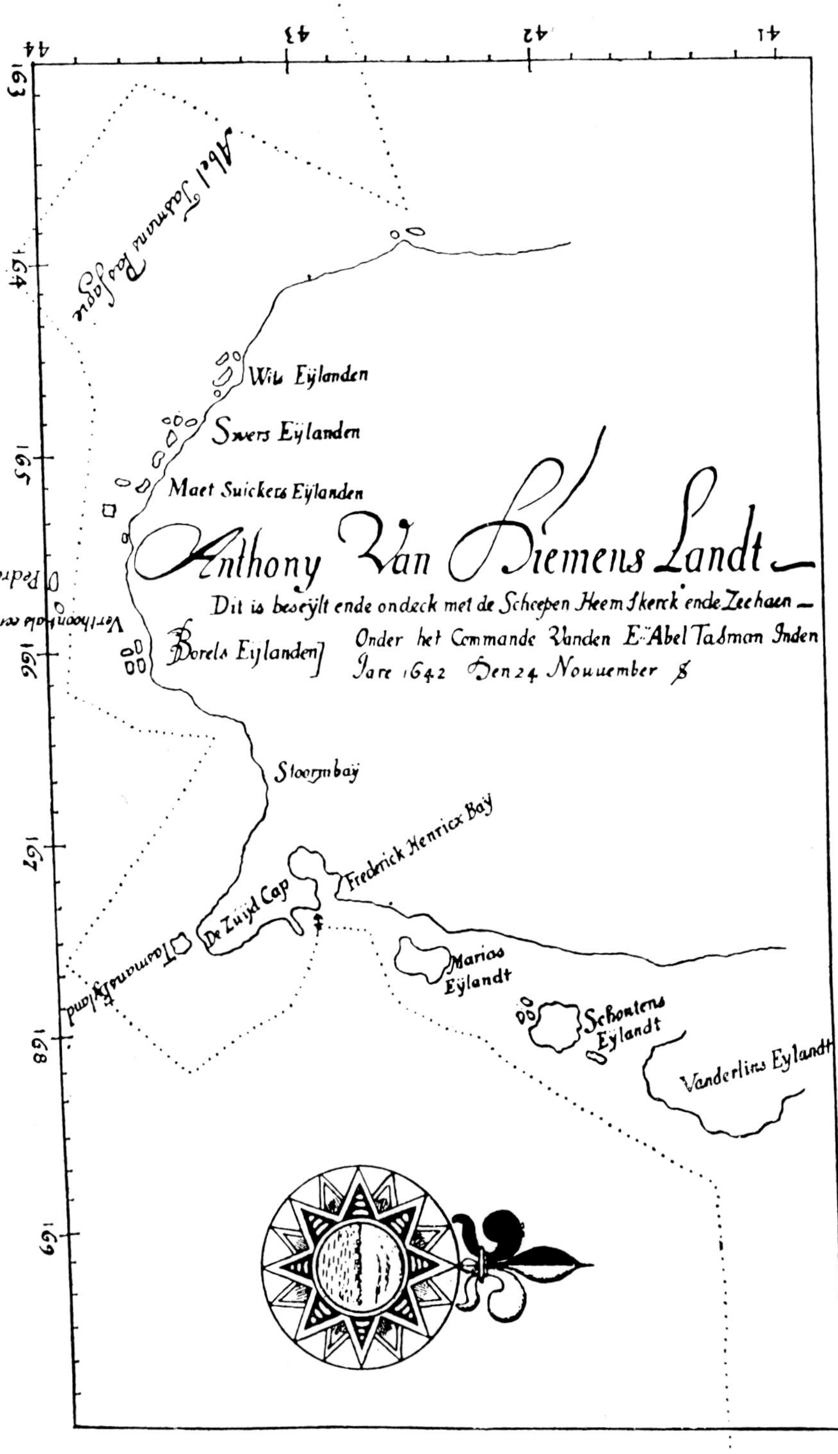

Abel Tasman's map of Van Diemens Land, originally made in 1642 and
here reproduced from Heeres' *Tasman*, 1898

Plate 1

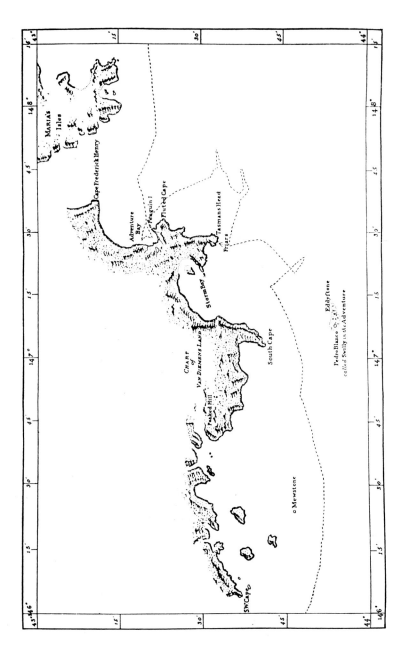

Part of one of Captain Cook's charts from *Voyage to the Pacific Ocean* showing
Van Diemens Land, 1777

Plate 2

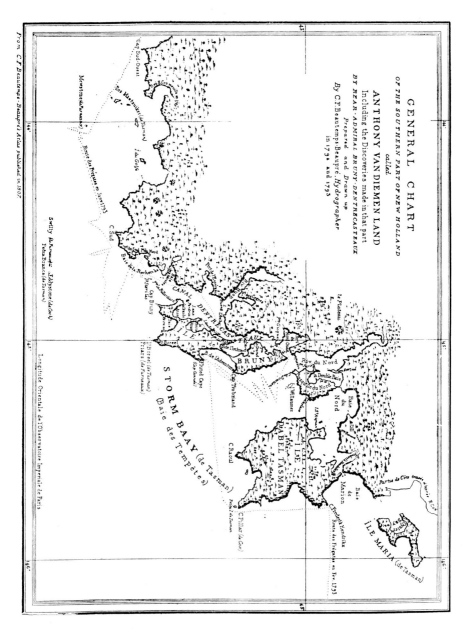

A map of Van Diemens Land drawn up in 1792–3 by C. F. Beautemps-
Beaupré

Plate 3

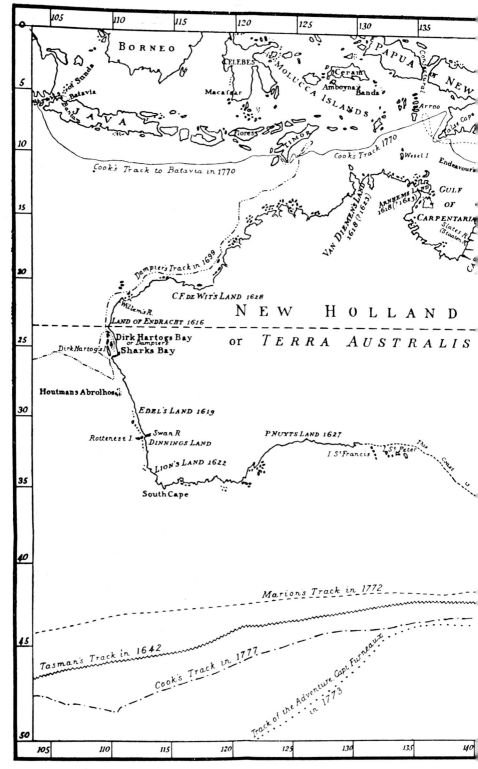

A map of Australia showing Tasmania as a peninsula rather than as an island, from a chart published in London in 1789

Plate 4

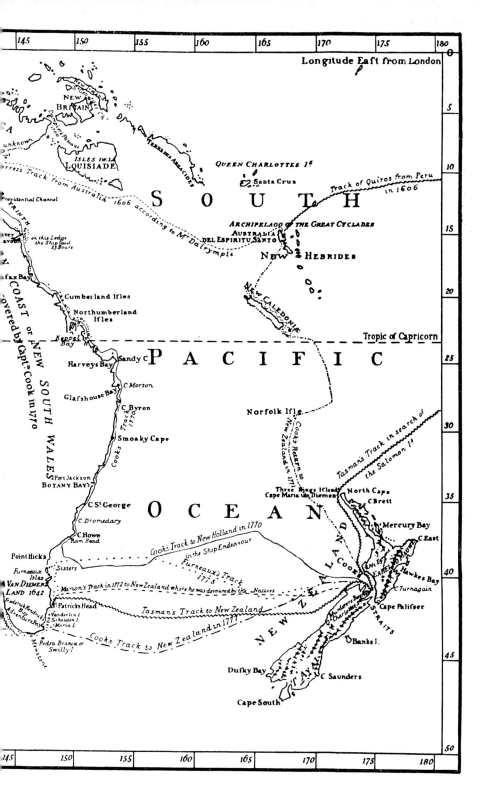

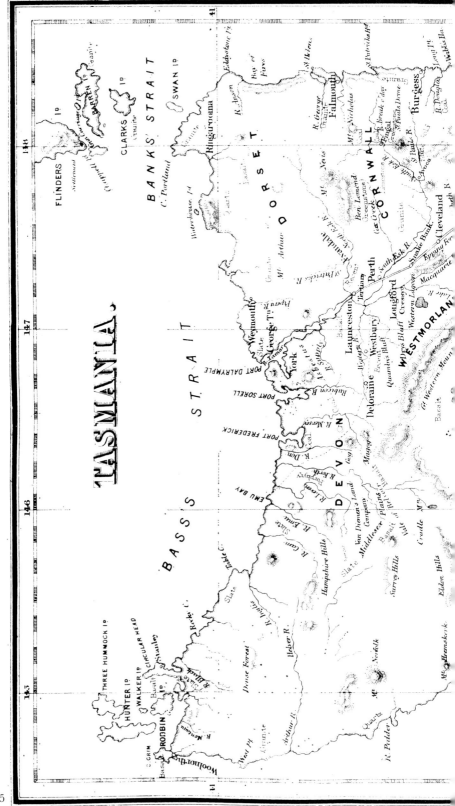

TASMANIA

Plate 5

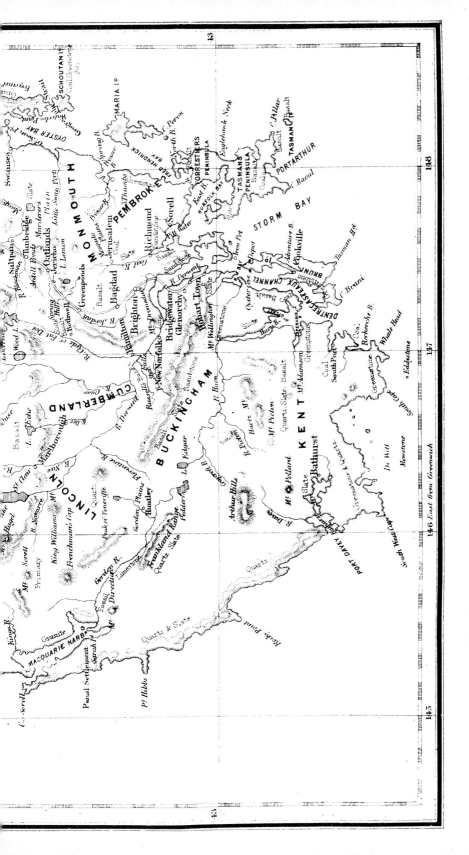

A very fine map of Tasmania published in the late nineteenth century as one of the plates for Bonwick's *Last of the Tasmanians*

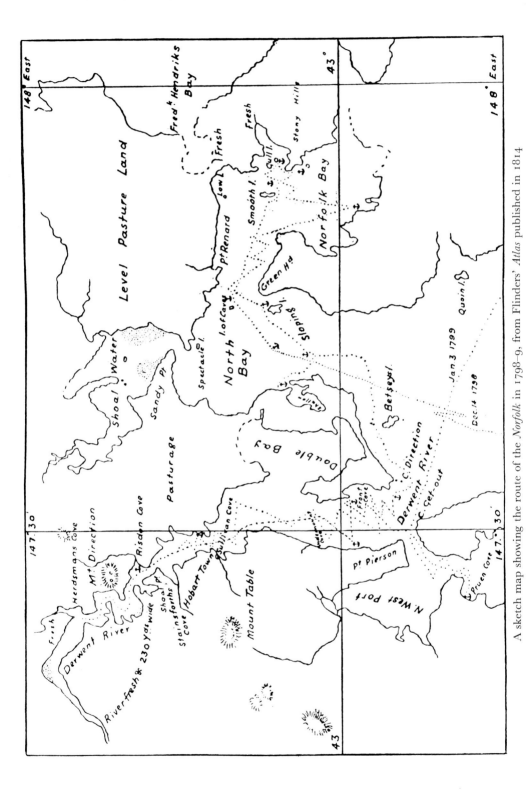

A sketch map showing the route of the *Norfolk* in 1798–9, from Flinders' *Atlas* published in 1814

Plate 6

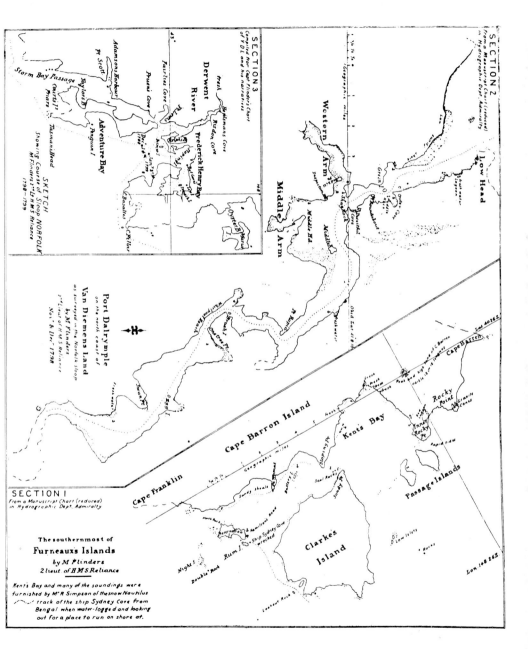

Three parts of the coast of Van Diemens Land as surveyed by Flinders in the *Norfolk*

Plate 7

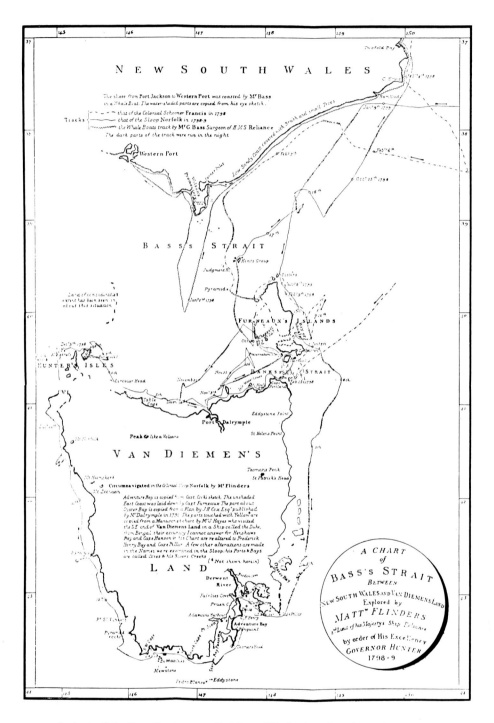

A chart of the Bass Strait, compiled from Flinders' explorations, that shows most of the coastline of Van Diemens Land. This chart was published in 1800

Plate 8

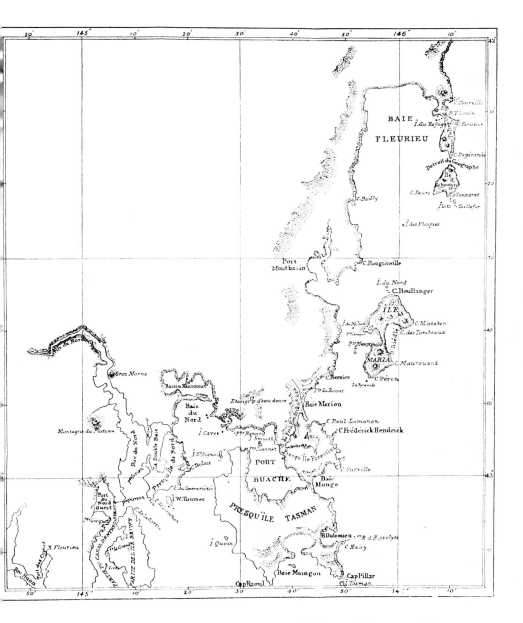

A sketch map showing the results of Captain Baudin's expedition to south-east Tasmania in 1802

Plate 9

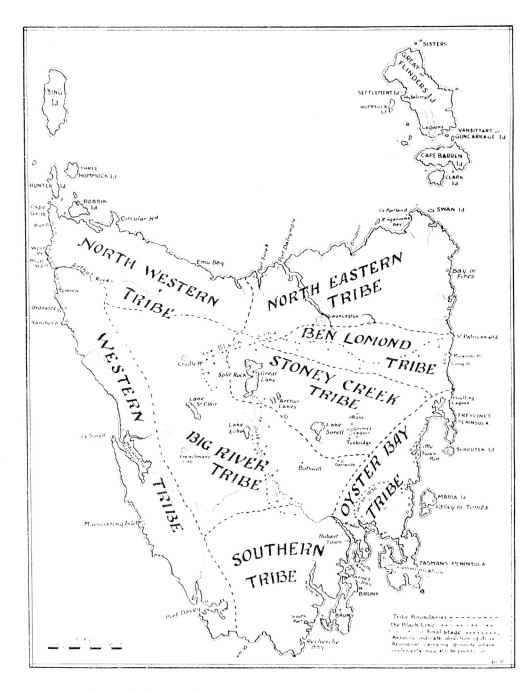

A map showing roughly the areas that the various Tasmanian tribes held

Plate 10

ordered, but tobacco was prohibited on the grounds that such a luxury was hardly compatible with such primitive peoples. Meanwhile, the sickness increased. Wooreddy, the Tasmanian chieftain, lost his principal wife and child, and another leading man and his two wives died. A sad story was told of another infant being found suckling at the breast of its dead mother. The cry went from this barren land: "No good—this bad place—no egg—no kangaroo—no like—all die."

But a severe trial was still to come, for "the Blacks" were to be civilized and to be the instruments for taming their wilder countrymen. Yet paradoxically, if they were to become "civilized", they were placed on Bruni in very close contact with some of the worst characters to be found in the colony. Mr. Robinson had repeated complaints from the women of cruel assaults and rapes by the convict woodcutters who, of course, had no women of their own. He observed indignantly, but passively, the casual assaults, kidnappings and seductions by the whalers, who counted it their right to use the gins for their sexual gratification, particularly as many of the women still went about naked.

At this time, the black whale came around the southern coast, and into the Storm Bay. As a result, several permanent whaling stations existed at the mouth of the channel. The whalers were, generally speaking, a rough-hewn class of men. Their full rations of meat, spirits and tobacco, provided a ready means of attracting the females whenever required. One interesting effect of this intercourse was that often after the woman had produced a half-caste child (which was promptly dispatched) she was apparently unable to produce any children after intercourse with men of her own race. This factor was often commented upon, even at that time, and quite obviously played a vital part in regard to their success as a species. No doubt too, the whalers were grateful that the Governor and the Government in Hobart Town had kindly brought all the naked black women of the island right to their doorstep!

The locality of the "Native Depot" did not allow Robinson to sufficiently isolate his charges. To prevent further trouble and sorrows for them, he applied for permission to remove the aborigines to Barnes Bay, and, as he stated in the official letter, "care will be taken that they have from now onwards no contact with the 'White Heathen' ".

But the troubles continued. The gins left the depot to seek out the company of the sailors and they would go off on the ships for several days at a time as supercargo. This created strife within the depot and also brought in venereal disease, if it was not already present. Mild expostulations and denunciations were alike of no service, and Robinson

6

wrote almost despairingly about "the moral pestilence". But it all appeared to fall upon deaf ears at Government House, for now they had no need to worry further—honour, or conscience, was satisfied, "natives" were being taken care of.

But the storms of war were again rising. Outrages and cruelties increased on Bruni Island. The Whites became more infuriated, and the Blacks more determined. The latter saw no hope and they resolved to die spear in hand: with another people and in another time, this would have been considered heroic. We can all sympathize with struggles for freedom, especially if they are Greek, and classic. But when colonists are brought into collision with the races whose lands they have seized without compensation or inquiry, the feeling is otherwise; the heroism of the foe is lost in the midst of selfishness. The resolve of the Tasmanians, therefore, seemed to be to make no peace with the possessors of their hunting grounds. This naturally, if unfairly, excited the indignation and displeasure of the colony. It was then that Mr. Robinson, sick of his miserable failure on Bruni, but still convinced that it lay in his power to do something more effective for the aborigines, proposed going after the wild marauders on a mission of mercy. The Aborigines' Protection Committee seconded his suggestions, and the Government sanctioned his objective.

Later, when Mr. Robinson was over seventy and a resident of Bath in Somerset, years after these events took place, he stated:

> "I considered that the Natives of Van Diemen's Land were rational; and although they might, in their savage notions, oppose violent measures for their subjugation, yet if I could but get them to listen to reason, and persuade them that the Europeans wished only to better their conditions, they might have become civilised, and therefore become useful members of society instead of the blood-thirsty, ferocious beings that they were represented as being. This was the principle upon which I formed my plan.*

A dozen aborigines had been captured by Mr. Gilbert Robertson, and others, and were lodged for safety in the Richmond jail. It was arranged to forward four of these to Mr. Robinson, though the latter was to rely more upon his Bruni aborigines. Black Tom, Pegale, Joseph, Doctor and M'lean (a European), were appointed to act as interpreters to his party. Eumarrah, with Manalagana and his wife, went with him later.

* But since their language was difficult to understand, and since interpreters were considered unnecessary, it was rather difficult to "get them to listen to reason".

But the one upon whom he most relied, and who proved a faithful and an efficient ally throughout his subsequent time in the bush, was the young Truganina. She was the beauty of Bruni, and for this reason had been nicknamed Lala Rookh by the Europeans. She was, in fact, the last of the Tasmanian race, dying at about the age of sixty years. Her picture (see plate C5) sadly shows her only as an old, sad and disillusioned relic of a once fine race: it hardly does justice to the young beauty of Bruni.

Many stories are told her her vivacity and intelligence. She was always full of fun and as coquettish as any French girl has ever been. Men of her own race found her irresistibly attractive, and she appears to have had many admirers among the Europeans, too. Her mind was out of the general run of the mill, fertile and wise, and she was courageous in difficulties. It has been said that she had the fascination of the serpent, and the intrepidity of the royal ruler of the desert. She was, moreover, well known for her sexual exploits, and might well be termed the Nell Gwyn of the Tasmanian aborigine world.

A lady described her appearance in 1832, and indicated that she generally wore no clothes, though occasionally a little dress was thrown loosely around her person. However, she always showed her small, beautifully rounded breasts, and the rest of her figure was most well formed. A dress, however small, was always worn with grace and a coquettish love of display. The *Courier* of Hobart Town noticed one characteristic in her portrait by M. Duterrau: "She is the very picture of good humour," it said.

Though she was a wife, she was never a mother, as is so often the way with real coquettes. Her older and more sober husband had always had some difficulty in restraining the erratic tendencies in his fickle partner. No one really knows why she bothered to persevere in following the Mission, so inconstant was she in other ways. She was a woman of the forest, yet she devoted many years of her life to difficult and perilous work on behalf of the Europeans, on journeys to entrap and secure her countrymen. It has been said that she became infatuated with Mr. Robinson, and that they were even lovers but, whatever the truth of this may be, she was without doubt much attached to him. Some have thought that vanity was her leading passion, and that the desire of distinction among the Europeans and the Blacks induced her to become prominent as a guide and interpreter.

Although her husband, Wooreddy (or "the Doctor"), consented to be one of Mr. Robinson's party, a story is told how, shortly after the departure of the party in January, 1830, and when they were well and truly out in the bush, as Mr. Robinson was sleeping near a large cave, the jealous husband arose in the night and, taking a weapon in his hand, was about to dash out the brains of Mr. Robinson when he was discovered. Yet Mr. Robinson does not seem to have had any ill feeling, for Wooreddy seems to have continued with the party. "At all Mr. Robinson's meetings with the Tasmanians, and many times, he was preserved from danger by the actions of this man afterwards . . . Manalagana as a warrior stood unrivalled among the aborigines and was considered a sage of his tribe," said the artist Mr. Duterrau, who painted several pictures of the aborigines, including the group that depicted Mr. Robinson in his rather strange dress (see plate A26). The artist, who was also a good friend of Mr. Robinson, goes on to say:

> "Such was the commanding influence of Mr. Robinson, that he possessed over these rather strange people, that, at first interview, Manalagana, left the bush, and from then on accompanied Mr. Robinson on all his 'Pauline' missionary journeys, throughout the island and he continued this faithful attachment to the conclusion of his service in 1835."

Manalagana then went to live on Flinders Island, where all the captured aborigines were taken. However, he died there very soon after, in 1836.

Often, in my visits to aboriginal peoples in various parts of the world, I have found them filled with a great desire to follow one. Once I had seven of them following me around and they would wait at my door for me to appear. They were often poor, skinny little men and the small pieces of bone through their septums was about all the ornamentation that they possessed. But they would have made good and faithful friends if treated correctly. Anyone from the "Great Outside" would be treated the same.

Mr. Duterrau also has something to say about Manalagana's wife:

> "This woman laboured incessantly to promote the objects of the mission. Tanleboueyer and her sister were originally stolen from their families by the sealers, as was the custom of those gentlemen, when they were little girls and kept for later use as slave girls and for assisting and cleaning the seals and the mutton birds. They were held in bondage until emancipated by Mr. Robinson in 1830. She was superior to the other aborigines both in person and intelligence, and possessed much dignity of manner, seldom participating in the

frivolities that the others indulged in. She was exceedingly attached to her husband. The feeling was mutual, for during the period of six years, they were with Mr. Robinson, they never were known to quarrel."

In the first instance his engagement with the Government was for a year, but he demanded payment in advance of one half of his year's salary, so that his wife would be provided for in the event of any accident, as things could be so very uncertain.

Mr. Robinson's work did not begin very encouragingly. For instance, the boat that had been provided for his passage to Port Davey, in the south-west, was wrecked, with the loss of nearly all his supplies. However, being a resolute man, he set off with a full rucksack on foot to reach Port Davey overland. Not long afterwards he was nearly killed. Walloa, a female Tasmanian, arose, like Joan of Arc from amidst the remnant of her race to deliver her people. She gathered a party of warriors around her by her courageous conduct in the field, something this is most unusual as, according to contemporary reports about the Tasmanians, the women were generally regarded as of small account. Walloa soon took charge of the Port Sorell tribe, and with them murdered Captain Thomas and many others. Hearing that Mr. Robinson was in her neighbourhood, she immediately sent her forces against him. However, unarmed and warned of her approach, he fled in great haste. For five days the pursuit continued. Just when he was almost cornered by this furious Amazon, M'Geary appeared on the scene with a large party. Being thus confronted by such a strong band of Europeans, Walloa retired with her forces to the fastnesses of the north.

During the last quarter of 1830, when the "Line" operations were taking place, the energies of the colony were entirely engaged upon this scheme, and it had much influence upon the Mission. That manœuvre, though not apparently in itself bringing destruction to the Tasmanians, caused much more lasting damage by breaking down their social and tribal structures; and it is probably not too strong to say that this breakdown was their death knell. The work of Mr. Robinson and his Mission was merely an extra knife in the dying body of the race.

Mr. Robinson in his first year travelled the whole of the western and northern part of the country. At Cape Grim, to the north-west, he met the powerful Bendoadicka, his wife Narraga, and his brother Peewee.

While the Line was out he was in the Cape Portland district, to the north-east. It was here that he heard of the capture of thirteen aborigines at one time, and twelve at another, by the party led by M'Geary and M'Kay. Disappointed in his own plans, it was then that he executed the first part of his mission by removing the young women and the female children from the sealers. That was fairly successful from his point of view, and a relief after all his failures. Perhaps the sealers realized what was going on—they had plenty of boats, and they knew that the intention of the Government was to put all the Tasmanians upon an island where, incidentally, they would have easy access to them. This would mean that they would eventually have a wider choice of females without competition from the other settlers. They had, by experience, learnt how to handle the males: those that would not bargain their women away for tobacco or flour could be coerced by other means. The only disadvantage to the sealers in this new plan was that they would have fewer people to clean the carcasses of their seals and prepare the mutton birds, for in the past they had relied on the female Tasmanians to do this work for them during the day. The sealers, when the season was over, passed their days in slumber and intoxication. Little ships would go among them trading, letting them have tobacco in exchange for the skins. It is difficult to know how many native women they had as they would dissemble at the sight of strangers. Having the authority of the Governor, Robinson visited some of the islands in the straits, and collected eighteen females from the sealers.

In 1831, the Governor gave Robinson's peaceful methods a trial. Mr. Robinson urged the withdrawal of the armed parties from the bush. His enemies declared that this was a plot on his part to secure the whole management of the captures, and therefore to deprive the leaders of the Line parties from their prize. He tried to get assistants to help him in his campaign of catching the Tasmanians without using any form of force, and high rewards were offered, but there was no response and he had to do most of the work himself. It was not until after the Line project had been abandoned that he gained so much assistance from the community, when the folly of the Line had been amply demonstrated. At this stage his salary was raised, from £100 to £250. There was then a strong force organized for the abandonment of the Line, as Mr. Robinson's was now considered the only way of tackling "the Black Problem".

As he had to forgo the use of physical force he had to think of other schemes and plans. His Tasmanian female decoys were decorated in gaudy ribbons to attract the eye of those still out in the bush, trinkets were distributed, and even marvellous wooden toys provided. An ex-bushranger said that he had found red feathers, red strings and other pretty looking objects hung in the trees of the far interior by the adventurous party. Among the feminine decoys were, to mention a few, Gooseberry, Violet, Molly and Truganina. It is said that they looked well in their fine feathers, and employed their arts and smiles skilfully to gain the confidence of their more innocent countrymen, those whom they gathered in being either sent off to the island depots or added to the Mission's strength. One or two of the gins may have had a sister or a brother who had attached himself to a neighbouring tribe, and natural affection urged the search after the lost one; for these women really thought that they were doing a service to their people, and were afraid that the Redcoats might capture the aborigines and probably shoot them if they remained wandering in the forest. Sometimes, too, a man wanted to seek a lost wife and thought that he might find her among the growing number of tribes-people that the Mission was gathering. They thought that they would then be draughted off to join their relatives and neighbours in the new and wonderful hunting ground that had been promised to them—they had not yet learnt about Flinders Island.

The first conquest of 1831 was the Stony Creek tribe. The chief, Moultehalergunah (as it is spelt by Mr. Robinson), had been a great hunter of the white man. Twenty came along with the Moultehalergunah when Mr. Robinson captured them, aided by M'Geary, M'Lean and Platt.

When the aborigines were brought in they would generally ask if some of their relatives were also there: one would ask for a son, another for a sister, a third for his wife. One man, Eumarra, met Mr. Robinson in the forest, rushed towards him, and grasped his hand. With him he brought five men and one woman. In June, 1831, in his official report Robinson was able to say that, through the efforts of his party, 123 had yielded, 236 had been communicated with, 110 had gone back to their hunting grounds, and that 16 had escaped after capture and no one knew where they had gone. During these activities he had also become acquainted with sixteen tribes, but it does not seem that they had many members: perhaps they were something like the tribes of northern Thailand where some have as few as eight people.

Towards the end of the year Mr. Robinson had even more success at bringing the aborigines in, as they were very much afraid of the power of the Redcoats. In this success he was ably supported by Manalagana, of whom Mr. Duterrau, the painter of the Tasmanians, said that: "He was a noble-minded savage, of superior intellect and courage, and of great benevolence"; an opinion borne out in the artist's pictures of him, for he is usually shown in some heroic attitude. Manalagana's son was murdered by one of the wild tribes but, showing restraint remarkable by any standards, he did not seek revenge but co-operated instead, apparently in good faith, to bring in the offending tribe without any bloodshed, so that they might be saved from destruction by the Redcoats. However, it must be said that on several occasions it was as much as the chief could do to prevent the Mission of Conciliation becoming a March of Massacre.

The Mission arrived at Lake Echo on November 18th. It was a strong party, consisting of Mr. Robinson, his son, an Hawaiian, a messenger and twelve friendly aborigines. They had ascended from the valleys of Central Tasmania and had reached the vast irregular plateaux occupying a position somewhat similar to the Deccan in India. The smoke from the fire of a tribal remnant was seen, rising in thin columns through the thick foliage. A rush was made towards this, but they were too late. The hunted creatures, always on the watch, with the stealth of all primitive peoples had discovered their enemies first, and had hastily retired to an even thicker region. Robinson urged on the pursuit. One aborigine, a female, knew the terrain well, but she became alarmed at the closeness of some much feared tribes that she knew were lurking around, and led the party astray: a whole month was lost on false trails. But on the last day of the year the tribe was contacted. Then Robinson practised his bushcraft. Sending forward some of his female decoys, he and the rest planted themselves in thickets of scrub, anxiously awaiting the results of the negotiations. What happened is described in his own words:

"In less than half an hour afterwards, I heard their war-hoop and I knew that they were advancing upon me. I also heard the rattle of their spears as they drew even nearer. At this moment Manalagana leaped to his feet in great alarm, saying that the Natives were coming to spear us. He urged me to run away. Finding that I would not do so, he immediately took up his spears and kangaroo rug, and walked away. Some of the other Natives were about to follow his example, but I prevailed upon them to stop. From their advancing with a war-hoop, the Natives as well as ourselves, considered that they were advancing upon us with hostile intentions in mind, and that they had either killed the Natives that had been sent from us, or that those Natives had joined the hostile tribes. As they drew near, I did not observe my people among them. The hostile Natives being a large body, I was rather anxious as to the result. It was not until they had approached very near, that I then saw my own people with them.

But they continued coming up in the same warlike attitude. I then went up to the chiefs and shook hands with them. Having explained to them in the aboriginal dialect, the purpose of my visit among them, I invited them to sit down, gave them some refreshment, and selected a few trinkets as presents, which they received with much delight. They evinced considerable astonishment at hearing me address them in their own tongue, and from henceforth placed themselves entirely under my control. The men were accompanied by the women; and, after taking their refreshment, I returned with them to their own encampment, where the evening was spent in mutual good humour, each party dancing alternately.

It was obviously a clever move on Robinson's part to be able to learn the languages of the people for, if the Australian aborigines' languages are anything to go by, they were extremely difficult to learn. In fact, he was probably about the only White who had this knowledge. Bishop Nixon (bishop from 1843 to 1863), the first Bishop of Tasmania, was considered a great missionary bishop, yet he appears to have had little contact with the really wild members of his see. We hear of his concern for a semi-civilized one, when brought to his notice, but as the bishop was ill he could do little more than express pious concern. There is also a photograph of him with a group of Tasmanians, but really one cannot help feeling that he was the first missionary to the pioneers and the settlers and that the original Tasmanians were ignored by him. He certainly did not speak the languages.

Another point indicated in the above quotation from Robinson's record is that the aborigines themselves did not really know the temper of their own people, as illustrated by the attitude of Manalagana, who was not going to stay around in the face of apparently hostile tribesmen. This uncertain temperament is found very often among the highlanders of New Guinea today. Perhaps Manalagana had been too long among "civilized" people and had forgotten the ways and the attitudes of his wilder kinsmen.

The capture of the Big River, or the Ouse River tribe, was recognized as the grandest feature of the Black War, and Mr. Robinson played the most important part in this affair. The leader and his party had ventured westward under the protection of the forests that lay at the foot of the Frenchman's Cap. The grim cone of this volcano rises five thousand feet above the uninhabited western interior that to this day is still partly unexplored. There, at last, appeared the tribe for which they had been searching. It was the last tribe of any note and was the

terror of the colony. Confident in their strength, the Tasmanians stayed
for the approach of the strangers, Mr. Robinson, his son, M'Geary, Mr.
Stanfield, and the Hawaiian Islander. We also know that among the
Tasmanians with them were Manalagana and Truganina. The
chieftain of the hostile tribe was Montpeliata, a stout but very tall man,
who carried a spear at least eighteen feet long. He stood there glowering
at them, backed up by fifteen powerful men, each with three spears
and a waddy and filled with all the hate and loathing for the white man
that the war had caused. Their bodies bore the evidence of wounds
inflicted by the bullets and bayonets of their enemy. It was hard for the
chief to keep them under his control as they rattled their spears, shouted
their battle-cries, and menaced the Robinsons' party. The women of
this wild party remained in the rear, but were holding a fresh supply of
weapons for their men. There were no children any more, it had got
beyond that stage; but one hundred and fifty dogs growled defiance
at the intruders upon their domain.

Robinson's party, European and Tasmanian alike, were terrified. A
single word from the chief of the wild bunch and every man would have
been transfixed with spears. M'Geary, who was a hardened veteran of
native-hunting, whispered, "I think we shall soon be in the resur-
rection."

"I think we shall," rejoined Robinson.

They moved further forward into the presence of the tribe, and stood
still before them. The chief advanced towards them, some sixty yards
in front of his tribe. He saw before him the tamed natives quivering
with alarm and the Europeans standing firm, though apparently they
appeared to be without their arms. This was most unusual.

"Who are you?" shouted Montpeliata.

"We are gentlemen," was the response.

"Where are your guns?" was of course the next question.

"We have none," said the leader.

Still full of suspicion, though astonished, the great warrior cried out,
"Where your piccaninny?" (This was the term for pistols, little guns.)

"We have none," was again the reply.

There was another pause. Their fate had not yet been decided upon.
The male guides in Robinson's party were now much alarmed. Bungena,
recovering himself, ran as fas as he could over a little hill. Montpeliata
called after him to come back, and said that he would not be hurt.
Meanwhile some of the courageous female guides had sidled round the
group and were holding quiet, earnest conversations with their wilder
sisters. However, there were still another few minutes of indecision

before Montpeliata walked slowly to the rear of his company, to confer with the old women (the real arbiters of war). The men pointed their spears in watchful guard, but the yelping curs were called off. With their amazing instinct, they retired and were instantly quiet.

As in many places and cultures, the women had the last word, and thus it was with them that the great warrior chief deliberated. Suddenly the old women of the tribe threw up their arms three times—the sign of peace. Down came the spears, forward with an accompanying sign of relief and an upward glance of gratitude came the little band, for the Tasmanians were not treacherous: once they had decided upon a plan of action they seldom reversed the decision, and Robinson's party knew now that they were safe. The impulsive Tasmanians of the expedition rushed forward with tears and cries as each saw in the others' ranks a loved one of the past. Eumarra recognized two brothers and his wife embraced three other relatives. The chief of Bruni grasped the hand of his brother Montpeliata. With great joy a festival followed, and as tears flowed at the many recitals of woe, a corroboree and pleasant laughter closed this eventful day, to be followed by the New Year.

This was the most difficult and the most formidable of all the tribes, and it had now been captured where the Line had failed. Nor had it cost the £30,000 that was spent on that venture, when the whole population of the colony had been placed under arms to fight an opposing force of a few men armed only with wooden spears. So can guerillas keep a large army pinned down.

European fears had made this Big River, or Ouse, mob seem like a mighty host: in fact it consisted of sixteen men and nine women. Knowing the terrible deeds done by these few, their incredible marches and their widespread acts of violence, their enemies could not deny them the attributes of courage and great military tactics. Most of the other savage hordes that had dared to attack the soldiers and the colonists of the Empire were much better armed than these, who had only wooden stakes hardened in the fire. Governor Arthur had rightly termed them a noble race. Though they thus submitted to a moral force, it was because they felt that their work was done. They had had a good try to alter things. They had fought for their soil, but had been vanquished. They had lost fathers, brothers and sons in the war. Their mothers, wives and daughters, harassed by continued alarms, worn out by perpetual marches, enfeebled by want and disease, had sunk down one by one to die in the forest. Their graves and their bones were everywhere. Now only a miserable remnant of the formerly proud tribe was left. Their children had been sacrificed to the cruel exactions of defending their native soil and had perished of cold, hunger and fatigue, or had been murdered by parental hands to save them from an even worse fate: they had even been smothered to prevent them from crying and thus giving away the camps of their people. But above all the Tasmanians did not want to breed any more.

Dr. Story says that the Line movement,

> "Struck them with such surprise, and displayed the powers that could be brought to bear against them, that Mr. Robinson had less difficulty in persuading them to accompany him to where they would not be molested by the Whites, and have plenty, damper, sugar, blankets. When landed on the north-east corner of the island, he, with his tame aborigines, followed the wild ones for some days before they would return to the boats with him. They had been terrified by the Line, saying it was 'pop, pop, all pop'. 'If,' he said, 'you go there, you get killed. Come with me you get plenty damper, I don't want you to come with me, but you get killed if you go there.' And thus he worked upon them, some going with him, and the others following after a time, he was a very shrewd person really."

Also, the Hon. J. W. Wedge said about the Line in a written communication:

> "Notwithstanding the want of success attending the expedition, I am impressed with the belief that it had a considerable moral effect upon the minds of the Natives, and disposed them to lend a more willing ear to Mr. Robinson's propositions, when he succeeded in getting near enough to have an interview with them."

It must be remembered, where Robinson is concerned, that the tribal members had yielded to him as friends rather than prisoners. But, somewhere in the process of their subjection, they were turned into prisoners just the same. It is true, also, that they laid down their spears, and brought out from various hidden places sixteen sets of arms which they had taken in the war, but the captors returned their spears so that they could still continue to hunt. Leisurely the two parties, the tamed and the untamed, proceeded towards the settlement of Bothwell, situated to the westward of the road from Hobart to Launceston. When they arrived there on January 5th there was great alarm among the inhabitants at the prospect of some wild aborigines coming into their midst. But Mr. Robinson guaranteed the peaceable behaviour of his wild charges.

While on the road, he had heard many tales of woe about the hardships that the wild ones had suffered before their capture, and many furious denunciations of the cruelties of the Europeans. They dwelt at much length on their wounds. "They all had dreadful scars," he says.

On arrival he went to the Bothwell Inn, where he had the use of a bed—an absolute luxury for him! He was not afraid that his charges would desert him in the night, such was the rapport between the wild tribesmen and himself.

From this stage onwards, if they had been handled properly, the Tasmanians could have achieved a position somewhat like that of the Maoris in present-day New Zealand, though they would never have been as numerous. They had, too, a different way of life, and territorialism seems to have been much stronger with them as hunter-fishers than with the Maoris who were given more to root crops and cultivation generally, and who form, therefore, a more settled and numerous community. The Tasmanians' way of life, being entirely dependent upon the hunting supplies, supported a very much smaller population.

From Bothwell, Mr. Robinson addressed the following letter to headquarters, on January 5th, 1832:

"On the 31st ultimo, I succeeded in effecting a friendly communication with these sanguinary tribes. Their whole number was 26, including the celebrated chief Montpeliata of the Big River tribe. I fell in with these people, thirty miles north west of the Peak of Teneriffe."

So they continued on to Hobart Town, much to the terror as well as the curiosity of the settlers. Mr. Robinson was greeted with an almost triumphal entry, for it was through him that the war had now really ended. His own house was in the main part of the town, and his wife and children were all out to see his triumphant arrival, as were most of the other inhabitants. With him were his own faithful fourteen aborigines and the twenty-six voluntary captives, the men still with spears in their hands. Shouts of welcome rose from the gathered crowd. The Governor was deeply moved by all this and greeted and entertained the party at Government House. Before the governor's feast came the presents, sweets, toys, pretty pictures, trinkets, and, of course, dresses. All were showered upon the wild ones in the hope that they would now be tamed. Two poems appeared to commemorate the occasion in the *Hobart Town Magazine*, 1834, the first reads:

They came, sad remnant of a bygone race,
Surviving Mourners of a Nation's dead;
Proscribed inheritors of rights which trace
Their claims coeval with the world! They tread
Upon their nation's tomb!

They came like straggling leaves together blown,
The last memorial of the foliage past;
The living bough upon the tree o'erthrown,
When branch and trunk lie dead.

The second went:

They are come in their pride, but no helmet is gleaming
On the dark-brow'd race of their native land;
No lances are glittering, nor bright banners streaming,
O'er the warriors brave of that gallant band.

They are come in their pride, but no war cry is sounding,
With its woe-fraught note, over hill and plain;
For the hearts of those dark ones with gladness are bounding,
And bright songs of peace breathe loud in their strain.

They are come—they are come, and a boon they're imploring,
Oh! turn not away from their soul-felt prayer,
But to high hope of heaven this lost race restoring,
For yourselves gain mercy and pardon there.

Implicit in the first poem is the understanding that the Tasmanian aborigines were on their last legs. Yet the colonists who, by the implication of the poems, were aware of this were still going to banish them to the lonely bleak island of Flinders, where they would be far removed from the life they were accustomed to, and where not only would there be the chance that they would succumb, but also they would have no positive inducement to stay alive: among many primitive people death is no more than giving up the perpetual struggle which is life.*

Colonel Arthur, the Lieutenant-Governor, pleased them with his

---

* There were, it would seem, no such things as conservationists in those days. The Tasmanians were not the only tribes to suffer, the Moriori people of the Chatham Islands were another race who also suffered. It was not the happiest of times for them to survive in. It was, too, an equally tough time for wild animals and birds as well.

courtesy and kindness. Seeing this, and anxious to please even more, he commanded the band to play. But the effect was not what he had expected. The wild aborigines screamed with terror and rushed to Mr. Robinson, entreating him to protect them from the terrible noise. It was a long time before they calmed down, but eventually they did and were even persuaded to touch the drums, though they did this as if they were testing the power of a noisy animal. A grand fiesta followed, during which their confidence increased, and, after being personally decorated with ribbons by the Governor, they were persuaded to show their strength and skill with weapons. Ondia put a crayfish on a spear, and at a distance of sixty yards brought it down with another spear. Thus hours passed in the Governor's garden, which was open to everyone for the occasion. But that evening Mr. Robinson took them to his own home, and they camped about his premises.

It was at this time that portraits of the Tasmanians, copies of which appear in this book as plates A27–A28, were painted by Mr. Duterrau. But, a few days later came the rub, for a vessel was prepared and the natives were induced to go on board, in order to go to the splendid hunting grounds that Mr. Robinson and so many others had told them about: a place, they were told, where their sadly reduced numbers would be safe; a place where no soldiers and no capture parties were to be found, and where they would never be molested. One wonders who were the most deluded, the settlers or the Tasmanians. The latter undoubtedly believed what they heard, unused to dissembling Europeans. But did the whites *really* believe what they said, or had they willed themselves to believe in order to appease their consciences?

On their way to Flinders Island, the aborigines suffered dreadfully from seasickness for they were never a seafaring people. They appeared also to feel themselves forsaken and helpless, and such was their feeling of abandonment and despair that some tried to jump overboard. This stark contrast to their treatment a few days earlier merely enhanced the cruelty of their situation. The children, with a few exceptions, had not been allowed to go to the prospective settlement, and the journey was made all the worse for the heart-rending separation which had preceded it. They were placed in an orphanage situated close to Hobart. This establishment had been started for the care and education of the children of the flotsam and jetsam of the convicts and any other abandoned children that were found around. The building was very large and the arrangements very suitable for the objective. Hundreds of children were deposited there, from small babies up to fourteen-year-olds—if they lived that long. Most of the aboriginal children, in the short while that they survived there, were remarkable for being so sickly and depressed. Indeed, the death rate among these children was so terrible that it was the only reason the camp did not become appallingly overcrowded. Those that did survive were, on the whole, cared for well.*

Great enthusiasm attended the reception of Mr. Robinson. The newspapers were loud in his praise, and the jealousy of his rivals yielded to admiration. Although his salary as conciliator, or head of the Friendly Mission, had been previously raised to £250 and a bonus of £100 bestowed upon him, some fresh demonstration of gratitude for his efforts was demanded. He himself wrote the letter presenting his claims, and the Committee for the Protection of the Aborigines was prepared to second him. A grant of £400 was made without hesitation and a promise given of a further £700 on completion of his wonderful mission. It is very hard indeed to find a similar example of such hypocrisy in the entire annals of the British Empire.

Very businesslike about the extermination in hand, we find him leaving on February 11th for Great Island, afterwards called Flinders Island, to report upon it as a suitable home for the captured ones. Then he returned to the main island and struck off to the west once more, as the poor hunted creatures had by this time left forever the central and eastern parts of their island. It should be pointed out that the western part of the island was then (as it is still, more or less, to this day) an unknown quantity. At Port Davey, twenty-six Tasmanians were found, several of whom were over six feet in height. One old man reminded Mr. Robinson of Abraham, with his white flowing locks and beard. This particular tribe had never really been active in war and had caused little trouble to the settlers.

More great conquests of the aborigines followed. At Birch's Rock, sixteen were taken; at West Point, six more; at Mount Cameron, five; at Surrey Hills, four particularly miserable wretches were captured and at Sandy Cape, thirty-seven. From the report of July 12th, 1832, thirty-two gave themselves up at Macquarie Harbour. The appearance at one place on the West Coast of a group of sixteen was so wretched that they were said to resemble orang-outangs rather than human beings. An old man belonging to this group had had his eyes put out

---

* It is interesting to note in this connection a report that appeared in *The Times* during September 1972. White Rhodesians are nowadays following almost exactly the same practice as did the Tasmanian settlers, by placing the children of the tribes whose land they have appropriated in an orphanage, thus separating them from their parents.

by the pepper shot fired by some Christian pursuer. Mr. Robinson was much moved by this spectacle, and exhibited the poor creature, one would like to think, as an example to the pursuing "Christians" to take more care; but, in keeping with the times, this motive seems unlikely.

However, a rather formidable difficulty was experienced by Mr. Robinson on the Arthur River in the inhospitable region of the north-west of the island. A strong band of aborigines had been brought to his notice by some of the tame Blacks, and a conference was held on the evening of September 12th, 1832. In spite of the appeals of some of the tame ones, such as Nestor, Manalagana and Mr. Robinson, in the best Tasmanian that he could muster for the occasion, the men of the forest distrusted them and rejected the advances of the Whites. There followed a night of fearful suspense as the Mission camped a little distance away from the group of wild men, constantly reminded of their presence in the dark by shouts, cries and the rattling of spears. The subsequent events were recounted by Robinson himself:

"At the earliest dawn of day they made a large fire, around which the men assembled, and began preparing the weapons intended for my destruction. At this juncture, one of the Wild Natives (a relative of one of my friendly aborigines) commenced a vehement discussion, and argued against the injustice of killing me, and asked why they wanted to kill their friend and 'protector'. I had by this time put on my raiment. My aboriginal companions were exceedingly alarmed, and on looking for their spears in case of trouble, found that the wild Natives had taken them away during the night. Several of their blankets had also been stolen, and even attempts had been made to tie up the dogs. In the midst of this discussion I rose up, and stood in front of them with my arms folded, thinking to divert them from their savage purpose. I said that if they were not willing to go with me, they could return again to their own country. Scarcely had I spoken 'ere they shouted their war-whoop, seized their spears, and proceeded at once to surround me. With their left hand they grasped a bundle of spears, while in their right they held one. My aborigines shrieked and fled. The Natives had nearly encircled me. Their spears were raised and ready to strike. The friendly aborigines were all gone. At this crisis I made off. Although I saw not the slightest chance of escaping without at least one spear wound, I pursued my way rapidly through some copse, winding round the acclivity of some low hills, and took a north east direction toward an angle in the river; on approaching, I saw one of the friendly Natives who had escaped, who, with much trepidation, said that all the rest of the Natives were killed. At the same instant she descried the hostile Blacks approaching, and in much alarm begged of me to hide, while she swam the river and went to the encampment on the other side. To have attempted concealment at such a crisis, would have been to suicide. And looking up (for the river hath steep banks on either side), I saw one of the wild Natives looking for my footsteps. At this instant he turned and I lost sight of him. I saw no chance of escape, except by crossing the river. This difficulty appeared insurmountable, for I could not swim! The current too was exceeding rapid, and it required time to construct a machine. The Natives now were in strict search after me, and I expected at every moment to be overtaken. The raft on which I came over upon was nearly a mile downstream. I was persuaded the hostile natives would be waiting to intercept me there. I therefore abandoned all thoughts of crossing on this form of machine. I made an attempt to cross on a small spar of wood, and was precipitated into the river, and nearly carried away by the current. After repeated attempts, I succeeded, with the aid of the woman, in getting across."

In 1838, at a public meeting in New South Wales, he gave full credit to Truganina for saving his life in this incident. It appears that Mr. Robinson tried to get across the river by straddling the log and paddling with his hands and arms but that the log kept rolling over, and he probably would have drowned had not Truganina helped him. When reminded of the incident towards the end of her days and living at Oyster Cove, she clapped her hands, danced about and was very merry for one so old.

When Mr. Robinson got back to camp he found several of his aboriginals missing. The wild blacks did not rush across the rapid stream and storm the camp, as it appears that, much like the New Guineans today, some of the tribesmen disliked water, and they were content to merely sit and glower on a little hill their side of the river. They cursed, they threatened, they promised that, if they caught the chief of the Conciliatory Mission, they would burn his body and make charms, which were to be worn round their necks, of his ashes. The Englishman replied by repeating again and again that he had no evil design against them and asked rhetorically if they would like the soldiers to catch them instead. His talk at least had the desired effect on Kyenrope, the daughter of the chief of the Piemen's River tribe, for she made her way across the river and joined the Mission. Old Wyne,

her father, watched her flight and denounced her folly in the choicest
of native oaths.

Of course Mr. Robinson did not feel very comfortable in the vicinity
of such neighbours, and made use of a ruse to get himself out of the
awkward situation. He ordered the Tasmanians that had remained
with him to make a great fire of damp wood and leaves that would
create a vast cloud of smoke, as if signalling for assistance to some
soldiers near at hand. The alarmed wild aborigines beat the retreat
and left the way open to the relieved members of the Mission. Robinson
was in fact over forty miles across the roughest of country from the
nearest British settlement at Cape Grim, and he made off to that place
of refuge as quickly as possible. He was lucky that there were now so
few wild Tasmanians left, so that his journey was untroubled by en-
counters with natives tribes.

In this instance, Robinson was unsuccessful in his work, except for
the young girl, but he seems to have left some impression upon the
whole of that wild band. For another Englishman, a Mr. Cottrell,
passed that way some months later and this extract comes from a letter
he wrote to Mr. Robinson on January 19th, 1833:

> "On the tenth, we fell in with the tribe that attacked you at
> Arthur's River. Old Wyne and Edick were with them. They remained
> with us all night, and agreed to accompany us to Macquarie Harbour;
> but when we had marched about four miles, the following day, they
> disappeared among some scrub."

In October, 1833, Mr. Robinson returned to Hobart Town, with his
son, and brought in thirty aborigines. These were entertained royally
at Government House before being taken on to their burial island,
Flinders. As if to cover himself, Robinson wrote:

> "It cannot afterwards be said that these people were harshly
> treated, that they were torn from their country. No; their removal
> has been for their benefit, and in almost every instance after all, of
> their own free will and consent."

Their numbers were now rapidly dwindling, but on February 28th,
1834, he succeeded in capturing eight more of their women, and placed
them for temporary safety on Hunter's Island, at the western entrance
of the Bass Strait. This was accomplished with the help of some sealers'
boats. Three others followed on March 14th, and a further nine on

April 12th. These twenty, which included five women and eight young people, were then conveyed in a barque called the *Emerald* to Flinders Island. They all came from the north-western corner of Tasmania, and were, in fact, the remnant of the tribe that had attacked Mr. Robinson on the Arthur River two years previously. They confessed that it had been their intention on that occasion to murder him.

Upon interrogation of the Tasmanians on Flinders Island it was learned that apparently there were now only two old men and their families left at large on the mainland. This information Mr. Robinson disclosed in a letter to the Governor. However, Colonel Arthur and the Colonial Secretary thought otherwise, and it proved later that they were right.

Robinson now switched to the western part of the island, which has about the most difficult terrain that one can imagine. Very few had ever gone through that area before. Besides having large areas covered with almost horizontal scrub, it had terrible swamps, with flies that go with such places. Punctuating all this at intervals there were razor-back ridges. It is said that the region is even forsaken by birds. When another governor, Sir John Franklin, undertook a western journey to Macquarie Harbour years later, he suffered terribly and several of the party were disabled for life. No wonder that only one party of prisoners that escaped from Macquarie Harbour convict settlement ever arrived safely in a civilized region. Many men who tried this escape route perished in the scrub, were lost in the snow, or were even devoured by their companions in a desperate dog-eat-dog fashion. However, this was the territory traversed by Mr. Robinson and his Judases, expecting to find here a remnant of the Tasmanians, who now had no other hiding place from the implacable perseverance of their pursuers.

They had a frightful journey via Cradle Mountain and over the lofty plateau of the Middlesex Plains. Robinson later described some of the horrors of the journey in a letter to Mr. Burnett. In the letter, written on October 2nd, 1834, he states that his natives were very reluctant to go over the dreadful mountain passes and "that for seven successive days, we travelled over one solid body of snow, of quite 'incredible depth', frequently the natives were up to their waists in the snow'. But still the ill-clad, ill-fed, diseased and weary band of men and women, including the always cheerful little Truganina, went onward. Their legs, we are told, were one mass of lacerations from the sharp rocks and the thorns of the scrub. But their labours were rewarded and the last free Tasmanians were caught.

These poor wretches, found huddled together on the extreme western bluff of the island, were captured on December 28th, 1834. The band consisted of four women, a man and three boys, with thirty dogs in attendance. They said that they had rather put themselves at the mercy of the inhospitable western forest than at the mercy of the White man. Mr. Robinson wrote to the Governor, describing the scene of the meeting:

"The moment these poor creatures saw our Natives advancing, they ran forward, and embraced them in a most affecting manner. To this truly affecting scene, a most interesting conversation followed."

In this "interesting conversation" as much alarm as affection was obviously expressed.

On January 22nd, 1835, the eight aborigines were brought into Hobart Town. The Mission had accomplished its work, and Mr. Robinson had finished his task. His tally of success was:

1830–31, fifty-four natives brought in,
1832, sixty-three,
1833, forty-two,
1834–35, thirty-six.

In the last two years the island was swept of its original inhabitants, and any future mention of Tasmanians implies the white interlopers, not the indigenous peoples.

The next important question was, what should be done for the man whom the nation delighted to honour? The promised cash from the Government duly came, as did a thousand acres of land. Public meetings were held to acknowledge his services, and the result of a public collection, said to be of several thousands of pounds, was presented to him. As a further honour he was made First Commandant of Flinders Island. This post, however, lasted only for a short time. To put it kindly, his administrative abilities were inferior to his bush lore.

Instead a new sphere opened for him. The Tasmanian settlers had, with their flocks, crossed the Bass Straits into Victoria, Australia, and the plains of Port Phillip were becoming dotted with their homesteads. Hardly surprisingly a "native difficulty" had arisen there. Cruelties were the order of the day on one side and "outrages" on the other. All the indications seemed to point to the imminent outbreak of another "Black War". Mr. Robinson received an offer of £500 a year to be "protector" of the aborigines of Port Phillip, and, by 1838, he had become a citizen of Victoria. It is not within the scope of this book to criticize the performance of his duties there. However, it can be said that in 1853 he sailed away to England. Advancing age subdued his former fire and vehemence, and he died in Bath in 1866.

chapter 9

"That-Me-Country"

The removal of the aborigines from the main island to one in the Bass Straits was being discussed even before the making up of the capture parties. The general feeling of insecurity, plus a little guilty conscience, prompted a wish for this removal—"out of sight, out of mind", as the saying goes. One influential person who spoke up against the idea was Chief Justice Peddar. He declared it to be an unChristian attempt to destroy the whole race; he felt that once taken from their old haunts they would all die, a belief which he was sadly, and all too soon, to prove right.

In 1826 the public were much excited and vexed over this question. Some were for entrapping the people and shipping them off to the neighbouring but unsettled shores of Victoria. Others objected to this form of treatment on two grounds: one, that it would be cruel to place them in the way of the barbarous tribes to be found there, as they might not get on well with them and be unable to protect themselves from attack; secondly, that unlike the Australian aborigines, they were not used to wresting a living from such a wretched, sandy and barren country, and so would be unlikely to have sufficient food.

As an alternative, it was suggested that they should be shipped to King's Island. This lies half-way between Cape Otway, on the coast of Victoria, and the north-west corner of Tasmania. It is thirty miles in length, and from twelve to fifteen broad. It was not inappropriately called "the dread of seamen", for there was a long list of terrible shipwrecks on its coast: for instance, the convict ship *Neva* went ashore there, and out of three hundred female convicts, only eight were saved; in 1845 the *Cataraqui* was lost on the south-west coast of the island, and only nine of the four hundred and twenty-three people on board survived.

The eloquent Bishop of Tasmania, who visited King's Island at the time of the accident, later revisited the scene of the tragedy and recalled the night of the *Cataraqui* loss:

> "The surgeon was the first to perish; the poor, unhappy girls were tossed into the ocean as they were, unclad and unprepared; the wild, screaming death shriek mingling with the wilder storm."

The bishop walked along the beach together with the sealer who had first found the wreck, two days after the accident. The sealer told him:

> "Yonder I dragged on shore the bodies of eighteen poor girls; some were locked in each others' arms, others tranquil as though still asleep, others bent and twisted in the most distorted way; and here I dug their grave and buried them."

In one place he had buried fifty, in another twenty and in a third two hundred and thirty-five bodies of the lost. In the end the ocean had accepted the unwanted of the land.

Such a place was in some ways favourable for the new Tasmanians' purpose of disposing of the old, as it would be most unlikely that the aborigines could get away from its difficult and treacherous shores to reclaim their own land and haunt the newcomers. But for the aborigines it was certainly not suitable as a home. It was too bleak and exposed and, if it was difficult for people to get off, it was as difficult for people to get on to, so that communications would be difficult, a further excuse for the colonists to neglect the people they had displaced. However, King's Island was eventually rejected, and they started to look for other suitable island sites on which to dump the aborigines.

The Kent group of islands named after H.M.S. *Kent*, presented some advantages at first, and was recommended by the Aborigines Committee as early as December 1st, 1829, but though the islands did possess wood, water, mutton birds and some game, they were completely isolated. Also, it was observed that at certain seasons the group suffered terrific westerly gales and were generally cold and wet.

Cape Barren Island, which lay south of Flinders, was also suggested by the Committee, on May 26th, 1831. It was later rejected because, though it was twenty miles long, it was found to be a hopeless country. Clark Island, not very far away and ten miles from the mainland, was examined next, but was found by Mr. Robinson to be without anchorage, water, soil or the means of food.

Maria was the one most suitable. When Tasman, the Dutchman, first saw its wooded hilly shores in 1642 he could think of no better way to name it than after the beautiful daughter of his Dutch superior, Maria Van Diemen. It was a lovely spot, abounding in picturesque scenery, noble forests, undulating downs and quiet nooks, with many mountains, streams and fertile valleys, so much like the best parts of Tasmania. But it was not to be. Fears were expressed that it was too close to the mainland—it was only three miles off-shore—and that the aborigines might be able to escape back to the mainland. In effect, it was considered too good for them.

When, however, the roving parties had collected together some of the unfortunate Blacks it became imperative to find a dumping ground for them, and Swan Island was selected. This lies between Clark Island and Cape Portland on the mainland of Tasmania, only three miles from the parent island. It had little in its favour, for its water was brackish and the soil exceedingly poor, and it was small, about a mile and a half in length. Mr. Robinson placed there twenty-three of those that he had befriended on November 20th, 1830, and a further thirty-three on December 13th, 1830. By some fluke, those that went there were not unhealthy on this bit of desolate granite rock. However, one little incident that happened illustrates the melancholy condition of the captives. Among the first batch was an intelligent female, Kyenrope, who had been one of Mr Robinson's more faithful and loyal "guides". When a second group was dumped on the island by Mr. Robinson, the earlier transports were eager to hear the fate of their friends. Among the many sad tales told by the newcomers was the news of the murder by the Whites of the two brothers of the guide. It was impossible to describe the harrowing sorrow of this unfortunate woman, or to describe her regret at the part that she had taken in the Mission's work. She heaped indignant reproaches upon herself, and upon the enemies that she now realized were bringing about the destruction of her race.

The limited area of Swan Island and the numerous arrivals soon compelled the Government to find another place for the flotsam. Vansittart (or Gun-Carriage) Island, which got its name from the supposed resemblance to a gun-carriage, was then discussed for the purpose. It lay half a mile north of Cape Barren Island and four miles south of Flinders. One is at a loss to understand the reason why the Whites should choose this place for the poor captives, for it is an extremely miserable little place, only half a mile broad, almost entirely surrounded by dangerous rocks, and with very strong surf. There was a further impediment here, as sealers had occupied the only suitable locality and were living there with their families: some of the aborigine women, when working for sealers, had been taken from there in the first place! In those days of despotism, Robinson was given the authority to have the sealers and their families removed. Sulkily, the sealers prepared for their departure, while in the meantime the impetuous Mr. Robinson brought his black charges (minus their children) from Swan Island to the Great Dog, a little islet between Flinders and Gun-Carriage. It seems that the aborigines were already on the downhill slope for they had to live on what they could scrounge and the meagre rations of bad beef and flour provided by the authority, which were enough to give anyone scurvy, let alone the bad stomach troubles from which they all seemed to suffer.

In April, 1831, the settlement took over the sealers' area, a little bay on the western side of Gun-Carriage, and a Dr. Maclachlan was left in charge of the sixty people. A Sergeant White was ordered there in June in charge of a small military party to organize and distribute the stores, to see that the females received the correct treatment, to keep off the sealers, and, of course, to govern in the absence of Mr. Robinson while he was searching for more wild aborigines to bring in.

It was not long before the utter unsuitability of the place became obvious to everyone. The unfortunate creatures had no reason for exercise—for very little game ran within the island's wind-swept narrow boundaries—and so used to sit day after day on the beach, casting tearful glances across the stormy sea towards the mountains of their native land. Of course, it would have done them no good to go back on their own accord, as they would only have been hunted down as escaped criminals. Instead, these denizens of the thicket and the forest, without any maritime taste, saw at every turn the restless and hateful waters that hemmed them in, and they pined in their rocky prison. Even their officers were dissatisfied with the dungeonlike residences in which they were required to live in order to keep watch on their charges. Strong representations were also made to the courts of power about the wretchedness of the climate: there were none of the woods and dells to provide the shelter that helped to make the mainland so much more amenable and hospitable. The aborigines were not used to wearing clothes and they would put sacklike things about their bodies which, in their ignorance, they would not take off when damp, further confusion being caused by the vehement assertions of the Europeans that it was wrong to wear no clothes. As a result, many died of lung diseases. Even more died of the all too prevalent stomach sickness, which can probably be ascribed homesickness, or total despair, which primitive people are known to die of.

No way existed to halt this terrible homesickness. As one old hand put it, "They died of the sulks, like so many bears" (an allusion to the koala, or tailless opossum, which rarely survives its capture, but mopes at its chain, refuses food and dies).

Such was the happy hunting ground chosen out by those at Hobart. No kangaroos were there, and the whole colony would have perished for lack of supplies had not a sealer's boat, laden with potatoes, most fortunately been forced to take shelter in the bay because of a storm. The much-hailed saviour of the Blacks, Robinson, was meanwhile doing his brave deeds on the mainland to bring more unfortunates to this miserable place.

This second refuge, too, had to be abandoned after a short trial. The sealers, whose huts and crops had been so cruelly and unnecessarily destroyed at the instigation of Robinson, were then able to return to their old quarters.

A new island had to be selected. It is quite obvious that the Government, a very grasping lot, were going to see to it that no good land was used for the purpose of housing and keeping the original people of the land, and Robinson seems to have had no interest in them after they had been caught. Their continuing welfare had none of the glory of their capture.

Finally Great Island, afterwards known as Flinders Island, was selected. This island is forty miles long, and twelve to eighteen broad, not very large when compared with Tasmania proper and most of it about as barren as the previous islands, but it did have a few kangaroos. It rises boldly from the sea, and has many mountain ranges, but almost everywhere it was extremely exposed. The place chosen on Flinders Island for settlement was called the Lagoons where, at the rear of a dreary tea-tree (Melaleuca) scrub nearly bordering the sandy shore, there was a salt lagoon. Fresh water was only to be found in the hollows of a granite rock, or dug for in morasses, or in the white sand where there was a submerged stream.

Robinson chose this for the future home of his captives. But what was he thinking of? He knew the kind of terrain he was taking them from, he knew the places that they chose for themselves—except when they were being hunted down and forced into more difficult terrain for protection. Captain Batman, the man who owned the boat that took them there, often described when he was back with his friends in

Hobart Town the despairing look of the people at their new home. A government surveyor, engaged on the island at the time when the first people were being taken there from Gun-Carriage Island, said that when they saw from shipboard the splendid country which they had been promised, they betrayed the greatest agitation, gazing with strained eyes at the sterile shore, hoping that it was merely a mirage that they saw. Their dismay when they realized it was all too real was agonizing; they uttered melancholy moans and, with arms hanging beside them, trembled with their convulsive feelings as they spoke in low voices to each other. They were not even reconciled when, on landing and making some small explorations, they found that there were a few kangaroos hopping about. Their habitation was to be on the south-western side, exposed to the ever boisterous western breeze, unsheltered by forests and unprotected by any rising ground nearby. The winds were violent and cold; the rain and the sleet were penetrating and miserable. With their health already suffering badly, chills, rheumatism and consumption diminished their numbers, adding force to their forebodings that they had been taken to Flinders to die. No wonder Robinson made himself absent!

Some settlers had been kind and had given the aborigines some sheep. These were taken to feed upon the salt bush that abounded there, so helping them a little with their food supply.

Old Sergeant White reigned on the island. He directed his soldiers to put up some long huts of wattle and daub, each about twenty-five feet long, leaving an entrance at one end and a hole in the roof to let out the smoke of their fires. The Blacks were expected to keep these clean. But the commander, however suitable to control military Redcoats, was not able to control the elements around him. Sergeant White was sixty-six years of age, but he still retained much strength and vigour, he had seen much service on the mainland hunting down the aborigines, a fact hardly likely to endear him to his charges or they to him.

Difficulties beset him at the very beginning for there had been feuds between some of the tribes for centuries—bitter quarrels leading to blows were a daily occurrence. The remnants of the Ben Lomond and Big River tribes were in open conflict and the western tribe would side with either, according to caprice. The Cape Grim mob, the most remote and barbarous of all, kept completely aloof from the rest. All was complete chaos. The aborigine women went about naked, and traded themselves for luxuries with the sealers and the soldiers, which led to trouble between those two bodies of Whites, for all women were at a premium anyway. The aborigines sought consolation from their sorrows in dissipation, increasing the general chaos. To add to their troubles, fresh people kept landing, and the best young lubras exchanged hands like shuttlecocks. Supplies of food were never flourishing, and above all, the climate put everyone in a bad temper.

The aborigine males disliked the Whites' attitude to their women and a rebellion broke out. The old sergeant adopted summary measures. He enlisted the services of the sealers, who mounted guard over the aborigines. He seized fifteen of the most powerful aborigine men and put them on a granite rock in the ocean, without food, water or wood. This was directly contrary to his orders which had been to employ no restraint, but, so he said, this measure was corrective punishment, to make them better citizens. Captain Batman, coincidentally, happened to pass with another load of Tasmanians and saw the wretched men, on the verge of dying, having been thus exposed for five days. Many later died. Their tale was a simple one: they declared that they had been carried off so that the soldiers might have no interruption in their indulgences with the naked black women.

Sergeant White's story though, was that he had discovered a rebellious attempt to upset his government and murder the Whites. He made a statement to this effect, which was certified by Robert Gamble and John Strange, and cited as evidence what an aborigine woman, Wild Mary or Piucommiuminer, had said. It reads as follows:

> "That Broom-teer-lang-en-er was the first who proposed taking a boat away that was on Green Island, belonging to the sealers. She, also, stated that Cantityer, her husband, meant to have put a firestick in the thatch of the hut where the surgeon sleeps—that they intended to call at other islands, and to take the females from the sealers, as also the boat belonging to John Smith, and to kill two half-caste children belonging to this man—to take his woman also."

The news of the "Great Rebellion on Flinders" reached the ears of the Government, and another Redcoat officer, Lieutenant Darling, was despatched to rule them. (His brother later became Governor of Victoria. He was attached to the 63rd Regiment and arrived in March, 1832.) He immediately adopted such measures as would help to restore harmony. The primary difficulty was the lack of water. This he relieved by digging in the lagoon, and in the white sand of the shore. His policy in regard to the sealers was equally determined. He ordered their absolute withdrawal from every part of the island and put up written notices on posts around the coasts warning them, under penalty of fire from his soldiers, against approaching the place.

Though a soldier of the times, he did try some humanizing processes. He tried to change the rough habits of his charges. He sought to engage the men in some form of employment and the women in domestic chores. In some of the earliest of his communiqués he says that he would like to have come out to the island good motherly women, who could instruct the aboriginal women in the useful arts of the home; he also added that "a great proportion of the women are young, and are willing and anxious to learn", but his advice was not heeded in Hobart.

It was during the period of his better government that two Quaker missionaries, Mr. Backhouse and Mr. Walker, paid a visit to the island, while travelling throughout Asia and Australia. They write in their narrative with a genuine display of simple fervid, Christian feeling, and matter-of-fact practical benevolence. They won the hearts of the aborigines and were very popular with them during their stay.

They found that the original settlement had been moved a dozen miles from the lagoons, to a spot called Civilization Point, or The Black Man's House, and formerly known to the sealers as Pea Jacket Point. There were twenty cottages for the aborigines; but eleven of these were tenantless. They were of wattle and plastered clay, well whitewashed, with roofs of coarse grass thatch. They were grouped in the form of a crescent, and placed about a quarter of a mile from the settlement of the Whites. There were forty-seven male adults, forty-eight female adults, seven boys and four girls, one male baby and four female babies under five years of age. They were not only protected from sealers there but also from strong drink.

In their report of their visit to the island the two "Friends" gave an account of a tea-party that affords much insight into the way of life on the island. The surveyor there, a Mr. Woodward, also said that every Sunday Lieutenant Darling and the doctor would invite some of the aborigines to dine with them. On this particular occasion a singular compliment was paid to the Quakers:

"A large party of aborigine women took tea with us at the Commandant's. They conducted themselves in a very orderly manner; and, after washing up the tea-things, put them in their places."

It is not usual, as Mr. Bonwick later pointed out, to invite company, and then leave them to wash up!

A formal report of this visit was made to the Governor, at his request:

"Little," said the reporters, "can be said of the religious state of the establishment," but they go on to say: "Nearly the whole of them are associated as married couples. No marriage ceremony is used among them; but when the parties agree to be united, they are henceforth recognized as husband and wife, and are not allowed to change."

The moral work being carried on attracted the attention of the Quakers and they digress upon this at length.

"The Catechist," they write, "has taken great pains to tell the aborigines of the existence and character of the Deity, and most of them now have some idea of these important truths. He has translated into one of their languages a large portion of the first three chapters of Genesis. The natives are daily instructed either in the house of the Catechist or in their own huts, amid the interruptions to which both these places are subject."

Sufficient was seen by them to know that civilizing influences were at work under Lieutenant Darling, and were not started, as Mr. Robinson would have everyone believe, by himself two years later. Added to the report were certain suggestions that they thought would add to the happiness of the Tasmanians on Flinders Island; such as a further supply of cows, of shoes for the wet weather, of boxes for clothing, and stools for seats. Naturally they also recommended that the women should have checked cotton bed gowns. Stuff petticoats, checked aprons, and neckerchiefs were also included in the list, as was the erection of a church and a schoolhouse.

In October, 1833, Dr. Ross, the editor of the *Courier*, played up the sunny side of the Flinders Island experiment, or the ultimate solution, especially dwelling upon the happiness and security enjoyed by the favoured ones there. However, the Reverend Dr. Lang of Sydney took him up rather smartly upon it:

"Happiness and security, Dr. Ross! The security of death you mean! The happiness of leaving their unburied bones to be bleached by the sun and rain in every nook and dell of that island, where they fell, unpitied, by the bullets of the Europeans! In thirty years—the period which it required, under the iron rod of Spain, to exterminate all the native inhabitants of Hispaniola—the numerous tribes into which the aborigines of Van Diemen's Land were divided have been reduced, under the mild sway of Britain, to 118 souls, imprisoned on an island in Bass's Strait! May the Lord long preserve this miserable remnant of a race so nearly extinct!"

In 1834, the colony went back to civilian rule, and Mr. Henry Nickolls was appointed superintendent, at a salary of £182. 10s.; Mr. Robert Clark, the Catechist, received £120; Mr. Loftus Dickerson was store-keeper and Mr. Allen (who later married the daughter of Mr. Robinson) became surgeon to the establishment. In that year there were thirty Whites on the island to look after the colony's 120 aborigines.

It is evident that Governor Arthur was still feeling unhappy about his prisoners being kept in the Straits. Was it a guilty conscience or that he was still afraid of them? He proposed to the Home Government that they should be let loose on the southern shores of the Australian continent, on the site of the present colonies of Victoria and South Australia. The Secretary for the Colonies, Lord Glenely, objected upon humane grounds. Varying his scheme, the Governor next proposed that Mr. Robinson, who had just brought in his last party of aborigines, should proceed to the opposite coast, with some of the Flinders Island aborigines, to civilize the wild Australian Blacks. That idea also being abandoned, he resolved to send Mr. Robinson to take charge of the island prison: he took command there in 1835, and with his accustomed energy threw himself into the work of reformation, though it appears that each successive commandant had been working on the poor aborigines in a similar fashion since they were placed there.

These are, in his own words, some of the reforming activities which he set about:

"I established on Flinders Island an Aboriginal Fund, which was raised from the proceeds of the work performed, and the sales of various articles prepared by them; such as salted mutton-birds, bird's skins, etc.—which were generally sold at Launceston. I also formed an Aboriginal Police, to preserve order, and to decide all disagreements which might arise among them. I also established a circulating medium among them, which was attended with the happiest of effects, as it gave them a knowledge of the rights of pro-perty; and lastly, and consequent upon the latter, I established a market, to which they brought their produce. Thus they acquired the habits of a civilized life, and felt an interest in the acquisition of property, which rendered them industrious and cleanly."

Dr. Ross intimated, in his *Courier* of October 8th, 1836, that

"Mr. Robinson has been the means of establishing a weekly newpaper among them. It is entirely written by the aborigines, and is published under the name of the *Aboriginal Flinders Island Chronicle*, on half a sheet of foolscap, every Saturday, price twopence each and profits arising from the work are equally divided among the editors."

Somehow this doesn't seem very convincing, for half a sheet of foolscap isn't really very much, and twopence in those days was quite a lot of money. Also, where did they get this ready cash from, as it appears that they were never given much to spend? Also, the field of readership, if, indeed, any could read, was extremely limited and in an essentially non-literate society the Tasmanians would have found verbal communication rather more satisfactory. Concerning this, the subsequent superintendent, Dr. Jeaneret wrote: "I have no knowledge of the newspaper referred to. None, in my time, were capable of such a work."

Mr. Robinson again as the speaker:

"At the periodical examinations in the School, some of the native youths were able to answer questions in regard to the leading events of Scripture History, Christian Doctrine and duty, Arithmetic, the principal facts of Geography, also on several facts of useful information. Some very fair specimens of handwriting were exhibited on such occasions; one in particular was worthy of notice, being an original address from a writer—a native youth of fifteen years of age, who was employed by me in my office—to his countrymen. It was expressed in simple and tolerably correct language, and breathed a warm spirit of gratitude to myself. In the schools they were taught various handiwork, such as knitting in worsted, sewing, etc.; and they proved to be apt and industrious scholars."

In his Progress Report dated May 17th, 1837, he wrote:

"The schools and religious services are still maintained, and the Natives are constant and regular in their attendance. They are rapidly acquiring industrious habits. The settlement is a very powerful tranquil state."

It seems somewhere along the line that he was suffering from delusions of grandeur. The School Report makes one feel this even if nothing else does.

7

Flinders State, according to Robinson's version of events, rose to its height like Athens under Pericles, but was left an empty shell at his departure. Much must be placed at the door of high talk, with which Mr. Robinson was always closely associated.

At a later date, just before coming away, he states:

> "The only drawback in the establishment was the great mortality among them. But those who did survive were now happy, contented and useful members of society."

Back in England, in 1861, when few aborigines remained, he saw the non-fulfilment of his prophecy. His incredible remarks when interviewed on the subject must surely sum up all the worst of colonialism, whether it is British or any other nationality:

> "The most serious drawback to the success of the establishment was the great mortality among them, which has continued to so lamentable extent, that at the present time there are but a small remnant living. Had the poor creatures survived to become a numerous people, I am convinced that they would have formed a contented and useful community."

In the process of becoming civilized they lost the life that they had. One of the legacies of this civilization was venereal disease. If this did not thin their numbers directly it weakened them still further for the numerous other diseases that picked them off. The Andaman Islanders, another rare group, were also carried off in a similar way, when they made a penal settlement there also.

Over-legislation did not help much either. Even the Committee of the Aborigine Society were at last sensible of the folly of this. In their report for 1839, they regretted that,

> "From the first, a system had not been applied more suitable to the habits of a roving people, instead of the highly artificial one, that has been referred to, and was imposed upon them."

The more civilized that they became, the more dependent were the aborigines upon their masters for supplies, and the less disposed they were to exert themselves to search for food. So they became listless which, to the ignorant and complacent authorities, was equated with being good. They needed energy to pursue the bounding kangaroo, or to clamber up the trees after the opossum. In a letter from Mr. Robinson, dated March 8th, 1836, we have the following announcement:

"It has been intimated to the Natives, that a ship will be in soon and therefore they will be shortly be supplied with fresh meat, which intelligence affords them much pleasure."

It would certainly have been a much better proposition if Mr. Robinson had utilized the sheep that had been given for this purpose, and were now several hundred strong upon the island. It would, at least, have given them something to do. The sheep had been there since 1833, and since then more cattle and sheep had been sent, and yet, not once in six months, did the aborigines eat their own beef and mutton! In 1838 there were still 1,800 sheep and 62 head of cattle on the island considered to belong to the aborigines.

Among the more obviously irritating habits of Mr. Robinson was that of altering the names of the aborigines in his care: it does appear that he tried to complicate the simple and leave the things that should be done alone, all the while trying to cover everything in a veneer of "decency". The aborigines had a host of white servants to watch over them, who could not, or would not, catch their long and liquid sounding words, so it might have been necessary to make a change, but hardly enough to warrant the formation of the absurd catalogue that he compiled. It would be interesting to know whose assistance he had in the formation of the lists—there may have been some quite educated convict on the staff at Flinders Island. But he evidently imagined he had performed an important and useful service to the community, even making it the subject of a special report on September 14th, 1836. He presented two lists—his own nomenclature, classical and grand; and beside it, the aboriginal name, or absurd English nickname. The following is a list of some of the males; it appears that some of the names in the list of the females were even more grand and ridiculous. It does seem that he suffered from delusions of grandeur and in such a peculiar way that he involved those under him as well.

List of Tasmanians on Flinders Island—Males

Alexander	Long Billy	Alphonso	Big Jemmy
Alpha	Doctor	Achilles	Rowlebauna
Ajax	Moultchelargene	Bonaparte	Little Jacky
Columbus	Lenerugirin	Daniel	Goannah

Francies	Big Mary's Jemmy	King George	Old Tom
Isaac	Problattner	Joseph	Rose's Jemmy
Milton	Penemeroic	Nimrod	Kangaroo Billy
Omega	Ballywinny	Romeo	Tomten
William Robinson	Pennebricke	Washington	Mackamee
	Walter George Arthur	Friday	

Among the double names of the females were:

Queen Adelaide		Queen Andromanche	
	Governor's Lubra		Larrentong
Agnes	Blind Poll	Princess Clara	Teddeburic
Princess Cleopatra	Kyenrope	Queen Elizabeth	Big Bet
Juliet	John	Jemima	Crank Poll
Louisa	Jumbo	Lucy	Mytermoon
Princess Lalla Rookh		Margaret	Bung
	Truganinna	Rose	Gooseberry
Patty	Goneannah	Semiramis	Jenny
	Susan	Lock Jaw Poll	

Some of these names stuck well and in the double form, such as that of the last of all the Tasmanians, Lalla Rookh or Truganinna.

The following is a list of the native names of the men on the island in 1834. They are given as spelt in the original document, according to Mr. Robinson, though later changes were, for example, "a" for "er".

There were Worethetitatilargener and Moulteerlargener, who were chiefs of the Ben Lomond tribe; Calamaroweyne, the supposed murderer of Captain Thomas;

Marenerlarger	Teelapana
Walentirloona	Panacoona
Wowee	Paropa
Nicamenie	Tymethie
Preropa	Nicamenie
Pyntharyne	Toinchone
Peey	Boobyinthie
Toindeburic	Rowlaplana
Toby Langta	Lamaima
Conapanny	Packabanny

and Wymeric.

The last three, who all died in one fortnight, were the husbands of Wild Mary.

Because of the difference of dialects, there naturally grew upon the island a sort of lingua franca, a mingling of the native and English tongues, almost their own peculiar brand of pidgin English. One marked difficulty which the Tasmanians had was to pronounce our "d" and "s".

While they were on Flinders Island the man who entered chiefly into the feelings and sympathies of the Tasmanians was the catechist, Mr. Robert Clark, whom the aborigines called Father Clark. He was in many ways a very remarkable man for, after several attempts, the missionaries themselves more or less abandoned the Tasmanians, believing them to be beyond redemption.

He was appointed to his position of schoolmaster and catechist in 1834, but after a while he gave place to the Rev. T. Dove, the Presbyterian clergyman, and assumed a secular office, without diminishing his efforts to help the Tasmanians. He was ultimately obliged to resign, rather than back schemes which he considered detrimental to the aborigines' welfare. He stayed at Hobart Town for about two years but then to the joy of most he was reinstated and stayed on Flinders Island until 1850, when he caught consumption—presumably from the aborigines, among whom it had been rife.

He gained the confidence of the aborigines by mixing with them and treating them seriously as human beings. He would sit on the ground with the men, smoking his pipe, and, as he had taught himself their languages, listen to their yarns of hunting and war, and then talk to them in their own soft tones about Christianity and the brotherhood of Man. With the gins, too, he was a favourite. His wife also was prominent in the work done with the women and children: indeed, she often played with the dark children, something apparently quite unheard of in those days. (Even nowadays, in some countries, if a white person takes too much interest in the natives he is considered to be fomenting revolution, or at least he earns the presumed insult of "nigger lover".) Captain Stokes, the explorer, when visiting Flinders in 1842, refers to the lasting effects produced upon the aborigines by Mr. Clark, "for whom they all continue to feel a great veneration, in a way that is due to a parent, in the way that they crowd around him".

The widow of the Rev. Frederick Miller, of Hobart, had in her possession a manuscript of Robert Clark in his capacity as schoolmaster, giving full particulars of an examination on Flinders Island in February, 1838. The Rev. T. Dove presided, and Mr. George Agustus Robinson,

Mr. Dickinson the store-keeper and Dr. Walsh were spectators: the missionaries, who felt that their hands were quite full enough looking after the convicts, sealers and settlers, were as usual absent.

Young William Robinson's class first of all came forward (the adults and the few children all went to school together) and consisted of the following remarkable characters: Isaac, Edward, Washington, Albert and Leonidas. Edward was pronounced imperfect in the alphabet, and went down; Washington attempted to spell; but brave Leonidas, more ambitious than the rest, made a trial of reading from the spelling book. Again Leonidas, obviously the hero of the class, repeated the Lord's Prayer, the Collect, the names of the months and the days of the week, in addition to counting up to one hundred.

In Charles Robinson's Class (these are the sons of the commandant, for he is like a patriarch!), Neptune attempted to read, and Peter Pindar was pronounced perfect in the alphabet. Neptune was fluent upon early scripture history, and his creed may be taken as orthodox of the period—at least for Flinders Island. Here are a few of the questions that were given to him and his rather quick answers:

"What will God do to this world by and by?"—"Burn it."
"What did God make us for?"—"His own purpose."
"Who are in Heaven?"—"God, angels, good men and Christ."
"What did you love God for?"—"God gives me everything."

Though apt in the general catechism, he failed to count beyond ten.

Bonaparte answered eight questions, and appeared to have a more decided and satisfactory faith than the emperor. Being asked, "Do you like God?" he promptly answered "Yes."

The boys' class taught by the catechist formed, of course, the prominent feature of the examination. Bruni, Thompson and Walter, the first two of whom died soon afterwards, could read, write and even add up a little. The last was certainly far above the average in intelligence for an aborigine: he could converse intelligently, and reason with ability. He had a wife and his own neat little hut.

The report of the female progress was briefer, and not so commendable:

"Clara reads—Daphne attempts to read—Emma attempts to read—Rose attempts to spell—Sophia attempts to spell—Sabina, imperfect in the alphabet—Henrietta imperfect in the alphabet— Lucy imperfect in the alphabet—and Wild Mary imperfect in the alphabet."

It may be gathered, though, that Wild Mary was several steps above Queen Adelaide in intelligence, as that lady, though present, did not enter the lists at all. Lalla Rookh or Truganina, one of the heroines of this book and the last of the Tasmanian race, was not examined in literature, her talents being more of a sexually athletic nature.

The senior women's class, under Mrs. Clark, distinguished themselves:

"Bessy reads the whole of the No. 1 spelling book. Patty attempted to read. Paulina spells the words of three letters. Juliet reads four easy pages. Semiiramis knows her English letters—a feat beyond the powers of the Assyrian Queen."

This was the end of the first day's examinations. A crowd of crowned heads appeared on the following day, and they at least distinguished themselves:

"King Alfred was perfect in his Alphabet, and could tell who made him. King George knew the first man, and who made the trees and the tall mountain, but was not troubled with more questions. King Alpha was content with playing ditto to his royal brother George, but Napoleon rushed boldly forth to the front, with ready replies after attempting to spell."

Sadly, the comment upon this conqueror was:

"This native attends school but very rarely, and is not improving. Mr. Dove addressed him very severely upon his neglect to be instructed."

He died very shortly afterwards.

The history of the last few years of Flinders is soon told. It is chiefly the story of death. Captain Stokes found that, of 200 that had been captured, 150 perished. Governor Arthur wrote home, on January 17th, 1835, deploring the rapid decline and adding: "Their number has been reduced to only a 100." To save the younger ones, fourteen were sent from the island to the Orphan School at Hobart.

One of the earliest victims on the island settlement was Mungo, the guide to the parties of Messrs. Robertson, Jorgenson and Batman. Manalagana, the noble chief who was painted so much by the artist Mr. Dutterau, died in March 1836. Dr. Tory is quoted as saying that "the deaths at Flinders Island and the attempt at civilizing the Natives were consequent on each other". In the end the greatest beauty of their race, Oura-Oura, though now old, was also brought to Flinders Island, "To die as they all die." As the surgeons put it: "It is a strange sickness of the stomach—in other words, home-sickness."* She was fortunate, her end was swift. She asked the surgeon to take her to the shutters and open them. In the foreground were the bleak and barren wastes of the island, but as the dawn light strengthened, clear beyond were the white slopes of Ben Lomond, on the mainland, its snows sparkling in the gleaming sunshine, and Oura-Oura with a shaking finger and arm pointed it out to him, in a trembling voice, in the pidgin English so patronizingly taught her by her nation's conquerors. Her last words were, "That–Me–Country." Ben Lomond still sparkled but she was dead.

It is said that Mr. Robinson was anxious, when he was appointed protector in Port Phillip, Victoria, to remove the remnant of the race from the island, and his suggestion was received with rejoicing among the pent-up islanders. A petition signed by the twenty-nine living men was addressed to the Governor, Sir John Franklin, on August 12th, 1838, begging for translation to Port Phillip. His Excellency's heart was moved, and he directed that a Mr. Montague, then colonial secretary, should open up a correspondence with the government of New South Wales about their reception. Some opposition being made, the question was referred home, and Lord Glenely objected to their removal.

After the departure of Mr. Robinson and the failure of their hopes of removal to Port Phillip, the aborigines sank into an apathy from which they never emerged. Captain Smith officiated for a time, and then a Mr. Fisher; but Dr. Jeanneret received the appointment of Superintendent in 1842 from Sir John Franklin, who gave out that he, like his benevolent and learned lady, was ever interested in the Blacks. How deep was their interest soon became shamefully apparent.

A beautiful Tasmanian girl had been adopted by Lady Franklin. She had dwelt in the colonial palace, had been taught, petted and trained to higher hopes. The novelty of possessing a black wore off and she was then left to grope her way to the grave, among the untutored of her own race and the ignorant and the vicious of ours. This comes from a report in the *Hobart Town Mercury*, about the beginning of the sad tale:

* Their tendency to "homesickness", for want of a better word, was particularly annoying in that, if a wife died, within a few weeks her until then perfectly healthy husband would also die, for no apparent physical reason.

"As there were no picaninnies at Government House at that time it was in some way arranged that an addition should be made to the family home. Lady Franklin visited the Black's temporary station, where she saw a pretty baby. It was ordered that the little wild girl should take her place as one of the family. The king's daughter carried no dowery with her, except for a single kangaroo's skin, a rush basket, a shell necklace or two, a pet opossum and her name— that was Mathinna, this means 'beautiful valley' in the Tasmanian language. She grew to be a tall and graceful girl, and here I am at a loss to describe perhaps one of the grandest specimens of our kind, that ever nature smiled upon. She stood when I saw her last, about five feet eight inches in height, was very erect, with a quick, thoughtless, or perhaps thinking if you please, toss about her head now and then. Her hair still curled short as before, but seemed to struggle into length, and was blacker than black, bright, glossy and oh! so beautiful! Her features were well chiselled and singularly regular, while her voice was light, quick, yet sighed a little, and was somewhat plaintive."

The reporter goes on with his sad narrative:

"When Sir John Franklin was ordered home, the Tasmanian beauty did not go with her ladyship. The medical men thought her unfit for the rough English climate. She was left behind. But, strangely enough, instead of her being placed with a household of respectability and virtue, where at least her happiness would have been consulted, she was thrust into the convict orphan school, where some black children had been sent to be educated or to suffer and to die.

"Poor Mathinna was, therefore, transferred sobbing and broken hearted from the tender care of one who had always proved far more than a mother to her, and the luxury and the grandeur of Government House, to a cold stretcher in the dormitory of the Queen's Asylum. She soon fell sick and was taken to a bed in the Hospital, she had no friends. All those fawners about Government House, who used to say kind things, and pretend to be proud to take her hand in the ballroom because it pleased the Lady Franklin, had all melted away; and her wan fingers beat upon the wall, she sighed and thought of the days gone by, and of the flocks of summer friends, who revelled in the sunshine of the hour, but vanished with its splendour."

When the Flinders Island establishment was removed to Oyster Cove, she was ordered thither. The sequel is soon told.

"Too soon alas! She fell into the habits of the rest; and, as they were permitted to wander about in the bush in all directions, among sawyers, splitters, slaughtermen, convicts and characters of the deepest depravity, all of life's flotsam and jetsam in fact, where her body was prized for a spell. One night, however, Mathinna was missing; and, although cooey after cooey resounded from mountain to mountain, and from gully to gully, no tidings were heard of the lost girl. In the morning the search was continued, till at length the wanderer was found. The little wild girl, with the shell necklace, and the pet opossum—the scarlet-coated, bare-headed beauty in the carriage—the protégée of the noblewoman—the reclaimed daughter of a great Tasmanian chief, had died, abandoned by every virtue and drunk, in the river."

Dr. Jeanneret was virtually the last superintendent of Flinders Island. He remained to see the embarkation of the Tasmanians under his successor, Dr. Milligan, all bound for Oyster Cove in D'Entrecasteaux Channel.

After the departure of the people, the island was let with the stock to Captain Smith, at a rental of £100 a year. The Bishop of Tasmania, moralizing over the past, in 1854:

"Nearly eleven years have passed since I landed on the selfsame rocks, with Sir John Franklin. How changed is the scene! Then, the beach was covered with the aborigines, who greeted their kind and beloved [!] benefactor with yells of delight; capering and gesticulating with movements more indicative of exuberant wild joy, than of elegance or propriety. Now all this is still. It was painful to witness the scene of ruin in the once neat and well ordered settlement. Desolation stared me in the face, wherever the eye was turned: the comfortable house of the superintendent, for instance, was rapidly falling into decay; the gardens well nigh rooted up; the range of buildings in which the aborigines were formerly hutted, untenanted, broken and tumbling down."

Such is the last sad scene of the Flinders Island drama. James Bonwick the author and, at that time, the authority upon the Tasmanian aborigines, sums up his impression in the following words when having often seen the island from a distance he finally landed on what had been for so long their home, but what now was quite deserted:

"Since the departure of the aborigines, I have passed by the island some half-a-dozen times. As I last gazed upon its storm torn coast, and my eyes rested upon its bleak and fantastic hills, the whole story, in all its varied and stirring phases came before me of men long since come and gone, the strugglings of the last of a race were there embedded."

chapter 10

The Remnant Return

The terrible mortality among the Tasmanians on Flinders Island excited the sympathy of their friends in Hobart.

Mr. George Washington Walker had, on several occasions, discussed the problem with others sympathetic to the Tasmanians' plight, who hoped that the remnant could be brought nearer the town. It was well known that this was the desire of the Tasmanians as well: they claimed that if they could only come to live in their own country once more, they would all be healthy and happy.

However, not everyone was kindly disposed towards the Tasmanians. One Hobart paper had a violent leader upon the subject, expiating upon the outrages committed in 1831, and predicting that a bloody renewal of atrocities would occur should the Blacks come back once more—as if twelve men, the number then alive, could light up the fires of the country homesteads and unearth their spears for slaughter, in the midst of a colony of eighty thousand Whites (Tasmania had become a very popular country for settlement).

The aborigine remnant did, however, obtain their wish. In October, 1847, forty-four of the surviving members of the Tasmanian race were removed from Flinders Island to Oyster Cove. The group was made up of twelve men, twenty-two women and ten children, though some of the latter were half-castes. The boys ranged from the age of four to fourteen and the girls from seven to thirteen. Sadly, though, Mr. Clark states that two years later, in August 1849, he then had with him only one child, six others having been placed in the infamous Orphanage School, which few who entered ever left alive.

Oyster Cove, their new home, was just a few miles away from

Hobart, and lies at the junction of the River Derwent with the ocean. Storm Bay opens to the south-east, and the narrow D'Entrecasteaux Channel to the south-west; these waters being separated by Bruni Island. Oyster Cove is the first little harbour in this channel, after crossing the mouth of North West Bay.

For a time, the new settlement seemed to prosper. Mr. Clark wrote cheerily:

"They are now comfortable and have a full supply of provisions; they are able to till their gardens, sow peas, beans and potatoes; seem anxious to earn money, of which they now know, to a certain extent, the value. They are thankful to the Lieutenant-Governor and the Colonial Secretary, for removing them from Flinders' Island, and to Dr. Milligan for all the trouble he has taken. The women now can all make their own clothes, and cook their food by boiling or roasting. Their houses too are comfortable and clean. They are as contented as possible."

But at the end of 1854 there remained of the original forty-four, only three men, eleven women and two boys at the station. The colonists found themselves charged with a rather formidable bill for looking after the last of the Tasmanians for, even though the establishment was rent free, the bill came to £2,006 8s. 8d.

When Bonwick visited the settlement at Oyster Cove in 1859, he recorded:

"A sad spectacle met my eyes. I simply now record what I stated to Dr. Nixon, the Bishop of Tasmania, on my return to Hobart. I went to him, knowing him to be really interested in the aborigines, and aware that a long and a painful illness, which subsequently led him to resign his bishopric, prevented him from helping to take a further interest in their welfare. Blame might naturally be attached to somebody. The blight had fallen upon the aborigines, and produced the disorders, doubtless, that had appeared in their midst. Mr. Dandridge, located with them, seemed kindly disposed towards them, but evidently regarded himself as a sort of ration distributor only, being, as he told me himself, convinced that he could do nothing to arrest their progress to the grave. He and his wife were then keeping a school for the children of the farmers and the labourers outside the reserve. Instruction was considered hopeless for the Blacks, as they are termed."

People were now quite apathetic about the Tasmanians: they had witnessed so many dying and so often for no apparent reason.

Mr. Bonwick continues:

"I saw a miserable collection of huts and outbuildings, the ruins of the old penal establishment, profoundly dirty, and fleas were swarming everywhere, as I found to my cost. The Superintendent said that he could not clean all the places by himself, for he had no manservant, and the Blacks had no inclination to do the work themselves. So it was not done. The buildings formed the sides of a square, enclosing a large courtyard. Even the officer's family were not well housed. The Tasmanians were in several contiguous huts or offices. The earthen floors of these were in a sad state. Some had parts of wooden planking still remaining. The sides of the huts were in a ruinous condition. The roofs were not all waterproof. Many of the windows were broken and the doors of some closed imperfectly. The furniture was gone. Here and there a stool was to be seen, or a log, but the women however preferred to squat on the floor, and that not always in the most decent of attitudes. The apology for bedsteads and beds was the most deplorable of all. I turned round to the Superintendent who was accompanying me, and expressed my concern at the frightfully filthy state of the bedclothes. In some places I noticed but one blanket as the only article on the shelf, and remarked about the insufficiency of bedclothing for the old people, and now at the cold season for the year. Mr. Dandridge seemed as surprised as chagrined, and, calling all the women, commanded them to tell where all the blankets had disappeared to. One of them quite cooly answered: 'Bad white fellow—him steal 'em all.' The Superintendent's explanation was that they were given up to drink and had sold for liquor the Government blankets, and even their very clothing, to the low population that were round and about. But could no protection have been afforded them from such ruffians?*

"The gardens so praised by Mr. Clark had all gone. There was no sign of reading material either in those wretched abodes. The cooking was managed, apparently, by boiling, judging by the big round pot I saw in each hut, and this was generally in the middle of the floor. Several times I saw the numerous dogs that were around licking from this vessel, for both brutes and human beings seemed to have the common bed and board. The weekly rations then were

* However, the clothing in fact contributed to the many deaths. Among primitive peoples cotton has harmed more than the sword.

14 lb. of meat, 10 lb. of white flour, 3 ozs. of tea, 14 ozs. of sugar, 3 ozs. of soap, 2 ozs. of salt and 3 ozs. of tobacco. For clothing, an allowance of blue serge, 3½ yards by 1½, was made, which they rudely made into some form of a loose garment. A flannel petticoat, red cap, handkerchief, comforter, cotton frock and jumper, were supposed to be provided, and some of these I saw in stock at the store. Hand-kerchiefs, at any rate, were not required, judging from their appearances, the sleeve was used. When expecting company, they were decked out suitably. Calico for chemises was at one time issued, and, doubtless made up by some in the old days. The polka dot jacket was gaily got up, though only worn on festive occasions. When I made a remark as to the paucity of clothes, and their miserable appearances in such weather, there was the repetition of the complaint of their selling for drink the dresses that should be keeping them warm, even though all had been stamped with some form of government mark."

In the time of Governor Denison they were happier, according to their own account, as that gentleman often paid them a visit, bringing along with some of his family, parcels of toys, marbles and balls for the Tasmanian children. He would spread out the treasure, join in their games, even playing at leap-frog with them. Then the visit would finish off with a merry laugh and a good feed. Lady Denison would occasionally ride down with some of her friends, and bring back many of the Tasmanians to the town for a change. One particular highspot was when the Governor sent the stage coach down to fetch some of them to Government House for a dinner and afterwards a light entertainment at the theatre.

Dr. Nixon, the learned and kind-hearted bishop, who towards the end of his working days was not very strong, and who would have otherwise have done more the the Tasmanians, often paid them a visit and never missed an opportunity to take sweets and tobacco for them. At times he would also bring them baskets of apples. However, the return home of the Governor and the illness of the bishop ended even these few happy moments in their later days.

When people went to visit them they spoke freely of their friends. But often their talk reverted to events during the "Black War" and the trouble that it had brought to them. Frequently their talk was laced with the terms "bad white fellows", and these still haunted them, stealing their clothes and making them drink, for their reserve was in the worst part of the suburbs of Hobart. In addition, little or no restraint was put on their movements as their numbers dwindled and the Whites no longer had any fear of them. They would often go on walkabout for days at a time, as do the Australian aborigines of today. Indeed, this habit seemed to improve their health for, after all, they were and always had been a nomadic people.

Maryann, the half-caste wife of Walter, was now a fine, upstanding example of an educated Tasmanian, and so a sad indication of the races' potential had they been educated rather than half-educated. An alternative would have been to have kept the remnant in the savagery that they were accustomed to, together with their dignity and their pride.*

Maryann complained bitterly about the moral conditions at the camp:

> "We had soul in Flinders," she said, "but we have none here. There, we were looked after, and the bad whites were kept from annoying us. But here we are thrown upon the scum of society. They have brought us among the offscouring of the earth [referring to the convict population of the area]. Here are bad of all sorts. We would be a great deal better off if someone would read and pray for us. We are tempted to drink and all bad practices, but there is neither reading nor prayer. While they give us food for the body, they might give us food for the soul. They might think of the remnant of us poor creatures, and make us happy, nobody cares for us."

It appears that the bishop had made some form of provision for their religious instruction, by requesting a neighbouring clergyman to give them an occasional service. But the parson was unpopular with the Tasmanians, and whenever his horse was seen on the hill, it was a signal for a general dispersal. There being no congregation, the services were never held.

When Robert Clark, the catechist, was removed from Flinders with the Tasmanians, he had hoped to spend a few years with them at Oyster Cove and to see them on their feet again. He still had forty-five

* When I was in Canada, in 1962, I saw one group of Indians that lived at Brantford in southern Ontario and had their own land; they were fine specimens of humanity. Then, the next day, in one of those never-ending streets that one finds in the big Canadian cities that look so good on paper but are an eyesore to be in (I believe it was Toronto), I saw a bedraggled group of people that looked just about as dejected as the Indians one sees in the cities of South America, like a group of gypsies that have been turned off a race track. Loss of pride affects not only the mind but the physique as well.

Tasmanians, enough to provide the nucleus for a new start. He had ideas about establishing them with a good dairy farm, and about making them popular with the people of Hobart. He would make them live on the fat of the land and save money besides. They would be employed and be interested in something now they were back on their home island, and then he hoped that they would not die at the terrible rate that they had on Flinders.

But there was no letting up of the fatal disease. They still sickened and died, and the rest were now beginning to lose heart. Yes, they thought, they too would die, they must die, they would all die soon. Then why should they till the ground and look after animals? For whom would the potatoes be grown? Then why need they trouble about dress—they the dying ones? Pictures lost their interest, even books were left unopened, or only looked at with glazed eyes. They read their fate. In such a mood they cared for nothing. They lost interest in all that was going on around them. Everything seemed to remind them of their end. It was not a bit strange, therefore, that when any form of temptation came their way they fell for it, and so often weakened themselves still further, merely hastening the apparently inevitable end.

However, Mr. Clark was spared the grief of seeing the worst. The health of his wife was affected by the bad quarters in which they had to live in close proximity to the aborigines. She moved to Hobart for a change, and died there. Her tender-hearted husband returned to Oyster Cove a changed man. He had lost a partner indeed. He strove at first to forget the past and try to live for the future, for he was still quite young, but the death of his wife was a very deep blow and those whom he was helping were also dying around him. The plethora of death affected him greatly and he became ill with the heaviness of it all.

He preferred to be with the aborigines at the end. It was Maryann that did most of the nursing, and she recalled:

"I attended him along with his daughter, night and day. But all the people wanted to do something for him, for all so loved him. And then he would talk to us, and pray with us. He would tell me to read to him from the Bible, when too weak to hold the book. How he would talk to us! When he thought that he was going to die, he got the room full, and bade us 'Good-bye'. He held up his hands and prayed for us. Oh!, how he did love us. And then he said, while he was crying, 'Mind you be sure and all meet me in heaven!' No one cares for the Natives' souls now that Father Clark is gone."

Father Clark, who loved them, was spared by death from seeing the extinction of the Tasmanians. His story provides some relief to the harshness and the selfishness that surrounded the Tasmanians; they did at least know kindness from such a really good man. It only heightens the tragedy to know that he entered it near the end and not at the beginning.

At the end of the 1850s Old Sophia, one of the oldest inhabitants of the settlement and a woman of great character, was apparently over sixty years of age. Despite her white hair, it is said that she had quite the most monkeylike face that ever could be seen upon a human being. (It is strange how the very young and the very old of many primitive tribes seem to go like this.) The recession of the lower jaw and the low forehead, coupled with the marked prognathism, seems to have been the cause. She was born on Bruni Island, and had given birth to two children. Wherever she went a troupe of mangy dogs accompanied her. At all times she held forth a long harangue with the curs, who answered in snapping barks of recognition. At night two would lie in her wretched bed with her in order to keep her back warm, a habit which reminds me of the practice in the highlands of New Guinea, where the very old are given a sow pig to keep them warm in their hut at night.

Another personality was Ragged Wapperty (see plate C7). She, too, was not exactly a desirable-looking old lady. Her country had been near to Patrick's Head, to the north-east of the island. Her native name was "Woonoteah coota mena", which means "thunder and lightning". There was nothing at all brilliant about her then. Her countrywoman, Flora, seemed to be about forty to forty-five years of age. Often when a visitor was being shown through the store by the superintendent, and receiving an explanation of the dresses worn by the ladies, Flora would appear at the door. She would suddenly untie a string, let fall to the ground her only serge garment and carry out a striptease show, then leisurely enrobe herself in one of the pieces of finery from the shelves of the store, being obviously gratified by the expressions of shock and surprise on the faces of the colonial mid-Victorians!

Patty, another personality, had the native name of "Cooneana", the "Ring-tailed Opossum". She may have been between fifty and fifty-five, although in the account of her death at Hobart Hospital, in July 1867, she was said to be seventy. After she died, only two Tasmanian women remained. Patty was the wife of Leonidas, of whom we have heard a little in the previous chapter, and belonged to the Kangaroo Point tribe of the Derwent. Her most distinguishing feature was a very broad nose.

Emma, rather younger than Patty, was of the Patrick Head tribe, and had been married to Albert. Caroline, commonly called Queen Caroline, was the consort of Roumetewah, or the wombat, the renowned chieftain of the Big River tribe. Her native name was Ganganinnanah. She appeared to be the most aged of the settlement people, and always sat away from the others, crying in a helpless, almost imbecile manner. She had been with the Coal River tribe since childhood, but seemed to have belonged to another tribe originally, until taken under their wing.

Bessy Clark (plate C15), named after the wife of the catechist, was then under forty years of age, and was probably the best looking of all the women to be found in the remnant of her race. There was no recession of the lower jaw, and her good humour gave a pleasant expression to her broad face. Her native name was Pinnano Bathae, or the "Kangaroo Head". She had not led a forest life with her tribe, having been taken from them in early childhood. On one occasion when Mr. G. A. Robinson was out with one of his sons and some others, seeking the whereabouts of the Macquarie Harbour tribe, a family was disturbed at their roaring fire so suddenly that the mother in her fright forgot the little girl, whom she left near the warm embers. The deserted infant was placed on the back of young Robinson, and was finally given to the care of a countrywoman on Flinders Island. When old enough, she was sent for education and training to the orphanage in Hobart. It was thought she would there be free from the temptations that usually struck the aborigines about the age of puberty. Subsequently she returned to Flinders, and there married Agustus. This is how she recounted her courting days:

> "He [meaning Agustus] tell me plenty times he love me, then he make love, then he ask me be his wife. I tell him go ask Father Clark. Father and Mother say, 'You marry him.' So I did."

Evidently some marriage troubles followed soon after, for he relaxed his attentions to his partner, as he wanted to go off on a whaling cruise.

This is what James Bonwick said about a visit he made to the settlement:

> "Laughing little Lalla Rookh, or Truganina, was my special favourite of the party. She acted amongst the rest as if she was indeed the Sultana. She was then much over fifty, and yet preserved some of those graces, which made her beauty a snare in the olden

days. She sadly tried the patience of several husbands. Her coquetry was like that of any French courtezan. Her features, in spite of her bridgeless nose, were decidely pleasing, to those that knew her in her younger days, when lighting up her sparkling black eyes in animated conversation. Though her nose was of the genuine saucy retroussé order, later in life it was not quite in keeping with a further fair moustache, and well developed curly whiskers, that were just beginning to turn with the advancing years. She was in 1829 the wife of the bold Wooreddy, the chief of the Bruni tribe. Her appreciation of the society of English people, was a sore trial to her more sober sided Tasmanian companion."

She was to be the very last of the Tasmanians.

Maryann (or Mary Ann), the half-caste wife of Walter (or King Walter), had, according to Bonwick, the appearance of her mixed race. Her delicate hands, her dark eyes, her nose and mouth, showed the Tasmanian mother in her; but her broad and lofty forehead indicated the European descent of her father. She was unquestionably a woman of weight, being some seventeen or eighteen stone, and often made the floor creak when she walked. She had an intellect of vigour, with a strength and independence of will that was stamped upon her features.

Maryann's mother, Sarah, had been stolen from the forest by one of the early sealers in the Straits, Cottrel Cockrane. He had not been cruel to her, nor had he been a neglectful father. But when Mr. Robinson made a raid upon the sealers in the Straits and carried off the dark-skinned partners, Maryann found a new home on Flinders Island. There she was cared for as the daughter of a black woman rather than the child of an Englishman, and her associates were therefore of her mother's race. But with her intelligence, had she been received into a respectable family and treated in a proper manner, she might have been a happier and more useful woman. As it was, she became the wife of Walter, a full blood who, though he did try his very best to become civilized, had not had the same advantages as his wife. Maryann and Walter never had a child.

There were some aborigines, it is obvious, who could have made up the nucleus of an educated group that might well have rescued their own people. But such an observation depends largely on hindsight and it would have required the life and the times that surrounded the Tasmanians to have been more enlightened; something which was hardly possible at a time when slavery was still rife. It is a great pity that Mr. Robinson was so vigorous about his work.

The masculine element of Oyster Cove was not very advanced. There was one called Tippo Sahib, no longer a terrible warrior like his Hindu namesake, but now old, feeble and blind. He was of the Coal River tribe, and claimed Flora for his bride. Agustus has already been mentioned as the husband of Bessy Clark. Then there was Willie, about whom the women of the settlement never seemed to tire of talking: he was the youngest living of the Tasmanians, and was just twenty-one. He was declared to be a fine young man "plenty beard— plenty laugh—very good, that fellow", but he was often absent on whaling voyages. As William Lanné he was the last of the Tasmanian men and died in 1869.

There was also Black Allen, Jackey, or the Leonidas of Flinders Island, the husband of Patty, the Ring-tailed Possum. He had associated with the Whites since boyhood, and had accompanied Mr. John Batman on his expedition after the Blacks in 1830. He was very advanced in one civilized habit, drinking, and this was to be his undoing and downfall.

Finally there was Walter, who was head and shoulders, intellectually and culturally, above the rest of the band. He was of royal blood, being the son of "King George", named after George Arthur, the Governor of the colony. He had no accentuated features, but appears to have had a very fine head. However, he seems to have suffered frequently from melancholy.

Walter at that time was employed to take passengers to and from the steamer, on its way from Huon to Hobart. He received the princely sum of one shilling a day for attention to the mailbags, and earned further money by the execution of other business commissions. He cultivated, at his leisure, part of his own little farm of twenty acres. Having been able to earn more than his countrymen, he had quite a civilized appearance, spoke English perfectly and wrote well. Many Europeans would go and take tea with him and his wife. In his little country cottage there was not a particle of dust to be seen, there were prints on the walls and several books. The daily newspaper was placed on the sidetable and the furniture was very similar to what one would expect to find in an English country cottage.

But the curse of drink had already fallen upon the little homestead. One evening, in May 1861, he and Jack Allen went on board their boat at the Hobart wharf, on their way to Oyster Cove. They had been to the pub and were seen by many in a state unfit for the voyage. After progressing for three miles in this state, the boat capsized when off Sandy Bay, and Walter and his mate sank to the bottom of the Derwent.

As an epitaph, Captain Stokes' description of him when they met on Flinders Island in 1842, serves well:

"Walter and Maryann, a married couple who had recently returned from Port Phillip, where they had been living in the family of the former Superintendent, Mr. Robinson, were so civilized and proficient in all the plainer parts of education, that they possessed great influence over their countrymen, who, incited by the contemplation of their superiority, were apparently desirous of acquiring knowledge. The Barracks in which the Natives dwelt formed a square of good stone buildings; but Walter and his wife had a separate cottage, with a piece of land attached. Maryann is a tolerable needlewoman and capable of teaching the others."

Mr. Bonwick had this to say of Walter and his affairs:

"I have before me the original letter addressed by Walter George Arthur when he sought to buy a piece of land near the aboriginal station of Oyster Cove. The letter occupies more than three sheets of notepaper, and had been rather roughly struck off in a hurry. It had been kindly presented to me by Sir Richard Fry, who thus permitted Mr. Surveyor General Calder to keep a certified copy in the office. Walter entreats Dr. Milligan, the Protector, to get a certain eight acres block for him, and, as he says, 'ascertain from the Government what they would charge for it, the 8 acres'. He gives his reason for the purchase, and is generous enough to use the plural number in the first person; for his wife, Maryann, being a scholar and weighing nearly twenty stone, was a partner demanding consideration. 'We would very much like to have it,' he continues, 'to make it a little homestead for ourselves. My reason for troubling you so much is that there is no distance from the water's edge, and that is more Dryer than the other Piece of ground up the Creek by Claytons', and not only that, if we put anything into the ground up the creek it either gets trodden to Pieces or otherwise rutted up by somebody, or spoiled in some way so we can't do any good by it.' He is too independent to solicit eight acres of the soil seized by the Whites from his nation, but adds: 'I mean for to buy it out.'"

Walter, believing himself possessed of sufficient means, also tried to obtain an assigned servant, and applied to the Government to this effect in 1856:

"I beg respectfully to apply for permission to hire a Passholder Servant man subject to existing regulations."

But this was refused. Although many a white man, who had been exiled for his country's good and who was utterly illiterate, obtained this privilege, it was not thought expedient to place a Christian Englishman under the authority of a savage, and for this reason the application was rejected. Mr. Calder, who knew him well, gives this report in 1868, in reply to a question of Bonwick's through a friend:

" 'Mr. Bonwick asks if the Blacks of Tasmania were capable of true civilization.' My reply is, 'Yes, undoubtedly'; and I give as an example the case of Walter George Arthur, a Tasmanian aboriginal, whom I knew well, who was captured when a mere infant, and brought up and educated at the Queen's Orphan School (at Hobart). His ideas were perfectly English, and there was not the smallest dash of the savage in him. He was a very conversible man, fond of reading, and spoke and wrote English quite grammatically. His spelling was also quite correct. This man had also a hundred acres of land, and knew his rights in relation thereto, quite as well as you do yours. An instance of this, quite creditable to his acuteness, sense of right, and of honourable feelings, was related to me by our old friend Bennison, the surveyor. One of Arthur's neighbours was a grasping and unprincipled fellow, who mistook Arthur for a person with whom he might do as he pleased, and encroached upon a cultivated part of his land, which Arthur had no idea of suffering. So, after expostulating with him to no useful purpose, he employed and paid Bennison to resurvey his land, which was done in the presence of both litigants. This operation proved that Arthur was right, and that he knew his proper boundaries quite well. And when he saw that his opponent was satisfied, he said to him, 'Well, Mr. . . . , though you have tried to wrong me, I will treat you very differently from what I believe you would have done to me, if I were in your place. You can come on to my land and remove your crop when it is ripe.' "

He was not quite civilized after all, for such conduct as shown by the above incident was scarcely that most generally adopted by the enlightened settlers!

chapter 11

White Contacts

The rough sealers of the stormy Bass Straits would form an interesting chapter in the early history of the colonies, even without their association with the aborigines of Tasmania and the part that they played in the Black War. These primitive Straits' men were mostly runaway convicts who had gone to such inaccessible places that the authorities had not bothered to go out and pick them up, and, in general, they avoided causing trouble for fear that it would bring the Government breathing down their necks.

On shore these people would, perhaps, have been bushrangers and defied the law, but on the sea, at the beginning, these bold spirits in their little homemade whale boats merely waylaid vessels, perhaps levying a tax upon the cargo. Occasionally they hovered near to some coastal settlement and invaded the unwary solitary settlers for supplies, a mild type of nineteenth-century Viking. But it was the seals and the mutton-birds that bore the brunt of their viciousness, and to a lesser degree the Tasmanians, for they relied upon the Tasmanians for their supply of female flesh. The women of the white settlers were often too well guarded. The women convicts were far fewer; indeed, many of them perished in the numerous transport wrecks around the shores of Australia, as has already been mentioned.

It was either force of circumstances or the development of latent honesty that finally led them to change their mode of life, for it was difficult for dog to eat dog, and most of the community in the early days was of convict origin. The growth of commerce pointed the way, and converted many of them into producers. The granite islands which form a "giant's causeway", from Victoria to Tasmania, provided at once a home and a field of labour. In sheltered nooks they raised cabins, as often as not of driftwood, enclosed a garden plot, obtained some goats and, at the beginning, frequently had no other companion than a dog. Hunting for seals in those treacherous waters for the sake of the skin and the oil was a perilous undertaking. Flinders, discoverer of the Straits' seals and Flinders Island, became indirectly associated with the extinction of that furred animal and the aborigine.

The mutton-bird, the sorrow of the blackbirded aboriginal captive slave of the sealer, is so-called from its supposed taste. To naturalists it is the sooty petrel. Web-footed, it skims with its long wings over the ocean for its food, which is chiefly plankton. It is smaller than a duck, but somewhat larger than a pigeon. It accumulates fat to an enormous extent, and gives, on merely being pressed, a considerable amount of oil. The time of incubation is towards the end of the year (bearing in mind that it lives in the southern hemisphere). The birds only then come to land, the female burrows in the sand of the shore or the decomposed granite of the islands, often for over a yard, and there deposits its one white egg which, in the course of incubation, becomes terribly stained from the excrement and the soil. These eggs were diligently procured by the female slaves and carried by the sealers, along with their seal oil, to Launceston and other markets. The dried birds were often taken too. The feathers were plucked and dried, being used for mattresses among other things. In the warm weather, a bed made of such feathers could produce a terrible musky odour. It took about twenty-five birds to produce a pound of feathers, which would be sold for sixpence. The sealers' women (as there were often several) had a clever way of catching the birds to procure their feathers and oil: in the very early morning, when the birds that had stayed on the island at night were not yet stirring, they would rouse the birds and drive them like so many sheep into a pit with a brush fence on one side which they had made in preparation.

The stolen gins were the slaves of the sealers. When stolen from the mainland they were taken to the rocky islets of the Straits, made to till the land, collect sea-birds, eggs and feathers, clean the carcasses of the mutton-birds, boil the bodies down for the oil, and do the same with the seals. They had to hunt the wallaby, and preserve the skins, pick up the nautilus shells driven on the sands by the storms and take their turn at the oar.

The history of old Munro, the "King of the Sealers", fits the times. For a quarter of a century he lived on Preservation Island near the mainland and in the Bank's Strait. There the old man held sway over his neighbours, both wild and tamed. The tamed were accustomed to go to the "Governor of the Straits" and refer to his judgement and decision in their disputes. An old hand declared that the secret of his superiority lay less in the strength of his intellect and the astuteness of his counsels, as upon the use of "a lot of crackjaw dictionary words and wise looks". There he had, at one time, three female Tasmanians, as well as a half-caste family. This patriarchal group was much esteemed by the sealers.

The darker side of the picture came before the public at the close of the Black War, when arrangements were being made to exile the aborigines to an island in the Straits. Mr. Robinson, armed with the Governor's authority, sailed among the islands to investigate what was going on there among the sealers, and to see if what he had heard about their harems of black girls was true, and to rescue them if possible.

The earlier the stories the more disgraceful they are. For some of the wretches used to boast of the tortures they carried out on the women before shooting them. Often they suffered long hours of beating. One woman managed to wriggle free while being beaten, as she had grease from the mutton-birds on her body. The sealer chased her all over the islet, and then shot her; when his companions asked him why, he replied "because she wouldn't clean the mutton-birds properly". There was another report that a wretched man called Harrington had stolen a dozen young lubras and had placed them on different islands to work for him. If he ever felt they had not done sufficient work, he would tie them to trees for twenty-four hours at a stretch, flogging them from time to time. He had also been known to kill them in cold blood when they opposed his will.

Captain Stokes tells of a brutal sealer who volunteered a passage of his autobiography:

> "He confessed, that he kept the poor young creature nude and chained up like a wild beast, and whenever he wanted her for anything, applied a burning stick, a firebrand from the hearth, to her skin."

When the government craft belonging to Flinders Island was lying off Circular Head, on the northern side of the island, a sealer's boat came out to it. In the stern was seated a young lubra who appeared quite intelligent and attractive, but with an obvious look of fear and sadness. The low tones in which she spoke, and the furtive glances that she threw from time to time at the sealers, indicated sufficiently the terror under which she lived. An aborigine from the ship conversed with her, and urged her to fly from the Whites and go to Flinders. Jackey, as she was called, was excited but declined to leave the whaleboat. Lieutenant Darling was on board, and, guessing the reason for her refusal, gave her to understand that he had power from the Governor to take her from the sealers. As soon as she understood this, she bounded up upon the deck with a burst of joy. Another Tasmanian woman rounded on her for her conduct, and went ashore with the sealers in her place, but she too ran away from them in the night, and came to the cutter with her little child.

Mr. Robinson gave a sad recital of his first Straits capture, the women that he took to Gun-Carriage Island, who told their tales of the past to him. One spoke of how she had been stolen by the veteran Munro, and another how she was bought for some skins, while a third spoke of her regular sufferings under the lash. Jock, or Ploic-ner-noop-per-ner, spoke of the way the sealers tied her up, used her and afterwards beat her. Another, Smoker by name, was given up to the sealers by her own husband for liquor, after she had given birth to several of his children. She had run away, was chased, caught and severely flogged.

At first it was with much difficulty that Mr. Robinson rescued some of the women as the sealers, aware of his errand, concealed them. Later, when they saw how easy it was to get them back again, they were not so concerned. Among those taken by Mr. Robinson were Kit, Sall, Judy, Mother Brown, Little Mary and Little Buck. He had, however, positive instructions not to take a woman away against her will. The sealers and the conciliator were far from friendly over this affair, but he made many a compromise with them. One was that if they helped him gather in the wild wanderers he would allow them to keep the women that they had. In his official report he declared that "the sealers were perfectly satisfied with the arrangements"; and, of course, they were. Not only did they have women, but when they got tired of those they already had they could always go to the lubra pool on Flinders Island for more. They did not have to search the mainland any more.

From the journal of Mr. George Washington Walker comes the following extract:

"From conversation with several sealers in the Straits, twelve of whom we have seen, and from the testimony of other persons, confirmed by that of Native women, who once lived with the sealers, but who are now at the settlement [Flinders], we cannot regard the situation of the aboriginal females amongst that class of men as differing materially from slavery, unless the circumstances of one man having only one woman and living with her in a state of concubinage, and holding himself at liberty to abandon her when it may suit his own convenience, constitute the difference. The objective of these men in retaining the women, most of whom it is asserted, were originally kidnapped, is obviously for the gratification of their lust, and secondly for the amount of labour that they can extract from them. In resorting to coercion in order to extort the services of these poor defenceless females, great cruelty is very often used, by their unfeeling masters, with few exceptions.

"At our request, a woman, named Boatswain by the sealers, with whom she lived some years, gave us some particulars relative to the treatment of women among them. This she did partly by words and partly by expressive signs, that certainly could not be misunderstood, except by the most dumb. Her statements were also fully corroborated by the other women who were present, and who had been similarly dealt with. She was requested to show in what manner they were beaten. She made signs that she would be nude, stretched out with her hands up against a wall, in the attitude of a prisoner tied up to be flogged, for the feet were tied as well, she made at the same time a doleful cry and personated the beater, in the course of his work on her. After this she described a different scene. She represented a person striking another over the back and the legs, and then herself as sinking down on the ground, while she repeatedly exclaimed, in a piteous tone, 'Oh, I will clean the mutton birds better', until at last her voice seemed to fail through exhaustion. It seemed that in the first scene, the purpose was for sex and the second was in regard to work. She said that the men beat with great sticks. Then she asked if certain men beat their women, she excepted four, the woman of one was weakly, and would have died if he had beaten her. On her observing of one of the men that 'he beat his woman' it was remarked with surprise, that she had an infant. To this she replied, 'Yes he beat her when the child was in her.' On inquiry being made, if she would go back to the sealers, she replied, in strong terms, that she would not, and the other women joined with her in making the same declarations.

"They appear to have made little or no progress in civilization or in anything other than that which contributed to the pecuniary advantage or the sexual gratification of their masters. They have even been encouraged to perpetuate their barbarous customs. What indeed, can be expected at the hands of men who live in such open violation of the humanitarian ways of life, and are so cruel to the animals that they destroy, in many cases, unnecessarily."

The subject of half-castes is one of the saddest of the many sad stories in the history of the Tasmanians. The Tasmanian half-caste, along with the Australian aborigine half-caste, if permitted to see the light of day, seldom lived very long in the tribe. This seems a pity, since we can see today that the half-caste Australian aborigines are very fine specimens, particularly the girls: they are often brown-skinned, honey-coloured blondes. The mother, to conceal her shame or repenting of her act, would often prevent the birth by abortion; or when unsuccessful, would practice infanticide. If motherly love led her to spare the child, there was always a husband or a brother who might avenge the family wrongs with a fatal blow.

There seemed to be several half-castes among the sealers, since they were not under tribal law. But Dr. Story says that among the Tasmanians living the tribal life he did not know of one instance when they were brought up within the tribe. There was a superstition amongst these people that the female who brought such a child into the world could never revert and would never again be able to bear full-blooded children. Likewise in Australia in those days it was exceedingly rare to see a half-caste. Then, as the missionaries found, "It was the rule to destroy the half-caste immediately after birth." Mr. G. A. Robinson and various other protectors said the same thing at Port Phillip in Victoria. However, one of these protectors was of the opinion that his experiences in both Australia and Tasmania indicated that the half-castes in any case mysteriously seemed to disappear around puberty.

The Government of Tasmania did try to save some of these half-castes. A sawyer called Smith had a black friend, Mrs. Fanny Cochrane Smith, who came to the notice of the Government through warding off an attack by the aborigines on her house when the men were away. They received £25 per year for their half-caste child. Grants of land were even made to reputed parents, subject to the life of the offspring, or contingent upon the orthodox marriage of the parents. But the tribes repeatedly avenged their honour by luring the child away from civilization or parental control and murdering it.

Perhaps the worst and most shocking aspect of the half-caste tragedies was the indifference of the English fathers to the future wellbeing of the offspring of their liaisons.

Before the half-castes existed in any number, or when mostly confined to the sealers of the Straits, many benevolent individuals had a faint hope amid the rising horrors of the Black War of their future utility. However, people who came to Tasmania had heard the reputation of half-castes in other parts of the world, and it was a case of giving a dog a bad name. Many of the people who could have helped drew back at the last moment, especially the religious ones. They did not understand that it was the environment that was to blame rather than the mixture of the blood. If the half-castes had been well cared for, as many could have been, and even if they had been no more than semi-educated, they could have helped their less fortunate kinsfolk. Instead, they were beset on both sides, and very few survived. When there were people like the Rev. George Taplin going about New South Wales saying: "They are generally very bad and low, especially the women!" there was precious little chance for them.

In Tasmania, the half-castes were certainly never numerous, yet Mr. Robinson, when depriving the sealers of their older women, acknowledged that a large number of their children remained behind, for they knew what their own race would do to them should they be taken to Flinders—they would not have lived very long, unless they had passed puberty before their arrival. One woman had thirteen children by a sealer. Maryann, the wife of King Walter, was one of five children by a white father and a black mother. Captain Stokes counted twenty-five on Preservation Island and the smaller islands nearby. But in 1846 Dr. Jeanneret reported that on Flinders Island there were forty-seven Tasmanians of pure blood and only five half-castes.

In November, 1868, the surveyor-general at Hobart, Mr. Calder, stated that there were between eighty and ninety half-castes. He adds:

> "This statement I make upon the faith of a letter lately received by me from Captain Malcom Laing Smith, formerly of the 78th regiment, I think, who interests himself much about them. They are stationed at some of the smaller islands of the Furneaux' group, between, or about, Flinders and the Cape Barren Islands."

Before Maryann's removal to Flinders Island she had lived at Launceston, being taken there by her father to the care of a friend. Although she was of superior ability to many white children there, her unhappy circumstances caused her to be thrown by the officials among the degraded blacks of the island, to her own moral and intellectual loss. Repelled in cold disdain by her father's side, she clung to her mother's kind, and finally contracted the childless marriage with Walter, the most intelligent and educated of the then living Tasmanians. Her sister Fanny, also a half-caste, many years younger than herself, married a European, and after five years of marriage, gave birth to a child. The Government had made the pair a grant of land of 100 acres, though this could never be sold. They seemed to live happily in Hobart to the end of their days.

Dr. Nixon, the bishop, went on an episcopal tour to the islands of the Straits, with particular reference to the condition of the half-castes there. His observations are very interesting. He baptized many of them and their children, besides marrying some; the marriages in many cases having been delayed because of the absence of clergy. In his interesting narrative which he terms *The Cruise of the Beacon*, he bestows a compliment upon one whom he describes as the greatest lady of his acquaintance, Lucy Beadon, a half-caste, twenty-five years of age, who weighed twenty-three stone. Maryann was also about twenty stone, and it may have been a characteristic of these half-castes, at least the women, to be on the heavy side. Lucy was very good humoured and kind hearted. He also says:

> "From the pure love of those around her, she daily gathers together the children of the sealers, and does her best to impart to them the rudiments both of secular and religious knowledge."

The father of Lucy Beadon, although possessed of sufficient money to have lived comfortably in a civilized society, preferred his rocky, storm-girt home on Badger's Island. His aboriginal wife and most of his children died before him and were buried on Gun-Carriage Island. In January, 1867, he was laid, at his own request, beside the body of the Tasmanian mother of his children.

On one island the bishop carried out some christenings, having this to say about one of the half-caste children:

> "One of them, a boy of two years of age, was as magnificent a little fellow as ever I saw. His large full black eyes, and finely formed features, would have done honour to any parentage."

These are the only favourable impressions that were recorded about the half-castes. The terrific prejudice on the English side did not take the violent form as towards the full-blooded Tasmanians, but it was just plain, hard, cold ostracism, which may also have sprung from a primitive source, anthropologically speaking, for Man is ever liable to term automatically evil those things that either he does not understand or which are in some way "different".

In that trip of 1854, the Cruise of the Beacon, he also visited Gun-Carriage Island. There he conducted a service, afterwards saying:

"It was with a solemn sense of the privilege conferred upon me, that there in that storm-girt hut, the winds and the waves roaring around me, I, as the first Minister of God that had set foot upon the island, from the dawn of creation until then, commenced the humble offering of prayer and praise to that creation's Lord . . . These simple half-castes, the last relics of the union of aboriginal women with the sealers, had taken the prayer book as their guide, and did not set up their own rebellious wills against its plain injunctions; their psalmody, too, was correct, and touching in its expressiveness. There was a deep, earnestness with which my half-caste congregation joined in several parts of the service, which I should be glad to witness in the more educated and polished gatherings of Christian worshippers."

The pure stock, in general, were not interested in religion.

Some of the half-castes had been noticed as possessing uncommon beauty, and travellers of those times, including Lieutenant Jeffreys and Captain Stokes, have sung their praises, propounding the theory that their beauty saved them even among the wild tribes. A writer in 1815 saw a half-caste child in the company of one of the male Tasmanians. Turning towards the man in question, he exclaimed, "That not your child—too white." The Tasmanian, as bright as they come, and willing to give a laughable turn to his woman's erring, claimed the little one as his own, but excused its pale colour because "My gin eat too much white bread."

In the early days a sealer of King's Island was drowned, leaving behind in his cabin two pretty little half-caste girls and an older boy. Some kind person, pitying the state of the children on the rocks, made representations to the Governor, and the *Gazette* appealed to the public on their behalf. A Mr. Fairfax Fenwick took the boy, who soon ran away from his guardians. Two maiden ladies, Miss Newcombe and Miss Drysdale, accepted the charge of the girls whom they called Kitty and Mary, and conscientiously performed their duties towards them, turning them into "well brought up young ladies". But they too were destined for Flinders Island. On being taken to the new colony across the Straits Kitty obtained a husband and, it is said, lived there respectably: the two old maids had done their work well. Kitty did not stay there very long, later going to Ballarat in Victoria (most of the Tasmanian half-castes seemed to have eventually headed for Australia). Her sister Mary was less erratic than Kitty, and settled down to be the wife of an Englishman, becoming the mother of a fine

above a group of some of the last Tasmanians, here dressed in European clothes. Note the dog in the foreground

right once again in European dress: from left to right, Truganina, William and Patty

Plates 1, 2

Three studies of Truganina, who was the last of the Tasmanians

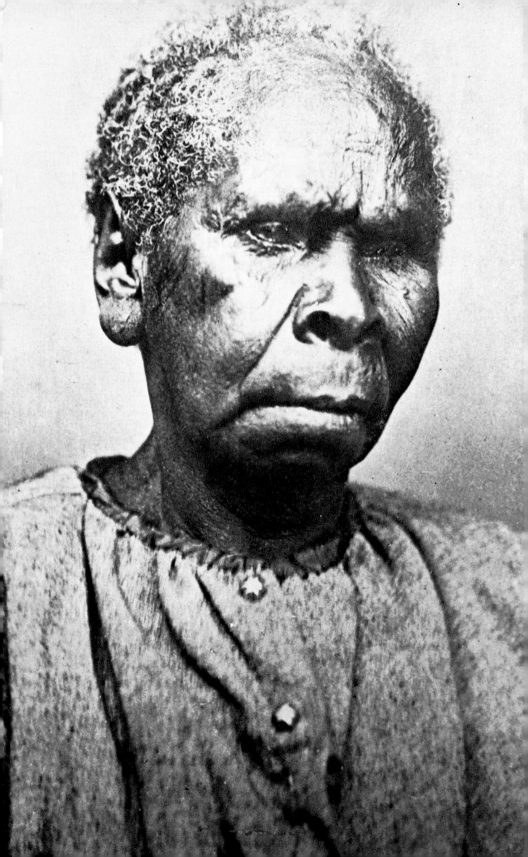

Three photographs of "Wapperty"

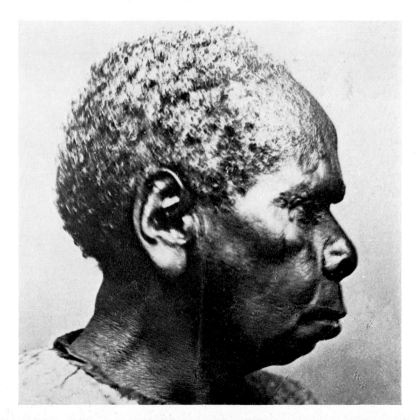

Plates
6, 7, 8

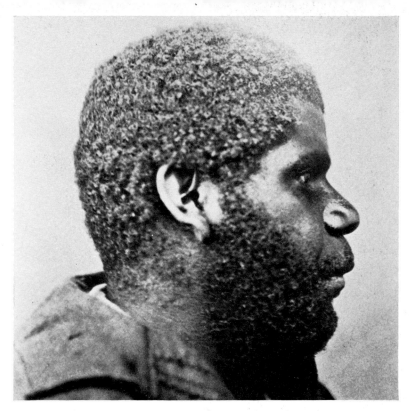

William Lanné, the last Tasmanian man. With his death all prospects of the race's continuance died

Three photographs of Patty

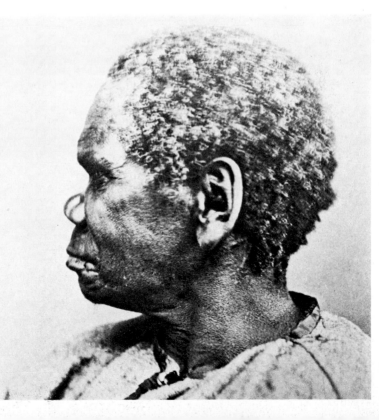

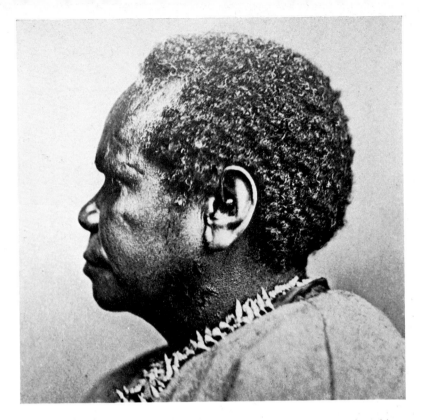

Bessy Clark, who was captured as an infant and reared among the whites

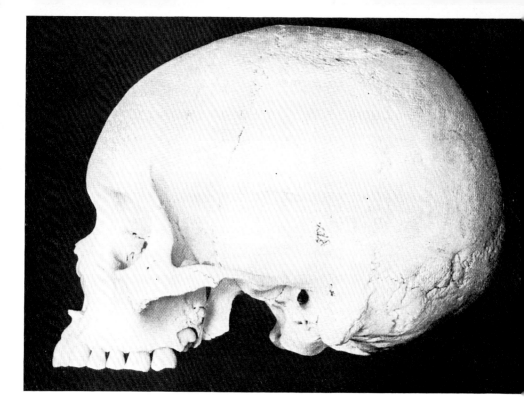

The Tasmanian skull, shown below under X-ray

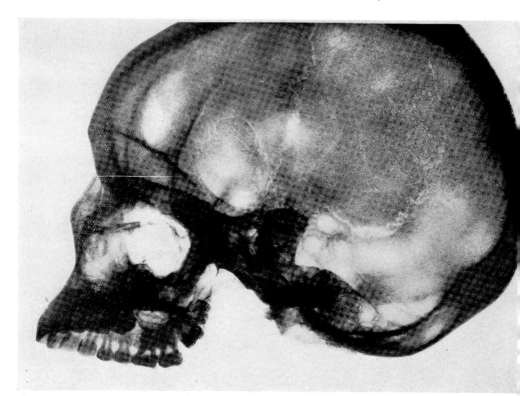

family. It is sad to realize that few bothered about the maternal feelings of the mother, or indeed even credited her with any, for she was eventually left in the cabin alone on the island, with her family all gone. Soon after her children had been forcibly removed from her, and surrounded by everything that reminded her of their presence, she died of a broken heart, a strong capacity which the Tasmanians appear to have shared with many other primitive peoples.

There is one romantic story connected with White contacts that still remains to be told. It is that of Miss Dolly Dalrymple, the first known half-caste in the colony, who got her name from being born (in 1808) near Port Dalrymple, the port on the River Tamar. She was seen by Lieutenant Jeffreys in 1820 and described as

> "Remarkably handsome, of light colour, with rosy cheeks, large black eyes, the whites of which were tinged with blue, and long, well-formed lashes, with teeth uncommonly white, and her figure was almost perfect."

She was then living with a couple in Launceston, who had no children and who had undertaken to look after her education.

Her mother Bong, a genuine Tasmanian beauty, had been attracted to and, for a time, lived with a young sailor in the Straits. He is said to have had respectable connections at home, but he was of "a wild and restless disposition". Dolly was not her only child; and it is in relation to another that she experienced a remarkable adventure. As may be expected, the men of the tribe were angry with the Whites who had stolen their gins, but especially indignant with those female members who preferred the society of the opposite colour. Many instances are known of killings on this account. The known attachment of Bong to the father of her children marked her as an object of their jealous fury. One evening, the sealer's party of which she was a member having been to Launceston for the sale of skins and the obtaining of supplies, Bong went to visit the house where her eldest child was. The boat had been anchored about ten miles from the town and, as she was returning through the bush with an infant at her breast, she was seen and tracked by a tribe that knew her. The child, the mark of her tribal crime, was seized from her and thrown into a fire that they had made. The furious mother snatched it from the flames, but not before it had received some burns, and darted off with it to the security of the scrub. Loud were the yells of the pursuers, and eager was the search for their victim. Aware of her inability to outrun the men, she very wisely sought the

8

densest undergrowth, but in a place where she could hear and see what was happening around their fire. Unable to find her track in the dark, the braves gradually gave up the chase, and returned growling to the camp-fire; and, after threats of revenge in the morning, gradually they all dropped off to sleep. The watchful mother, when she saw they were unconscious, hastened her flight to Launceston, reaching the town by dawn. But, sadly, her little child was so badly burned that it only survived a few days.

When the Conciliatory Mission was formed under Robinson she attached herself to the party, and proved of very valuable service, for she was all out for revenge upon the wild ones who had burnt and thus caused the death of her child, as they had other half-caste children. But when the war was over, Mr. Robinson, instead of recognizing the claims of family ties, harshly ordered her to go to Flinders Island with the other Blacks instead of permitting her to live with Dolly, or with another daughter of hers who lived in Launceston.

The beautiful Dolly, predictably, was exposed to many temptations, as Launceston was the centre for sailors, but history is silent on her career after the age of twelve, until she turns up again living at the Dairy Plains, as the companion of a stock-keeper named Johnson. A man called Cupid, having been speared though not mortally by the Quamby Bluff tribe, ran for shelter to Dolly's hut. She had no sooner extracted the spears from the body of the wounded man than the tribe surrounded the place. She knew that she would receive no quarter, so she fought very hard. For her gallantry in beating off the attack she received a grant of ten acres in the township of Perth (Tasmania), and the Governor promised Johnson another ten acres and a free pardon, as he was at the time a convict, if he became legally married to the brave woman; but Cupid, although the cause for Dolly's heroism, seems to have received nothing for his activities.

They were married and the beautiful children she had were legitimized. She lived to bring up a family of beautiful girls, celebrated all over the country for their loveliness, one of them having perfectly ash-blonde hair.

In colonial times, aboriginal peoples did not seem to have much right to the land that they were born into. As a Red Indian put it, "The French claim all the land on one side of the Ohio, the English claim all the land on the other side; now where does the Indian's land lie?" The Tasmanians were having the same sort of deal, even when they had all gone to Flinders Island, for the flocks and the herds that belonged by law to them were rented for £100 per year.

In the transfer of his country, the Tasmanian, according to Count Strzelecki, "has been allowed no more voice than the kangaroo". The Government declared in proclamations at various times when there were contacts with the Tasmanians that the tribesmen were British subjects and should be treated by law as on equal terms with the Whites. Was it so? Could they retain any portion of their country? Could they, if committing a fault, be tried by their peers? Would their evidence have any weight in a court of justice? Even Spanish law made special provision to treat natives as minors. English law, however, made them, as the Tasmanians themselves said, "neither Black nor White". The Tasmanians had unwritten laws, definite and binding national customs; yet these were scorned and trampled on by our rulers, who, to make further wrongs, took no pains to teach the wild tribes the new laws.

Governor Arthur, however, wrote the following in his despatch to the British ministry in 1835:

"On the first occupation of the colony, it seems a great oversight that a treaty was not, at that time, made with the Natives, and such compensation given to the chiefs as they would have deemed a fair equivalent for what they surrendered."

When John Batman afterwards made a treaty with the Australians of Port Phillip, with substantial gifts as tribute, shouts of ridicule from the authorities greeted his act.

The Tasmanians were a primitive people: they had advanced to a knowledge of cooking and fire, thereby hardening their stakes—for these primitive hunting implements could hardly be termed spears. But why had they gone no further along the path of progress? William Buckley, an Englishman of the nineteenth century who lived for thirty-two years with the Australian aborigines, showed them some improvements. But they were not accepted; instead he became as one of them, living as they did, hunting as they did and making fire in their primitive way with firedrills and fire saws. The aborigines apparently learnt nothing from contact with him. Does progress then only come from association with a power able and ready to impress others?

What did the Government do for the Tasmanians before the Black War? Nothing. What did the colonists do for the elevation of the race? Nothing.

When something was attempted, on the so-called Mission Settlements, only failure resulted. The Whites sought to impose their entire civilization upon the aborigines at once. They had to wear clothes as did the Whites, eat like them, have a similar education, work like them and pray like them, but they were in an entirely different dimension. Sadly, we learn very little from such past mistakes. Recently the Americans have been trying to impose their own form of high technology upon a race of low technology, the Vietnamese, and they wonder why it does not work. Ninety-five per cent of the Vietnamese work on the land and the country is agriculturally orientated, five per cent of the Americans work on the land and the country is urban orientated, and they still wonder why their methods do not work. So they try force. If, in their other aid programmes, they sought some form of *intermediate* technology, something not quite so sophisticated then, instead of the latest super high-powered tractor that requires great skill and knowledge to operate and repair, some simple tractor such as the iron horse, that with a few hours' instruction any villager could cope with and operate on his own ground, could be used. We expect too much, too soon, and prefer to impose progress with force and threat rather than gently and gradually.

The Tasmanians were treated as marionettes. When Europeans pulled the strings they moved; without the pull they were still, and then when they did not move by themselves, they were pronounced stupid and unimprovable. Where, in any case, was the drive coming from for their advance? Food and clothes were given to them at Flinders; so why should they work? They had become a childless race; so for whom were they then to toil? The Tasmanians loathed their very lives; school lessons, catechizings in abstruse doctrines of faith, long prayers, sermons. The well-meaning Whites were shocked and disheartened at the failure. Yet instead of recasting everything and admitting that they had gone wrong in their way of dealing with this unusual people, they joined in the arrogant cry of how utterly hopeless these people were and how useless the task of improvement. This view was shared by the outside world. Would there be any chance for them on the mainland, where they were wide open to the worst elements of society and their *bête noir*, strong drink? But there had been cases of success among the aborigines: Walter and the protégée of Lady Franklin were only two out of many. However, circumstances and the Whites had been at fault for, due to lack of care and effort on the part of the interlopers, these two were among the exceptions and not the rule.

The teaching of religion, too, was a failure. They were taught to prattle like so many parrots, without any real understanding of the phrases they were mouthing. It was only a veneer, a "skin-deep Christianity", taught more for the benefit of the pious consciences of the settlers, than for the souls of their charges. When the missionary spirit despaired of success among the adults, attention was turned to the young. Lord John Russell said in a despatch to the Governor, "The best chance of preserving the race lies in the means employed in the training of their children." Sadly enough, the babies were to be taken from their parents, lest example operate against the lesson. These sickly, limp-looking objects were often described before they sickened and died by the inhabitants of Hobart Town, where they were seen mingling with the offspring of the prisoner population, standing apart from their white schoolmates, listless and weary. The teachers usually said that they could learn, but took little or no interest in class work. Very few, in fact, lived to return to Flinders. Most had an early grave, for, in many ways, they had been really dead for many years.

A wealthy settler and government minister gives a very interesting account of how he caught a young aborigine and brought him up in his own house as one of the family:

"The little wild fellow never having seen the Whites before took some time to quieten down. I did not allow him to associate or live with the servants but had him to live with me in my tent. He accompanied me in all my surveying excursions, during which he always met with the greatest kindness from the settlers, and was allowed to sit at their table whenever I dined with them. His conduct was always correct and well behaved, and would compare favourably with most European boys of his own age. On one occasion when he was in Hobart, he was presented at a mixed party of men and women. During the evening, one of the gentlemen present tried to persuade him to kiss one of the young ladies present. He hesitated and said, 'No-good, no-good', meaning, not right. But having been further persuaded for some time, he watched his opportunity and went behind the girl, and gently touched her neck, and then kissed his fingers. Having acquired our language tolerably well, I was on the point of teaching him to read, when the severe inflammatory attack of the lungs carried him off. He was faithful and became very much attached to me."

This account, though probably well-intentioned, sounds all too like someone describing the keeping of some exotic pet.

In 1841, Mr. Robert Clark had four fine youths under his care, and from them could still have been hope for the Tasmanian race; but there were no Tasmanian girls with which to mate, so they all went childless to tragically early graves. Often, when they had been semi-educated, they felt that they could not take a member from their own wild, or semi-wild, race, and as the half-castes in most cases led a very lowly life, so there were few possible spouses for the one or two which had received some education. They felt that they could never be white men for they were set apart, and yet they could never again be aborigines for the term had developed into something derogatory, so they were left in a vacuum.

chapter 12

Decline and Extinction

It is impossible to separate the decline of the Tasmanians from the advent of the Europeans. The Red Indian spoke of his people as melting like the snow before the sun when the palefaces came. The Tasmanians were hurried and harried from the face of this earth by the poison of European contact and the sword of destruction. Unable to merge with the European colonists, unable to withstand them, they perished. As early as 1830, the Secretary of State in England wrote to Lieutenant-Governor Arthur and mentioned that, due to despatches received, it appeared obvious that the Tasmanian aborigines would soon become extinct.

The Puritans of America were not alone in the belief that aborigines, wherever they were found, were a kind of Canaanitish people, who were doomed to be exterminated by the chosen people as the scourge of God. Even Mr. Threkeld, the missionary to the aborigines of New South Wales, when faced with the rapidly diminishing number of his charges, seems to find some comfort from feeling that it "is from the wrath of God, which is revealed from heaven against all ungodliness and unrighteousness of men". He utters this sentiment when standing in a colony originally founded by and for criminals from Britain, who were rapidly filling the land with their prolific descendants.

The Tasmanian aborigines perhaps suffered less from strong drink than the Australian aborigines have done, because they were less social with the Whites and, when they were on their way out, there were less Whites about. But still the liquor trade was the cause of much misery. Whalers, stock-keepers and sealers used it to gain their ends with the lubras and the gins—getting them drunk added to the sport. The

"Tame Mob" that hung around Hobart in the early years of the colony were dissolute and drunken. The unhappy remnant at Oyster Cove deplored their exposure to drink's curse; and, while decrying their passion for the excitement in their dull lives, spoke feelingly of the cruelty that subjected them to the temptation. Dr. Jeanneret, sometime superintendent of the aborigines on Flinders, states:

> "This was, perhaps, unavoidable under so sudden a change, from a life of hazard to one of comparative indolence, without precautions which experience alone could indicate. Many of them were aged. Several suffered still from the effects of their wounds, and few prepared to adopt the means of graduating their exchanged position. The temporary necessity of resorting to a diet of salt provisions might also possibly operate prejudicially."

He speaks of a pseudo-civilization "increasing an inherent tendency to pulmonary and inflammatory infections". What they suffered from imported diseases such as venereal disease it is impossible to tell. It seems to have gone like wildfire through their settlement. Many regarded as dying from tuberculosis probably died of venereal disease, only they did not understand it then as we do now.

One of the principal causes of their decline was the absence of children. From information received from nine women at Oyster Cove at the end, only two had ever had a child. All had died years before. One said when asked: "What for? Blackfellow, him all die." Some, with a scientific turn of mind, struck by the non-fertility of the Australian and Tasmanian aborigines, have supposed that some mysterious effect was produced by their sexual intercourse with white men. Count Strezelecki advanced this theory about aboriginal women:

> "She loses the powers of conception, on a renewal of sexual intercourse with a male of her own race, retaining only that of being fecund with the white man."

Whatever the exceptions, births with aborigines after intercourse with Whites were, as a rule, unknown. There were instances of white women having liaisons with the Tasmanian men. There was one case in the region of Mount Gambier (Tasmania), about 1834, and there had been other examples.

Dr. Story, an inhabitant of Swanport at this time, declared:

"The deaths at Flinders Island, and the attempts at civilizing the aborigines, were consequent on each other. If left to themselves, to roam as they were wont, and undisturbed, they would have reared more children, and there would have been less mortality. The change to Flinders induced or developed an apathetic condition of the constitution, rendering them more susceptible to heats and chill, attendant on their corroborees, inducing a peculiar disease in the thoracic viscera."

Mr. Solly, then Assistant Colonial Secretary, showed what like causes produced in Australia, saying:

"Many of these lubras would prostitute themselves on every occasion and on any opportunity, for clothes, tobacco, or white money, and in such cases, I question whether they would bear children any more than white prostitutes."

Floss and Bartell, the physical anthropologists who were active in Australia around 1912, were convinced that the aborigines had their own technique of contraception that they practised freely, and it seemed a very safe method. Perhaps the Tasmanians had a similar method. This does not, of course, mean that it was only the aborigine women who may have practised birth control; perhaps the males practised it too, and when they saw their race going downhill they lost all urge for family life.

It is evident that the Tasmanians suffered from heart sickness as well as home sickness, and some instances of this have already been mentioned. Mr. R. H. Davis refers to their residence on Flinders:

"They have been treated there with uniform kindness; nevertheless the births have been few, and the deaths numerous. This may have been in a great measure owing to their change of living and food; but more so to their banishment from the mainland of Tasmania, which is visible from Flinders Island; and the aborigines when I am there have often pointed it out to me with expressions of the deepest sorrow depicted on their countenances."

Dr. Barnes, sometime medical superintendent of the settlement, was conscious of the same antagonism to his medical treatment:

"They pine away, not from any positive disease, but from a disease that they call 'home sickness'. They die from a disease of the stomach too, which comes on entirely from a desire to return to their own country."

Perhaps this they felt subconsciously was their only weapon once they had come in contact with a superior culture.

When Governor Arthur wrote home about the terrible decline of the Tasmanians, even before the great conflict of the Line and the subsequent battle strife, Sir George Murray replied in a despatch, dated November 5th, 1830:

"The great decrease which has of late years taken place in the amount of the aboriginal population, renders it not unreasonable to apprehend that the whole race of these people may, at no far distant period, become extinct. But with whatever feelings such an event may be looked forward to by those of the settlers who have suffered by the collisions which have taken place, it is impossible not to contemplate such a result of our occupation of the island, as one very difficult to be reconciled with feelings of humanity, or even with feelings of justice and sound policy; and the adoption of any line of conduct, having for its avowed or secret object the extinction of the native race, could not fail to leave an indelible stain upon the British Government."

It was too late to attend to the benevolent cry of Lord Glenelg, "Rescue the Remnant!" It is noticed in the glens of Tasmania that the beautiful tree, the Exocarpus, or native cherry tree, flourishes beneath that of other forest forms. When the taller trees are cut down, this particular tree begins to sicken, and gradually decays. It appears that the Tasmanian aborigines were of a similar nature.

The end of the final few came in the late eighteen-sixties, and they died at Oyster Cove. Their passing was recorded in the local papers. Patty died early in 1867, Wapperty was then also dying, leaving only two others of the female population alive. The last of the Straits' aborigines, known as Mrs. Julia Mansell, died in July, 1867, on Sea Lion Island. She was sixty years of age. Her large family of half-castes were scattered throughout the group of islands: her husband, a White, was sixty-four.

One man only remained, William Lanné. In October, 1864, the *Hobart Town Mercury* printed this paragraph:

"At the last ball at Government House, Hobart Town, there appeared the last male aboriginal inhabitant of Tasmania."

Mr. Bonwick has this to say:

"When I went over on a visit to Hobart in 1867, William Lanné had just returned from a whaling voyage. Truganina had mentioned his being a sailor, when talking to me about him 'him such a fine young man'. I therefore sought him out. Once I caught sight of him, but he was too drunk to talk with. My friend, Mr. Woolley, then gave me one of his excellent photographs of the poor fellow, a copy of which appears in this work."*

William Laney, Lanny, or Lanné, alias King Billy, the last man of the Tasmanian aborigines, was, strangely enough, the last child of the last family brought from the wilds to Flinders. He afterwards lived with his own people at Oyster Cove. He had many friends among the sailor fraternity, and he became a whaler, for years sailing from Hobart Town. Jolly in habits as well as appearance, he was always a favourite with his fellow seamen, and was received with enthusiasm by the old ladies of the settlement whenever he made an appearance. As he was the youngest and the handsomest of their tribes, they were always loud in his praises. In January, 1868, dressed in a blue sailor suit, with a gold lace band around his cap, he walked proudly with Prince Alfred, Duke of Edinburgh, on the Hobart Town regatta ground, conscious that they alone were in possession of royal blood.

Only two months later William Lanné went whaling again. He returned in February, 1869, bloated and unhealthy, and for the next few days he complained of sickness. The following Friday he was seized with choleric diarrhoea and, his system worn out through dissipation, he was unable to bear up against the attack. The next day, March 3rd, he attempted to dress himself, intending to go to the hospital for treatment, but the exertion was too much for him and he fell dead on the bed. He was only thirty-four years of age, and it was considered that his excessive drinking had killed him.

Dr. Crowther of the hospital vainly applied to the Government for permission to send the skeleton to the Royal College of Surgeons in London. However, a rather macabre note was struck at Lanné's funeral, for it was found that the head of the corpse was missing. During

---

* And in *this* work also: see plate C9.

the night after the burial the rest of his body was dug up and several parts removed. Crowther was blamed for the removal of the head and his honorary appointment as surgeon at the Colonial Hospital terminated, but it is interesting to note that the Council of the Royal College of Surgeons awarded him during 1869 a gold medal and a Fellowship of the College, the first instance of an Australian having been given this honour. One might be forgiven for suspecting that this was his just reward for having sent the head to them.

The last of her race was Truganina, or Lalla Rookh. She died in May, 1876, a long time after the others. She had been married at least twice, and was a little over seventy at her death. For some years she had lived with a Mrs. Dandridge and created much interest as the last survivor of the Tasmanians. After Truganina's death Mrs. Dandridge petitioned the Government to continue the allowance that they had paid for her upkeep, stressing that the care the old lady had required had been for some years onerous and at times distasteful.

Within seventy years of settlement the entire Tasmanian race had become extinct. Though they left a mass of various stone implements behind, little is known of how they were used or what they were used for: little is said by those who met the aborigines about the use of stone implements—in fact, the Whites often indicated that they were not in the habit of using stone tools. Perhaps the settlers were ignorant or unobservant. The remains are very similar to the tools of Mousterian Man.

Extinct. And have we learnt since then?

PART FOUR

Epilogue

chapter 13

The Physique and Culture
of the Tasmanians

Apart from the few photographs which are reproduced in this book, there is very little visual evidence or record of the Tasmanians' appearance. Their demise pretty well ante-dated the camera, certainly the appearance of the camera in the Antipodes. So, apart from these few photographs, whose subjects may through no fault of their own represent degenerate members of the race, we have only skeletal remains, the sketches and the paintings made by travellers, and a few artifacts, which include some of their crude stone axes. Otherwise we must rely on contemporary written descriptions, a rather unreliable source, as so often they are comparative and not made by scientists or other trained observers.

At a glance, from a distance, the Tasmanian aborigines appear to have much in common with the Australian aborigines. However, on closer examination there were many differences, one of the most obvious being the hair. While the Australian aborigines' hair is wavy, the Tasmanian's was woolly, closely resembling the hair of the negro or negrillo peoples of bushman type, and the inhabitants of some isolated islands in the southern Pacific, such as the Solomons, New Caledonia and, of course, the highland peoples of central New Guinea. According to Mr. Backhouse, a witness of their times, they looked Jewish, and the New Guineans have also been considered thus.

The Tasmanians were even more primitive in appearance than the Australians. Facially the chin of a Tasmanian was even less apparent than that of the Australian. The legs, too, showed a marked difference.

The Australian aborigine has virtually no calves to his legs, probably as a result of centuries of dwelling in almost flat regions where well-developed muscles for traversing rough terrain are unnecessary. The Tasmanians, on the contrary, like their cousins in New Guinea, lived in rough, rather mountainous country and had good calves to their legs, again probably as a result of many generations of living in an environment that was fairly uniformly rocky. Several contemporary observers commented on the good movement of the Tasmanians, remarking that they were of stouter build than the Australians, but better proportioned.* M. Peron writes that "Their thighs were generally muscular, but at the same time almost everyone has the extremities slender, long and weak." Some have considered their limbs like those of the negro, i.e. rather longer than the European. In old age the legs presented a stick-like appearance; otherwise Count Strzelecki's opinion of "their strong legs" stands true.

The Tasmanians' feet were flat, broad and turned inwards, lacking the delicate heel and high instep of more advanced civilizations. M. Maury, of the French Academy, when he saw them in 1830, considered them to be similar to the Papuans. The two races also had, in common with other peoples of the region, the habit of sitting on their heels, with their remarkably knobbly and crooked knees close into their armpits.

Their hands, however, were well formed, delicate in structure and rather small in size, having long tapering fingers and beautiful nails that Europeans might well envy. These possessed great facility and were ever-nervous in movement. The narrow palms could never equal the grip of the European races. In the character of their hand, the Tasmanians resembled the Indian or Hindu, a feature often noted in other primitive peoples: the hands for work, the hands for conquest must be sought among other races. In this context it is interesting to note that peoples with an inferior organization often have smaller than average hands. In medieval days the Scots and Irish, for example, had hands markedly smaller than the English, as swords and daggers dating from those times show.

Another French eyewitness, Captain Freycinet, said: "They differed

* A chief, captured on the Shannon River and confined in Hobart Town Gaol, exhibited wonderful feats of fitness and strength. He would spring five feet into the air and reel round and round like a top. Having no spear, he threw a broomstick through a hole in a sentry box from a range of twelve yards, the circumference of the hole being hardly greater than that of the broomstick. The children were trained early in physical skills and fitness. Lieutenant Breton saw a child of 5 throw a stick through a ring affixed to the wall of the gaol with great precision.

from all other known people." Dr. Knox, an ethnologist, had a similar opinion, adding that "the whole shape of the skeleton differed from ours". Count Strzelecki, a Polish explorer, observed, "Compared with the negro he (the Tasmanian) is swifter in his movements and his gait is more graceful." They were said to be able to cover forty-five miles in a day—a feat that the Australian aborigines were not capable of.

Opinions about the race differed, however. In 1823 two men observed the race and had different impressions. One, a missionary, was shocked at what he referred to as "the caricature of humanity" that he found in Tasmania. Probably his opinion was biased by the fact that the Tasmanians showed not the slightest interest in Christianity, nor indeed, in religion at all, a lack that is very rare among the races of mankind. However, even clerical opinions about the Tasmanians differed. The second observer, the Rev. Haughton, in 1823, noted:

"What I have seen and heard of the original inhabitants of Van Dieman's Land convince me that they are in every respect the most destitute and the most wretched portion of the human family, indeed, the shape of their bodies is almost the only mark by which they are recognised as our fellow men and were it not for the force of other evidence besides that which their condition and habits presents to the eye of the beholder I should without hesitancy affirm that they are a race of beings altogether distinct—looking more like Orang Utangs than humans."

Others referred to them as "gingerbread men, only bearing the shape of human beings". However, Dr. Ross, the editor of the *Hobart Courier*, when he saw a tribe for the first time in 1823 said, "We could not help admiring their upright and even eloquent gait, which would be a pattern to any Bond Street lounger! Their air of independence was quite charming." This, of course, would sufficiently annoy some of the new Tasmanian settlers to cause trouble between the two groups. Mr. Robinson dressed a few of the youths in European clothes and when people saw them "clean in person, healthy in appearance and cheerful and smiling" they were impressed by their fine appearance.

As for the Tasmanians' colour, Captain Bligh, of the mutiny on the *Bounty*, had something to say on this score, and some agree with him. He remarked that, what with the soot, charcoal and grease with which they plastered themselves as well as the accumulated dirt (for the males rarely washed), it was hard to see what colour they really were. This is another trait they had in common with the present-day highlanders of New Guinea, who seldom wash, fearing that the devils will get at them if they expose their skin. Opinions also differed as to the skin colour of the Fuegian Indians, another tribe little given to washing. They were said to be black by some, copper-coloured by Admiral Fitzroy and dark brown according to Captain Snow.

Dr. Anderson, who was with Captain Cook, described the Tasmanians as being dull black, but not quite so deep a black as some of the African negroes. They have been referred to by other explorers as being "blue-black". Dr. Miller, the sometime protector of the aborigines of Tasmania, refers to them as dark brown, or nearly black. There were some with whitish streaks caused by attacks of scurvy, a sorry comment on the diet they received in captivity or in association with the Whites. The protector Parker says of his Port Philip Blacks, whom he considered to be lighter than the Tasmanians, "I never met with one to whose complexion the word [black] would really apply. The most usual colour is chocolate brown." Mr. Angus, the artist, talks of a purplish-copper tint observable in their skin.

There were equally varied descriptions of the facial features of the Tasmanians. The eyes struck M. Marion as being small, but this may have been due to the fact that they had shaggy brows and deep-set eyes, as is found in so many primitive peoples. Another says they had small hollow eyes. Mr. R. H. Davis describes the Tasmanian eyes as "dark, wild, and strongly expressive of the passions". Others were struck by the brilliancy, and compared them with the eyes of Mediterranean races, particularly the Italians. The whites, according to general opinion, were never as clear as in Europeans, and the iris was always dark in colour.

There was, apparently, an air of melancholy about their eyes when in repose, which contrasted strikingly with their intense energy, animation and power when excited. For instance, the children always attracted strangers by their intensely expressive eyes. Even in old, sad age, the way in which Truganina's magnificent eyes still lighted up when reminded of her younger days was enough to draw many comments. Often the eyelids were half closed, and that gave the eye an almost hooded effect.

The Tasmanian's mouth was wide, the lips though full had not the negro's dimension. Dr. Milligan says they were slightly thickened, the jaws were strongly set, though the chin was inferior to that of the civilized races and in women, in particular, very small and receding (see plates A9 and A29). The lower jaw projected, according to Dr. Anderson. M. Labillardière noticed that in the children it projected, but generally receded as they matured. In other words, in the child the jaws appeared normal, but later in life, as the rest of the face developed, the chin did not. Dr. Pickering would have it that it is an error to suppose that it was a prognathous face like that of the negro. But Dumontier's photographs (plates C8 and C11) show the jaw in projection, a fact corroborated by the drawings of a Mr. Glover. Lack of chin in early and primitive types of man is usually equated with primitiveness and thus with lack of mental development. If this is indeed a valid criterion of judgement, then the almost total lack of chin in the Tasmanians, caused by the very receding jaw, must indicate that they had little in the way of mental abilities.

The nose of the Tasmanian was likened by contemporary observers to the button end of the "brougham" type, so they could be well described as button-nosed. The physiologist, Dumoutier, calls it prodigiously developed, for though not longitudinally developed its latitude was considerable, the nostrils being exceedingly wide, full and distended. The terminance of the nose, though virtually something of a pug, had, especially with females, a slight tendency to the retroussé. The most remarkable feature of the Tasmanian's nose, though not entirely unique in this respect, was the depression that occurred at the commencement of the organ, giving the feature something of a pyramidal shape. The root of the nose, like that in so many of the hill men of New Guinea and, of course, the Australian aborigine, had little or no bridge to it. The photograph of Patty or the Ring-tailed Possum (plate C14) gives a good illustration of this facial feature. The countenance of the women was considered masculine.

The ears were not flat as in primates, nor enlarged like those of some of the primitive Brazilian Indians, nor did they have an oblong slit as did those of the Easter Islanders. Nor did they make slits in the lobes and insert ornaments that would weigh the lobes down to the shoulders, as is the practice with the Dyaks and some tribes of South American Indians, according to pottery figurines as well as modern observations. They had, on the whole, well shaped and well proportioned ears, generally larger than those of the negroid type, which are inclined to be small.

The teeth were large and powerful, to such an extent that they appeared almost disproportionate. Their strength is evidenced by the fact that the Tasmanians used them to straighten out wood for spears. The remarks of Mr. Pardoe, a contemporary observer, are noteworthy:

"They had large crowns, thickly covered by enamel, even when they had much wear. Much thicker was this enamel than in Europeans, the canines were not so deeply seated as with Europeans, the gums were much thicker and therefore made up for the loss. Their colour was a very clear white, which made the French visitors envious and remark much about them in their reports about the natives of Tasmania. Very few of the natives had defective teeth, from the constant use of shell fish, but the majority were possessed of a magnificent masticatory apparatus."

Some teeth of Tasmanians in our museums show them to be much worn, frequently the entire set. They often show the state of taurodontism. In one case at the British Museum (Natural History) in the R.C.S. section they were worn down to the stumps (Grade Pedersen 3). But decayed teeth were so uncommon that Mr. Ronald Gunn sent this description with a skull for the R.C.S. collection: "The continuous part of the 2nd bicuspid and the 1st molar of the left part of the upper jaw were decayed which is a rare occurrence in the race."

Two skulls in the B.M. have only three incisors in the lower jaw and there is no trace of there ever having been a fourth. Dr. Jeanneret accounts for the soundness and the size of their teeth through constant vigorous employment on hard, tough material, i.e. roots, breaking open shell-fish, etc. The incisors were always stout and rounded, in fact rather similar to the rest of the teeth. This trait is also seen in other people who use their teeth for much more than just eating, such as the Eskimaux.

The Tasmanian aborigines did not practise tooth evulsion as did the Australian aborigines. None of the Tasmanians' jaws have their lower front teeth knocked out, as is so often seen in the jaws of the Australian natives.

In stature they were fairly well developed, the northern tribes in general taller than the southern tribes. Dr. Milligan saw "many of them above the usual height". Mr. Robinson found some at Port Davey about 2 metres in height. In 1819 a man 6 ft. 2 in. tall was killed. Dr. Story says that "the general height of the men was from 5 ft. 2 in. to 5 ft. 5 in.; the women, in proportion to the men of course were smaller". He adds, "Balawenna was a fine athletic man, more than six feet. His wife was in proportion to that height." They were not, generally, as tall as the Australians, though stouter in build. Among the Australians Captain Stuart found one 7 ft. in height. Their skeletons indicate vigour without coarseness. Peron, the Frenchman, refers to their broad shoulders and strong loins. But when he applied the dynamometer to test their physical strength, he found them inferior to his countrymen. It is quite likely, however, that the aborigines being tested exerted less force from want of practice with the instrument. Freycinet, some years after, gave a statement of power in kilograms, putting down the Hawaiian at 60, the negro at 57, the Maori at 51 and the Australian at 45.

Marion, another observer, supposed the shoulders of the Tasmanian to bend out of the straight line, a feature very similar to the Red Indians, who were not as upright as many believe. It is not unusual for primitive, forest people to have a slight stoop, which probably arises from the spear-throwing position. Count Strzelecki thought the race strong and square-built. The French noted the big belly, salient and formed like a balloon. This development is not restricted to primitive, isolated tribes!

Dr. Barnard Davis, who was an anatomist at the R.C.S. early in the nineteenth century, had several remarks to make about the skeleton of the female Tasmanian. Of the pelvis he writes "that it is remarkable for thinness, slenderness, and the delicacy and lightness of the bones. The central part of the iliac fossae is diaphanous, the pubae is thin, the ascending ramus of the ischium slender, and the obturator foramen large and of a triangular form. The spinus processes of the ossa pubes are strongly developed." This is very similar to the Asiatic Indian. Professor Acker from Germany also refers to the remarkable slenderness of the bones. Camper talks about the "peculiar pelvis" and regards it as different from that of the Aryan race. Strzelecki terms it unusually narrow, and therefore, in the eyes of a comparative anatomist, of a low type. Weber informs us that the pelvis of the European is oval in shape, round in the American Indian, square in the Mongolian and oblong in the African. M. Dupont affirms that the part is very strong and somewhat different from the pelvis of the European, and similar to the skeletons of the Palaeolithic peoples.

The breasts of the females turned a little outwards, as indicated in the sketches of Mr. Gould. According to Strzelecki the breasts instead of being spherical are in "marriageable persons, periform, and soon after marriage become flaccid and elongated". Often the female aborigine, when carrying a child on her back, would throw one of her pendulous breasts over her shoulder for the child to suckle as they went along. Mr. Knox asserts that the reproductive organs in the Tasmanians are said to be quite peculiar. There are some recorded instances of the genitals being tied up, though Labillardière saw the Tasmanians' relatives on New Caledonia wrap the genitals with bark or leaves. About the

Tasmanians' physique he observed: "In many the navel appeared puffed out and very prominent, but we assured ourselves that this deformity was not occasioned by a hernia. Perhaps it is owing to the too great distance from the abdomen at which the umbilical cord is separated." Circumcision, though practised by most tribes in Australia, was unknown among the Tasmanian aborigines.

Some of the colonists considered the Tasmanians but one remove from the brute. Dr. Weisbach, physical anthropologist, studied them and came up with the idea that "this singular race presented the most numerous simian similarities, in the length of the foot, and the smallness of the legs, the broad nose and mouth, the elongated arms, the broad feet, and the calf muscles". Many tried to make it similar to the orang-utan, and some even picked on the most hideous of all the monkey tribe—the mandrill.

The skin was not the most agreeable part of their person. People spoke of its harsh, dry feel. Even the females appeared to have a skin allied to that of a rhinoceros, and the aged ones, especially, were repulsive to the touch. Without doubt the scorbutic white lines in bends upon their bodies did not increase their attractiveness, but the skin itself seemed as if one could strike a match upon it, so rasp-like was its surface. The older colonists were accustomed to refer to the natives as "scabby sheep". The Dutch explorer, Mr. Modera, said of the Papuans, Australian aborigines and Tasmanian aborigines that he met: "some of them have an ugly looking disease of the skin, by means of which the entire surface of the body and limbs is rendered scaly". A Dr. Copse who was on the same voyage described them as if covered with scales.

The odour proceeding from the natives, though not regarded by some observers as being as marked as the negro's, was very pungent and somewhat musklike. There is a possibility that this smell might have been influenced by the diet of constant shell-fish.

The cicatrices on the skins of the Tasmanians and Australians are connected with the physical adornment. Plates A1 and A8 show some of the patterns used. Labillardière thus describes the people he saw in Tasmania in 1792: "Almost all of them were tattooed with raised points, sometimes placed in two lines, one over the other, much in the shape of a horse-shoe; though frequently these points were in three straight and parallel lines on each side of the breast; some were observed, too, toward the bottom of their shoulder blades, and in other places." He also noted that some of the women had marked their abdomens with large, semi-circular incisions, one above another, to remove, as he thought, the wrinkles caused by frequent pregnancies. These cicatrices were different from true tattooing, by needle pricking the application of a colouring substance, as found amongst the Maoris. The Tasmanian women, too, were often less marked than the men. One observer, who saw the infliction of the adornment upon a girl, described her screams and groans from the process: "Her head was secured between the legs of a very strong pale fellow, while another carried out the operation on her slowly." The boys would not cry out at all, being proud to stand unflinchingly as the long, deep cuts were made with the sharp obsidian knives. The wound was kept open with wood ashes and, when healed, the raised scar remained for life. A gash in one girl is described as being one inch long, three-sixteenths of an inch deep, and half an inch from its neighbouring wound, the cuts extended from the breast to the shoulders. Some Australians put grease instead of ashes into the cuts, and the Papuans use fat or clay.

The Tasmanians did not generally have as many cicatrices as some of the Australian tribes. The shoulders and breasts were the parts most frequently subjected to the operation. Labillardière mentioned that these "tubercles were symmetrically arranged, exhibiting sometimes lines four inches in length; at other times parts spaced at different distances". Captain King, who visited many of the north-western parts of Tasmania, saw that the aborigines there had in front incisions every three inches in horizontal lines, each an inch in diameter and having an elevation of nearly half an inch.

The skull of the last Tasmanian male, William Lanné, would not be typical of his race, as he did not have the usual Tasmanian features. In fact, it is scarcely safe to say that there is any type-skull of this race; they vary so much. A similar situation occurs with the highlanders of New Guinea, where sometimes one finds types looking extremely advanced alongside others who seem as equally primitive. These facts favour the theory that forty or fifty thousand years ago the primitive Neanderthal type and the more advanced Cro-Magnon man lived side by side; the latter, being more advanced, displacing and ousting the more primitive type.

Dr. Meigs, after examining 1,125 Tasmanian aboriginal skulls, declared that he could find none typical of the race. Professor M. J. Weber acknowledges that "there is no proper mark of any definite race form of the skulls so firmly attached that they may be found to represent this race". Dr. Paul Topinard seems to favour that view too, when describing some Tasmanian skulls in the Musée de l'Homme, Paris. One of these in particular seemed to be of a very elevated character. Even Dr. Pickering exclaimed after examining a Tasmanian aboriginal's skull, "His head might compare with an antique bust of any great philosopher!"

An inspection of the portraits of Manalagana, Wooreddy and Walter George Arthur, three prominent male Tasmanians, would make one doubt the low estimate of Tasmanian cranial development. Certainly, a comparison of their heads with the representation of the head of the German philosopher, Emmanuel Kant, as given in Von Baer's work, would not illustrate the superiority of the latter, which has a more retreating forehead with a far greater mass behind and before the whole of the ear, which is considered a very primitive trait. It leads one to conclude with Professor Clelland that "There is no foundation whatsoever for the supposition that the lower races of mankind have a forehead less developed than the more civilized nations". There is, in fact, remarkable contrast in the Tasmanian skulls, remarkably developed ones appearing alongside and contemporary with those of a much more primitive nature.

The volume of the brain is usually regarded as the index of mental power and development of intellect. Thus the Tasmanian's small brain has been taken as evidence of their lack of mental development. Mr. Williamson, an anatomist, put the Tasmanian's brain at seven-tenths of the size of the Englishman's. Dr. Barnard Davis, however, put it at nine-tenths. Professor Weights even speaks of the savage of Van Diemen's Land as having "uncommonly large heads". It is known that many races have larger brains than the refined peoples of Europe.

Prognathism (protrusion of the middle third of the face) is particularly interesting in the Tasmanians and is often found to extremes. It has been held to be a simian feature. The Nicobar Islanders, Andamanese and New Guineans also show prognathism in some of their people. Most of the Tasmanians had prognathism, leading some early observers to class them as a type of Negro, and others to describe them as members of the lowest levels of humanity. Yet this "defect" is found among many inhabitants of the remoter parts of these islands, notably Ireland and Wales. In earlier days it was also well in evidence among London's poor, doubtless due in many ways to a bad diet. Prognathism is said to be found among peoples who have to tear at their food. Of all the tribes of Tasmania, the Port Sorell tribe showed this characteristic most strongly, hardly having any chin.

No account of the physical condition of the Tasmanians would be complete without reference to that physical change in their make up caused by the advent of the Europeans and alleged to be the true cause of the women's barrenness. Count Strzelecki, the Polish anthropologist, mentioned that the Europeans' arrival had a poisonous effect upon them, subsequently depriving the Tasmanian woman of the ability to bear the children of a man of her own race after frequent intercourse with, or rape by, the newcomers. He contended that examples of this general principle were to be found in both hemispheres. There may be some truth in this: it is repeated many times in the material and records concerning the Tasmanian aborigines. The women were evidently very attracted to the European men, despising men of their own race if there were any of the newcomers around, as did the Indians of South America. The results of these unions were the half-castes, which all the Tasmanians despised, with a resultingly high rate of infanticide. The women, afterwards, were apparently unable to bear children of their own race again, even when returned to their tribe or family.

This was, of course, only one of the causes of their extinction. Others were their contraction of venereal disease and tuberculosis, and the removal of their children, which caused both parents and children to pine, often fatally. There was also the terrible home sickness which they seemed to suffer when taken from their tribal lands by the Europeans. This sickness seems to have affected them in their stomachs, and there is corroborative evidence of this from the records of the slaving ships which plied between the west coast of Africa and the southern states of America. The death-rate of slaves from what was most often described as home sickness and/or a stomach complaint was high, to such an extent that some crew members were employed almost solely to go round and try to prevent any of the slaves getting melancholy, the first indication of the sickness.

There may have been other causes for the women's barrenness, as suggested by Dr. T. R. H. Thomson, R.N., who lived contemporaneously with the last of the Tasmanians. He accounts for their sterility as the result of self-inflicted abortion, and the physical deterioration of the women as due to "moral causes", in their acceptance of the white man's comforts and thus, all too often, the recipient of his vices. He further remarks, "She returns to her tribe with a broken down constitution, probably past the usual time of life for conception (as they seldom bear children after thirty in these aborigines), to prove, in some instances, sterile." The Tasmanian men did not bother themselves about the European women, as their gins did over the European men. In fact it is stated that the Tasmanian male was not very highly sexed. A similar comment was made centuries earlier by the Spanish about the male

DR. TOPINARD ON THE FACE OF THE TASMANIANS

MESURES CRANIOMÉTRIQUES

	TASMANIENS No. 7								Australiens No. 10	Bas Bretons No. 13
	1	2	3	4	5	Moyenne	6	7	Moyenne	Moyenne
Projection verticale maxima de la tête (crâne et face)	192	—	183	—	—	187·5	171	—	188·0	188·8
CRANE										
Circonférence antéro-postérieure verticale (A) — Partie cérébrale du frontal	115	115	113	110	102	111·0	119	110	107·2	115·9
Partie pariétale	133	130	130	126	128	129·4	110	120	126·7	126·9
Partie occipitale supérieure	52	45	60	58	57	55·4	52	60	62·9	65·6
Partie cérébelleuse	65	64	52	60	—	60·2	52	—	51·7	53·8
Longueur du trou occipital	34	37	32	33	—	34·0	32	—	35·5	36·0
Distance du *point basilaire au point sus-orbitaire* (G)	116	111	108	106	—	110·2	105	—	110·8	110·0
Total	515	502	495	493	—	501·0	470	—	502·0	508·2
Circonférence transverse (B) — Courbe sus-auriculo bregmatique (C)	310	295	296	293	286	296·0	282	296	283·4	307·6
Diamètre transverse bi-sus-auriculaire	129	124	126	116	124	123·8	117	126	111·6	125·1
Total	439	419	422	409	410	419·8	399	422	395·0	432·7
Diamètre antéro-postérieur maximum (D)	191	187	176	179	174	181·4	177	187	180·9	187·3
Diamètre transverse maximum (E)	149	139	140·5	139·5	131	139·8	132	134·5	131·5	145·2
Projection verticale maxima, moins la hauteur des condyles occipitaux (F)	132	—	127	125	—	128·3	118	—	131·6	128·3
Rapport de la circonférence B à la circonférence A = 100	85·24	83·46	85·25	82·96	—	84·23	84·89	—	78·68	85·14
Rapport du diamètre E au diamètre D = 100 (indice céphalique)	78·01	74·33	79·83	77·94	75·28	77·07	74·57	71·92	72·64	77·51
Rapport de la projection F au diamètre D = 100	69·11	—	72·15	69·82	—	70·36	66·66	—	72·74	68·49
Partie de la circonférence horizontale maxima *antérieure* à la courbe C	255	247	236	237	236	242·2	238	258	235·0	242·0
Diamètre transverse frontal inférieur ou minimum	93	95	94·5	90	90	92·4	95	95	94·3	95·4
Diamètre transverse frontal maximum	116	115	115	109	107	112·4	107	113	108·1	121·0
Partie de la circonférence horizontale maxima *postérieure* à la courbe C	315	287	272	237	262	275·8	276	257	267·5	285·3
Diamètre transverse occipital maximum	113	105	121	105	104	109·6	103	110	105·8	113·0
Diamètre antéro-postérieur iniaque	193	187	174	176	171	180·2	177	186	175·0	181·5
Diamètre transverse du trou occipital	31	28	30	29	—	29·5	26	—	29·7	30·5
Angle dit de Camper	75°	76°·5	71°	75°	—	74°·1	80°	74°	71°·0	75°·3
Capacité de la cavité crânienne (en centimètres cubes)	1520	1424	1332	1255	—	1382·7	1103	—	—	—*

* La moyenne de 384 crânes Parisiens de M. Broca est de 1437.

MESURES CRANIOMÉTRIQUES *(continued)*

FACE	1	2	3	4	TASMANIENS No. 7 (5)	Moyenne	6	7	Australiens No. 10 Moyenne	Bas Bretons No. 13 Moyenne
Distance du point basilaire au point sus-orbitaire (G)	116	111	108	106	—	110·2	105	—	110·8	110·0
Distance du point basilaire à la racine du nez	100	98	96	93	—	96·7	103	—	97·3	100·0
Distance du point basilaire au point sous-nasal	102	93	100	94	—	97·2	93	—	93·3	92·2
Distance du point basilaire au point alvéolaire supérieur	103	96	105	99	—	100·7	95	—	100·2	94·7
Distance du point basilaire au point mentonnier (H)	117·5	—	118	—	—	117·7	99	—	106·6	111·0
Distance du point sus-orbitaire à la racine du nez	20	20	17	16	18	18·2	19	19	19·3	15·6
Distance du point sus-orbitaire au point alvéolaire supérieur	89	81	78	79	—	81·7	80	98	85	87·8
Distance du point sus-orbitaire au point mentonnier (I)	138	—	120	—	—	129·0	120	—	127·5	135·3
Diamètre transversal ou bi-zygomatique maximum (J)	140·5	131·5	132	123	123	130·0	124	136	126·6	129·4
Angle sus-orbito-mentonnier formé au point basilaire par les distances G et H	72°	—	64°	—	—	68°·2	72°	—	76°·0	76°·0
Rapport du diamètre transverse maximum de la face ou diamètre J à sa plus grande hauteur ou distance I = à 100	101·8	—	110·0	—	—	100·07	103·4	—	99·29	95·63
Intervalle des orbites	25	22	25	21	21	22·8	21	24	22·3	22·7
Profondeur de l'échancrure de la racine du nez (K)	10	05	06	07	—	07·0	07	04	—	—
Hauteur des orbites	30	32	25	31	29	29·4	31	38	32·3	32·0
Largeur des orbites	39	41	38	37	37	38·4	37	41	40·5	39·3
Saillie du rebord obitaire supérieur au-dessus de l'inférieur	+11	+11	+04	+03	—	+07·2	+06	00	* -·01	* —
Longueur des deux os propres du nez (sur la ligne médiane)	13	10	11	10	—	10·7	07	08	10·0	12·6
Largeur des deux os propres du nez (sur la ligne médiane)	16	14	10	17	—	14·2	13·5	19	17·0	23·2
Distance de la racine du nez au point sous-nasal	51	51	43	49	42	47·2	45	60	49·5	53·0
Largeur du maxillaire supérieur	70	63	70	61	65	65·8	59	61·5	63·0	59·2
Hauteur du maxillaire supérieur ou distance du point alvéolaire supérieur au point sous-nasal	14	13	18	19	—	16·0	14	19	16·2	17·6
Largeur du maxillaire inférieur (aux angles)	95	—	92	—	—	93·5	92	—	95·7	98·8
Hauteur du maxillaire inférieur (sur la ligne médiane)	29	—	32	—	—	30·5	25	—	31·2	32·2
Hauteur de sa branche postérieure	50	—	52	—	—	51	39	—	57·7	61·1
									4 Australiens	*1 nègre du Soudan*
Prognathisine facial	14	12	23	17	—	16·5	12	—	22·5	26
Prognathisine alvéolaire supérieur	02	04	04	06	—	04	04	—	10	14

* Le signe – indique que c'est au contraire le bord orbitaire inférieur qui dépasse l'inférieur chez ces Australiens.

Indians of South America, where the Indian women seemed to prefer the Spanish men to their own kind: as a result very few pure-bred Indians remain at the present time. Thus it was that, in the majority of cases, Tasmanian women consorting with the European males became barren. However, if they remained with just one European man, there would often be a family.

Strong drink, as with so many peoples unused to it, led to a general decline in their standards and demoralization. Venereal disease, of course, took its toll. The spread of this disease while they were on Flinders Island further sapped the virility of the male aborigine, on which drunkenness and premature decay had already had its effect.

The "self-inflicted abortion" commented on by Thomson may well not have been self-inflicted. There is evidence from West Africa that even as late as 1925, when Europeans were no longer a new phenomenon, a cause of the declining population of native tribes was the very high "abortion sickness" suffered by pregnant women. These entirely spontaneous natural abortions, together with other pressures, effectively restricted the population's growth. This is interesting as it casts doubts on both the Tasmanians' alleged practice of infanticide as well as their barrenness. But whatever the cause, for the Tasmanians the result was sadly the same.

The original Tasmanians were far more disorganized for any defence than were, say, the ancient Britons when the Romans arrived. The Britons did at least have tribal unity, whereas the Tasmanians moved in little family groups that owed allegiance only to the head of the family. Not until much later did the necessity for self-defence force them to form mobs.

Their material technology, culture and weaponry were very primitive: they had no bows and arrows, no nets or proper boats, only an apology for a canoe made of bark to enable them to make short trips across water from one place to another. Their foe was far more sophisticated than the legions of Rome, being equipped with firearms, and of course the Tasmanians were far fewer in number than the original Britons had been.

Early explorers tell us that the natives practised polygamy, with the difference that they never kept more than one spouse at a time, instead regularly going through a simple form of divorce. The chief would have a string of wives one after the other in fairly rapid succession. Later on, when men were comparatively few in relation to women, bigamy and polyandry were practised.

They were a kitchen midden people, similar in some ways to the Jomon culture of Japan, the first pottery from whose middens is dated around 6000 B.P. The women carried all that was movable among their possessions in opossum and kangaroo skin bags on their shoulders. Occasionally they had a small opossum skin cloak for their shoulders, the rest of their garb consisting of no more than a few shells and a string round the waist.

They had spatulas of wood for opening the shell-fish that they ate. Drinking vessels were constructed from leaves of kelp crudely fashioned at each end. Bags and baskets were made from rushes, and were consequently not very serviceable, and the implements and knives were made from granite and resembled those made from flint in the earliest palaeolithic cultures. Their weapons were the waddy and the spear. The waddy was a short piece of wood, reduced and notched towards the grasp and slightly rounded at the point. The spear was nine to twelve feet long, straightened by the teeth and balanced with a great nicety. They would poison the tips by sticking them into a dead and rotten carcass. The spearman, while poised to throw with the right hand, held others in his left ready for immediate use: the accuracy was exceptional at a range of about sixty yards. Labillardière describes the throwing well: "The warrior grasped it in the middle; raised it as high as his head; drew it towards himself with a jerk, that gave a tremulous motion at the extremities, which accelerated its progress, and tended to support it longer on the column of air; it was darted at one hundred paces, and remained in a horizontal position for three fourths of that distance."

The beehive huts mentioned by most of the early explorers were made of branches, the thicker end of each being planted in the ground so that the fan of the upper part formed the roof of the hut. The skeleton so formed would then be covered with bark. The beehive huts in general contained about six people.

Their appetite was voracious on occasions and, like the Eskimaux, they probably stuffed themselves whenever food was available. One woman was observed for a day during which she consumed, besides a double ration of bread, more than fifty eggs about the size of a duck's. One settler, a Mr. O'Connor, saw a child of eight eat a kangaroo rat and then a large crayfish. Before being eaten, game was cast into the fire and there singed, the entrails then being removed before the rest of the body was returned to the flames to be warmed ready to eat: the food was thus only half-roasted. When hungry they would tighten their waist with a thong of kangaroo skin. They detested fat, and one of their most interesting food customs was that some tribes would eat only female animals, others only males. On occasions they ate a few vegetable products, such as kelp and fern roots, native potato, mushrooms and the root of the grass tree, but in general their diet was purely carnivorous, including insects such as caterpillars and ants. The mainstay of the diet consisted of kangaroo and wallaby.

They obtained liquor from the cider tree, tapping it as a maple is tapped. The juice, which is like molasses, trickled into a hole at the foot of the tree which they then covered with a large stone. By natural fermentation the juice became slightly intoxicating, and was in the early days much approved by the stockmen as well as by the natives. (Very few primitive people are without sources of alcohol.)

The Tasmanian would move his fire every day, never lighting another on the same spot in case bad luck caught up with him. This is a belief very similar to that of the Laplanders.

In summer they wore no clothes, but in the winter the shoulders and waist were covered with the dry skin of a kangaroo: the women's dress was the same with the addition of ruffles. They were greatly distressed by the clothes of the Europeans and would wear such garments only when observed. They were more sensitive to cold than the Europeans, and would huddle over their fires, one at the front and one at the rear, to stay warm. These fires that they often lit, however, not only kept them warm but frequently gave away their position when they were being hunted.

Nearly every tribe covered the body with patches of ochre and grease (from the opossum) as a basis for dress. With obsidian knives they made several different cicatrices on the neck, shoulders, face and other areas of the body, such as the buttocks. In some cases the cicatrices resembled epaulettes, in others eyes. The incisions were kept open with grease until the skin became raised, the process then being complete. The accompanying pain they bore with great fortitude and affected indifference. When Penderome, the younger brother of the Western Chief, underwent the operation at the hands of a woman with a piece of obsidian, it is said that the flesh of his shoulder opened like a split fish. All the time that the operation continued he amused the bystanders with jokes and laughter.

They wore grease on their head mixed with ochre, plus bits of wood, feathers, flowers and the teeth of kangaroos (in New Guinea the natives use the teeth of the cus-cus in this way). The hair was separated into tufts, rolled and matted together into long locks.

They suffered **from** several diseases which were **often** fatal, and it appears that most were of a rheumatic origin as with the highlanders of New Guinea. Rheumatism and inflamations were cured by incisions; leprosy, from which like the New Guineans they also suffered was relieved by wallowing in ashes. Catarrh was frequently fatal in certain seasons: in one instance an entire tribe with the exception of a single woman perished on the Huon River. Surgery was simple, gashes being cut with crystal. A snake bite was treated by boring the wound with a charred peg and stuffing the hole with fur which was then singed off to the level of the skin: in fact, almost by cauterization. They had great faith in charms as medicinal preventatives and curatives: thigh bones were specially useful, and were fastened to the head of the sick in the shape of a triangle, apparently with excellent results. The sick were often deserted: their tribes could neither convey them nor wait for their recovery. Food and water were usually left within easy reach of them and, when able and if they had survived, they would follow their kinsmen.

When they felt the approach of death they were anxious to expire in the open air, and asked to be carried outside, feet first. They believed that the spirit lingered in the body until sundown. The French naturalists in 1829 were the first to record the burial practices of the aborigines, as follows:

"A fire was made at the foot of a tree. The body of the infant was placed in it. When the body was decomposed by the flames the skull was taken up by a female, probably the mother. It was then worn for a long time round the neck.

"The body being wrapped in a kangaroo skin, the couple would carry alternately the memento of their child. They would deposit several of the skulls together in a final resting place. [This sounds similar to the clutch of thirty-three skulls found together at Offnet in Hungary, dating from palaeolithic times.] During the carrying out of these rites they were jealous of spectators, and would take offense if any approached their dead. In other tribes bodies were placed in hollow trees and closed in by underwood."

These bodies are frequently found to this day in Tasmania. Backhouse records a striking funeral: After the death of a woman the body was placed on a pile of logs, over which a guard was placed throughout the night. At dawn the logs were ignited and the aborigines covered their faces with the ashes from the pyre, sat down and lamented until their faces became furrowed by the courses of their tears through the ash.

In another case an aborigine, just after capture, told his tribe that death was at hand: they prepared the funeral pyre and he died that night. Despite the complexity of the burial services, the Tasmanians had no traditions of ancestor worship.

The tribes to the westward were the finest: those from South Cape to Cape Grim had better huts and wore mocassins for travelling. Those on the east of the Launceston Road were confederate: towards the end the Oyster Bay tribe committed their children to the care of the Big River tribe rather than see them sent to any orphanage—many of the males of the latter tribe had been slaughtered by the English. It was the general conflict between the tribes that increased the difficulties of their conciliation: not only had they to be reconciled to the English but also to each other.

Territory and women were the chief causes of wars between the tribes, and in the latter days it was common for a war to start through the whites having driven members of one tribe on to the territory of the other.

chapter 14

Origins of the Tasmanians

A hundred years ago there were more peoples like the Tasmanians than there are today, although there are still pockets of similar people, particularly in the western Pacific. The largest group left are the highlanders of New Guinea, to which the Tasmanian aborigines had many affinities. The Semangs and the Sakai of Malaya are also probably related, as are the Andamanese and Nicobar Islanders of the Indian Ocean and those aborigines in the remoter regions of the Philippines. In fact any extremely primitive people were probably of the same stock, as if many thousands of years ago that region of the world was populated by the Tasmanian type. The Australian aborigine which lived relatively close to them, differed in several ways. Possibly on the large land mass of the Australian continent there were peoples similar to the Tasmanians, perhaps living in similar environments, and when the Australian aborigines reached the continent, from a different direction to that from which it is believed the Tasmanians came, the newcomers wiped or drove out the previous inhabitants, who were similar to the Tasmanian aborigines. We know that quite a lot of this occurred in that region of the world, even in historic times. Taking New Zealand as a case in point, when the present Maoris came in from the South Pacific, due to population explosions in that area, they found an earlier people already established in New Zealand, the Moriori, who they destroyed, possibly cannibalistically, very quickly. Unlike the Tasmanian aborigines the Maoris were markedly cannibalistic, as indicated in legends and the physical indications of the skeletons, etc., particularly when the remains are of Moriori origin.

Again, in the latter part of the eighteenth century, the explorer

9

Flinders (who gave his name to the island that was to become the notorious settlement camp for the Tasmanians), visited many of the islands around New Zealand, discovering the Chatham Islands. They, too, had primitive inhabitants, apparently not unlike the Tasmanians, although possibly rather plumper, for when Flinders visited the islands the one Maori among his crew, as soon as he saw the plump and rather indolent looking islanders, immediately remarked "Good, we shall have plenty of food!", going on to say that he would tell his fellow country-men of the "plenty fat sheep" on the neighbouring islands. And, in fact, when further explorers reached the Chatham Islands about three years later, they found that the Maoris had eaten nearly every one: as well as being plump the islanders were also pretty helpless, only having stone weapons to defend themselves against such calamities as meeting up with the Maoris. About 1,500 lived in 1832 but, as reported in 1860, only 100 remained.

The closest people to the Tasmanian aborigines (geographically speaking) were the Australian aborigines. In some respects the two races do resemble each other, although superficially the latter is taller and slimmer and has wavy hair in contrast to the more robust figure and woolly hair of the Tasmanian. It seems likely that the Tasmanian aborigine had a southern Indian ancestry, probably Dravid or Vaddah, who, in the distant past (50,000 B.P., according to Sir Douglas Mawson), crossed the land-bridges down to Indonesia, Australia and into Tasmania. It seems unlikely that he came any other way, for like his closest kin, the highlanders of New Guinea, he was very fearful of water. (This fear of water prevents them crossing even the larger rivers, so would certainly seem to militate against their ever having attempted to venture on the ocean.) They feared that if they entered the water, or indeed even washed, the dirt which had accumulated on their bodies, together with the animal fat and charcoal which they themselves applied, would be removed, thus allowing the devils and evil spirits to get at their bodies more easily. It would therefore seem that they did not come across the ocean as the Maoris did. In turn, this suggests that their arrival in Tasmania must have been very early, while the land-bridges still existed. Nor did they bring any refinements, culturally or socially, with them, suggesting that the civilization from which they came had reached no great degree of development. Even the Australian aborigines brought the dingo with them, but the Tasmanians only acquired dogs from the Europeans, although they then took to them very readily. In fact one group of nineteen aborigines brought in by the Line had 150 hunting dogs with them.

As mentioned elsewhere, the Tasmanians had many customs and habits in common with the present highlanders of New Guinea, although pressure of increasing population has meant that the New Guineans have had to adapt, and are food-gatherers no more. Instead they have adapted from their original hunter-fisher economy and have taken to gardening: the sweet potato, animal and birds as sources of food have become very scarce, and almost entirely restricted to the most inaccessible regions.

One point about their ancestry seems clear: they owe little to their place of origin. If they did in fact derive from Dravid stock (of southern India), it must have been well before the advent of other races of Indians. The land-bridge must have been pretty complete for these timid water-haters to have come across. There are other theories as to their origins which perhaps possess validity, albeit to a lesser degree. It is possible that the Tasmanians came from nowhere, growing like Topey in their island, which acted as a cradle land for their race. Evidence in support of this is suggested by other isolated regions, where the indigenous peoples become entirely creatures of their environment. Further support to this theory comes from the reports of recent finds (*Nature*, November 10th, 1972) of fossil man on the shores of Lake Mungo, dating back to 32,000 B.P. These people had a special type of burial custom, part cremation, part inhumation, which was also found among the Tasmanians. Other evidence suggesting that a people rather like the Tasmanians inhabited the Australian mainland before the arrival of the aborigines comes from remote areas of bush, where there are still a few aboriginals who, in their hair and build, resemble more closely the Tasmanians than the Australians.

Then how is it that there are so many pockets of Tasmanian type peoples (mostly as remnants) still remaining in the most inaccessible places of southern Asia and the Pacific today? Negritos they could be called, like the people of the Solomons, New Caledonia and New Ireland, etc. (by some these are termed Macro-negritos).

Tasmania is separated from Australia by the Bass Straits, the formation of which, according to Sir Douglas Mawson, occurred about fifty thousands years ago. Probably the Tasmanian aborigines crossed over a little prior to this time. In any case they were only 184 miles from the Australian mainland and there were stepping-stone-like islands in between. However, the Tasmanian males, at least, hated water and seem to have had no art for the building of boats of any kind.

Via the Bass Straits must have been their way of entry for in every other direction there is very deep water. On the northern side of

Tasmania the depth of the ocean is only fifty fathoms. This all seems to indicate that the Tasmanians are a race of great antiquity, who came over when there was a land-bridge, and before the dog was in association with man.

There are also ideas that other, perhaps even earlier, peoples inhabited the island long before the European ever reached Tasmania. This rather curious article comes from the Robert Town *Gazette* of September 2nd, 1872:

> "A small copper coin has been ploughed up at Newtown, which, however unwilling as we may be to indulge in chimerical fancies, certainly gives rise to many interesting conjectures. It bears the appearance of great antiquity, and the die or stamp which impressed it must have been very deep or crudely engraved, the figures being in high relief. The obverse is a crowned head, which bears no resemblance to anything European in kind. The countenance with a beard is in profile, the facial angle of which is greater than we usually find in the aboriginal race; but where are the circumstances to fix his origin in this island, we do not think that of itself it would subvert it.
>
> "There are on the side four or five letters or characters which we cannot decipher, nor ascertain to what alphabet they belong. The reverse shows a naked figure, that resembles an aboriginal native when he is in the act of throwing a spear. The coin has been kindly placed in our hands by the finder, whose character for veracity is indisputable. We know two men, both unfortunately unable to read, who discovered sometime since a stone covered with characters, in a cave in the bank of the river Styx, which they broke and destroyed. We ourselves have, we must confess, seen various figures and emblems cut or drawn on the inner part of bark composes the rude huts of the natives; but whether they, or the characters on the stone above alluded to, were engraved by the inhabitants, or by some runaway prisoner who had associated himself with them, we do not take it upon ourselves to determine."

If a connection did exist between India and Tasmania in more recent times, this may account for the coin, while the stone and bark characters seem certain to have been made by the aborigines. One of the greatest anthropologists of the nineteenth century, Latham, says "the aborigines of Van Diemen's Land, commonly called Tasmania, have a fair claim, when considered by themselves, to be looked upon as a separate species of mankind". It would be true to say that the Tasmanian aborigines have a closer affinity to the highlanders of New Guinea and the peoples of the Solomons, New Caledonia and New Britain than the Maori-types of New Zealand.

The Tasmanians themselves may give us fuel for the theory that there were many cradle-lands and that people in those lands just developed spontaneously, showing peculiarities and adaptations suitable to their environment. Should the climate, indigenous plant and animal life, and other ambient factors ever be the same in these cradle lands, the peoples in them, even though widely separated, would develop along similar lines. Only in certain particularly suitable areas did man, essentially a lazy animal, progress. It would be true to say that he is unlikely to develop without strong pressures from outside forces, such as the violent climatic changes in early Europe at the times of the ice-ages, which forced the primitive men then in existence to compete for food and shelter with the equally hard-pressed animal species. It is unlikely that many men survived each of these great changes, but those that did would have been the strongest, most able and most adaptable. Thus each time the race would have become a little more refined and a little more developed, probably resulting in Cro-Magnon man and, finally, *Homo sapiens*. However, where food and shelter are sufficient for the tribe's needs, and quite readily obtainable, there is no need to adapt, invent, or even think too much about its collection. Thus, as adaptation and invention are unnecessary, men do not indulge in them, which is probably the reason why we find these isolated pockets of primitive peoples to this day. This theory is borne out by the evolutionary evidence of the one-cell animal which was forced to become a two-celled creature because of the harsh elements with which it had to contend on the sea-shores that were its habitat.

This does not, of course, mean that the Tasmanian aborigines were, or the Australian aborigines are, in any way less than the other races of man. In fact they showed a marked aptitude for languages and mechanical things, often more so than Europeans. Among the Australian aborigine children this is particularly noticeable at school.

Socially, of course, they have not been subjected to the generations of disciplined conformity that marks the Europeans' culture. Thus, regardless of what they are doing, they will go on "Walkabout" when the mood takes them, often for five or six months at a stretch, hence of course, putting themselves at a disadvantage, educationally and by repute, among the more conformist, settled population.

A very strong argument that they inhabited Tasmania from very early times is the fact that they had no water-borne transport. On th rare occasions when they wished to cross a large river, they would search for a dead tree, and gingerly manœuvre across on that, with much concentration in case they should fall in. They were known to make extremely crude reed "boats" (see plate A24). But this, apparently, was an infrequent occurrence.

Another hypothesis for which quite a strong argument may be made out, is concerning the botanical development of Australia and Tasmania. As the existing forms of plant life bear a remarkable resemblance to those of the Tertiary period of Europe and America, it could be argued that the existing man in Australia and Tasmania would be contemporaneous, thus suggesting an earlier appearance here than elsewhere. Dr. Weisbach, who esteemed the Tasmanians as being little above brute animals, and who preached the continued refinement and ultimate perfectability of the human race, would approve the the suggestion of the aborigines' prior appearance as bearing out his theory that they were the lowest level of humanity, and being, with some groups of negro, the examples of this type of unprogressiveness.

The Tasmanians were great shell-fish eaters, and there are great mounds of shells to be found around the shores of Tasmania, which indicate that these people collected shell-fish for many thousands of years. In fact they are very similar to the kitchen middens of Denmark and those of the Jomoan culture around the shores of Japan.

Mr. Wallace, of Wallace Line fame (or perhaps notoriety), considered the Tasmanian aborigines very similar to the inhabitants of the interior of many of the islands of Indonesia, and to be perfect examples of the Papuan type. In the ethnological chart of the Novaro expedition the Papuans are recorded as being throughout Australia, New Guinea and Tasmania, except in its eastern province and a small area on the south-west coast.

Messrs. Lesson and Garnet, two French explorers, have further expressed a view in their *Sciences naturelles*, when they described the Papuans, including Tasmanians, the New Hebrideans and New Caledonians in these terms: "Their hair is black, very thick, moderately woolly; the nose a little depressed, no bridge to that nose, the nostrils transversely enlarged; the chin is little and well made; the cheek bones are projecting; the forehead is raised; the lips are thick and long; a beard is rare." They refer to the aborigines as being of a "deep black colour", their hair as short woolly and very curly and the facial angle as moderately acute. They regarded as Papuans all those who used red henna for the hair, had cicatrices on the body, roasted food, and lay on the ground by fires.

The Tasmanian aborigines were, from all accounts, much darker than the Australian aborigines, which is the more remarkable because they lived in a temperate land. This suggests the possibility that the early inhabitants of the world were dark-skinned. Pritchard, a contemporary anthropologist, regarded the Australian and Tasmanian aborigines as being of separate races, saying that "they are of decidedly pelagian negro stock". The compressed, elongated forehead with prognathous jaws is recognized in the skull, and shows that the fellow Papuans of the neighbouring Indonesian islands had a similar cranium, in the ample size of the coronal ridge, from which the head slopes down on each side, in the convexity of the parietal bones, in the narrowness and lateral compression of the forehead, which is very narrow between the two temporal ridges.

The New Caledonians, under the protection of the French, and no more to be tamed by them than the Tasmanians were by the British, have been described by some as the origin of the Tasmanian aborigines, but there are several manifestations of greater progress among these people, possibly as a result of contact with the more advanced brown race of Polynesia, that distinguish them from the other orders of aborigines. The physical differences, in spite of woolly hair, mark them as being an impure race. Labillardière, in 1792, was the first to recognize the similarity. "Their hair is woolly," he tells us, "their persons are of medium stature, and their complexions are as black as the natives of Van Diemen's Land, and the general type of their countenance is similar to that of the last mentioned people." M. Domény Rienzi, in his *Océanie* of 1835, referring to a heathen people, speaks of them as being Papuan by origin, but the last variety of that race, as those of Maricolo and New Caledonia. Nearly all these aboriginal peoples wherever they are found are to be identified as being even *pre*-Stone Age, wooden stakes hardened in fires being the nearest they came to making spears. Another distinguishing feature of such early peoples is their lack of gods. A few, perhaps more advanced, may have believed in some minor spirits who are animistic. Generally, too, they have no pots, they are hunter-fishers and wanderers, building no more permanent construction than temporary windbreaks as the need occurs. These windbreaks were made by the Tasmanians and are still found among the Papuans, when they are on the move, and among the South African bushmen.

Alfred Jacobs, another French writer, lumped the Tasmanians and New Caledonians together and gave an unflattering account of both:

"Their physiognomy is brutal and gross; the women, above all, with their woolly hair, their stupid countenances, their hanging breasts, their deformed extremities, resemble beasts more than human beings. The men are entirely naked, excepting that they envelop their sexual parts in a shred of cloth; as to the females they cover the middle part of their bodies with a girdle a foot in size, to which is attached behind a garment which descends from the shoulders to the calf of the leg.

"There is, in fact, in New Caledonia a mixture of this abject aborigine of Tasmania and the finer races of Melanesia. It appears that among the Tasmanians, the men were of usually quite good physique, while the women were short, squat and generally ugly, and with no waist. This seems exactly parallel with today's highlanders in New Guinea, as does the treatment meted out by the men to their women, who were, without exception, treated contemptuously as beasts of burden."

There are observations from contemporary travellers that some of the Tasmanian women were remarkably superior and fine-looking. One example was the girl taken in hand by the Governor's wife. This, too, happens in New Guinea, where suddenly a great beauty appears in a tribe, almost as if she were of an entirely different type to the rest. The dress and religious beliefs of the two peoples also have much in common.

Mr. Logna, the anthropologist, is reported to have stated that "it may then generally be said, that, both in their physique and the construction of their language, the aborigines present a type similar to the negritos of the Papuans, Tasmanians and others, as well as to the nearer negritos of the Molucca, Nicobar and Andaman Islands".

Many of the Tasmanians' superstitious practices are still found among the hill-men of southern India and New Guinea. Similar types of fish-trap also occur in these three areas.

The fact that crisp-haired Papuans are found on islands all round the Australian coast, and over such a very large area, ought certainly to indicate their migration prior to that of the Australian aborigines as we know them. It might be asked how a small intrusive party could drive them from the whole continent. But this would probably not be difficult, as there is little evidence to suggest that the climate has altered very much, thus suggesting that the original inhabitants would have been spread thinly. Also the contest would have taken place over many thousands of years, even until relatively recently, judging by remains found in a few isolated areas of Australia. Though not identical with the Tasmanians, they bear a greater resemblance to them than do present-day Australian aborigines. Finally, it may well seem incredible that after so many centuries of apparent isolation that the Tasmanian aborigines did, in fact, retain human characteristics.

What have the Tasmanians left behind them for us to see? R. W. Legge of Tasmania has brought together a remarkable collection of Tasmanian stone implements, and A. L. Meston has found rock carvings on the northern and eastern coasts. The stone implements (see plate A12) definitely indicate that these people are of an arrested culture, their artifacts close to the Palaeolithic.

Appendix I

Extract from My Home In Tasmania

The following is an extract from Mr. George Meredith's book *My Home in Tasmania* (during a residence of nine years) by Mrs. Charles Meredith, London, John Murray, 1852. It indicates the attitude towards the aborigines of the times: when it was written there were only nineteen left. It was soon after the time of an outcry among the white settlers against the plan to take the remnant of the aborigines from Flinders Island to Oyster Cove on the mainland.

"Seven or eight years before my arrival in this colony, the aborigines had been removed to Flinders Island in the Bass Straits, where large and comfortable dwellings were erected for them [note what Bishop Nixon had to say about these], and they were well clothed, fed, and instructed at the expense of the Colonial Government, under the care of a resident medical superintendent, until the year 1847, when His Excellency Sir W. T. Denison Bt., our present Lieutenant-Governor, imagining that they might be rendered more happy, and be more efficiently superintended here, caused those remaining to be brought again to the colony, and a new establishment has been accordingly formed on the west shore of D'Entrecasteaux Channel where they now are. Of the charitable and humane feelings which actuated Sir W. Denison, but one opinion can be entertained. How far he was justified in gratifying them by making this change is a separate question, as the colonists, especially those who had formerly suffered such fearful experience of the aboriginal ferocity and cruelty, were strenuously opposed to the measures—on the grounds that every adult man among the natives [at most nineteen!]

had been actively engaged in many, some of them in hundreds, of the most brutal and unprovoked murders, and that in all probability a return to their old haunts would lead to a renewal of the horrors which, since their removal, have been unknown, but which in former years rendered a residence in the colony one long series of alarms, suffering and loss, with the daily imminent peril, of a frightful death.

"Mr. Meredith's experience of the habits and needs of the aborigines extends over many years, and from the notes he has made for me, and our frequent conversations on the subject, I shall compile the information in my book on them from his own words. Many a time, contrary to our usual primitive country hours, has midnight found us still seated by our glowing hearth; I intent on hearing and he relating the horrors, and terrors, and hair raising escapes of his younger days in the colony, when every bush within spear throw of the house was a source of danger, and to stir beyond the door sill unarmed was nothing short of *felo de se*. The plain relation of easily proved matters of fact may perhaps tend to dissipate erroneous ideas as to the original enmity between settlers and the aborigines, who for some years after colonization of the island lived peaceably together, the natives visiting the houses and the stations of the colonists in the same amicable manner as the Blacks in New South Wales do now, camping near the homes of the white people with the consent of the latter, receiving food and presents and other things.

"In considering this subject it should also be borne in mind who and what the earlier settlers were. They were neither pirates nor robbers as were many of the early settlers in and usurpers of new countries in days of yore; but British farmers and country gentlemen, not usually considered a desperately ferocious and blood-thirsty class, nor by any means disposed to commence hostilities against quite unoffending people, but purposing to till their ground and feed their sheep without injury or molestation to the natives. In fact the natives gained rather than lost by the arrival of the settlers, in the food that was given to them by the settlers. The deadly enmity exhibited by the natives, through a series of years, towards the colonists and their servants, was in the first instance, unprovoked by the white population.

"I remember distinctly the first act of violence of that long and fearful tragedy—it was perpetrated by the natives, under the direction of 'Mosquito', a native of Sydney, who had been tried there for the cruel murder of a white woman. By an act of mistaken humanity on the part of the Sydney Government, Mosquito was reprieved from the gallows, and sent to this island where he was set at liberty, and was suffered to roam about unmolested. At first the natives here showed some jealousy towards him, but they ultimately became friendly, and gave him a gin, named Goosberry.

"I know of only one instance, in which a native lost his life by the hands of a white man; the occasion was this: my father had lost three horses, and two men were dispatched to look for them. During their search, they fell in with a tribe of natives, who instantly gave chase; one of our servants was armed with a pistol, and the other with a gun. The natives ran in two lines, one on either side of the men, with the view of surrounding, and when parallel with them, began throwing their spears. The man who had the pistol then cocked it, and pulled the trigger, but it missed fire; on this the natives yelled, and ran with increased energy, calling each other to close the lines [clever to know the language], and surround their victims; at this juncture the man who had the gun fired at the foremost native, and shot him dead; the others ran to their fallen companion, and our men escaped.

"The natives under the guidance of Mosquito, commenced and carried on what they intended should prove a war of extermination, both of man and beast. They spared neither sex nor age; the aged woman and the helpless child alike fell victims to their ferocity; and the feelings of the whites towards them in consequence may be easily imagined. For the space of some months, during which time I noted down their proceedings, the number of murders of white people which came to my knowledge averaged eight a week; and many doubtless occurred which I never heard of.

"The disappearance of all the young children among the natives compels us to the inference that they were destroyed; doubtless on account of the difficulty of conveying them about the rapid flights from place to place which the blacks now practised in the perpetration of their murders.

"Colonel, now Sir George Arthur, arrived here as Lieutenant-Governor in 1824, shortly after the first murders, and my father went to him immediately to propose plans for the temporary coercion of the natives, warning him that unless some sort of effectual means were at once adopted, the murderous habits of the latter would for a time be fearfully destructive to the colonists, and eventually cause their own extermination. His good advice was disregarded.

"Another instance is as follows: Within a fortnight from the time of Gay's murder, the same tribe went to my father's whaling station, at the mouth of Swan Port; they hailed the boats, and the men took them in, and, thinking they would gain some reward for capturing the murderous savages, pulled across the bay homewards, and then kept the native party, consisting of six men and four or five women, for two or three days, intending to send them by vessel to the governor; but whilst arrangements were being made for conveying them safely and unharmed on board, they effected an escape— some ran away, and the pursuit was in vain, but one woman slower than the rest, was slightly hurt in the confusion, and rushed into the sea where she swam and dived for some time, but she was caught in the end. Her wound was carefully dressed by a surgeon, who chanced to be passing. Surely I need transcribe no more; I do it in the hope of making known something of the real state of affairs as formerly existing between the aborigines and the colonists, which is so greatly misunderstood in England; where as I know well, the white people are most erroneously believed to have been the aggressors. I shall close this chapter with Mr. Meredith's brief account of the final capture of the blacks.

"The outrages committed by the natives continued without any attempt on the part of the Government to suppress them, beyond the formal publication in the Government Gazette, of a proclamation commanding the natives not to pass from the west to the east of a certain imaginary line drawn through the island in a north and south direction. The use of such a medium as a printed proclamation in a Gazette to address a horde of savages, who could not speak the English language far less read it, would not have occurred to any governor less gifted with sagacity than Colonel Arthur; and with that notable experiment he contented himself until the year 1829, when the whole male population of the colony, capable of bearing arms, was called out for the purpose of driving the natives on to Tasman's peninsula. Many whose better sense informed them of the impossibility of such a scheme succeeding, joined in 'The Black War', as it was called. The Black War proved an utter failure, and cost the colony £27,000. Except in the transfer of large sums of money to the contractors favoured by the government, matters remained as before the expedition was undertaken, until a person named Robinson, bricklayer by trade, undertook and performed the singular service of bringing every aboriginal, man, woman, and child, quietly and peaceably, and willingly into Hobarton. Whence they were shipped to Flinders Island, which is between forty and fifty miles in length, twelve to eighteen in width, and abounding with the smaller kinds of kangaroo, etc. The coasts are plentifully supplied with fish, and in addition to this abundance of their natural food, the natives were provided at the expense of the colony with dwellings, ample rations of flour and meat, bedding clothes, garden implements, seeds, fishing tackle, and all things which could be necessary for their present or improved condition; besides medical attendance [all in fact, except *water*]."

Appendix II

Numbers of Tasmanians

In 1802 there were estimated to be 20,000 natives up and down the country, and a slightly later survey (1803) showed that some 6,000–8,000 were women. By 1817 there were 7,000 aborigines left in all, and by 1824 there remained 340. The figures over the next forty-five years are as follows:

1825: 320
1826: 320
1827: 300
1828: 280
1829: 250
1830: 225
1831: 190
1832: 176
1833: 122
1834: 111
1836: 116
1837: 97
1838: 82 (42 males, 40 females, including 14 children)
1839: 68
1840: 58
1841: 49
1842: 54 (in seven years only 14 children were born)
1847: 48 (10 of these were children)
1848: 40 (12 males, 20 females and 8 children)
1854: 16

1855:	15
1856:	16
1857:	15
1858:	14
1859:	14 (5 males and 9 females)
1860:	11 (4 males and 7 females)
1861:	8
1863:	6 (1 male and 5 females)
1864:	6 (this is when plates C4 and C6 were photographed)
1865:	5 (1 male and 4 females)
1869:	1 (Truganina)
1876:	0

In 1834 the proportion of males to females was six to one, as the female babies were the first to be sacrificed. Towards the end the imbalance between the sexes increased: for example, on Flinders Island, from where the women only were removed by the sealers, in particular young female children. One woman was worth about five seal carcasses at this time. When they arrived at Oyster Cove the imbalance reversed, since the women were by now old and not considered worth stealing. Possibly, also, the males were more delicate and consequently more susceptible to the ravages of civilization.

Bibliography

Arnold and Clough (1866): *N.Z. letters of Arnold with further letters to Van Diemen's Land, 1847–51*

Australian Association for the Advancement of Science (1924): **S.A.** Vol. 17, Adelaide

Backhouse, James (1843): *Narrative of a visit to the Australian Colonies*, London

Balfour, Henry, F.R.S. (1925): *The Status of the Tasmanian Among Stone Age Peoples*, The Prehistoric Society of East Anglia, Vol. 5, Part 1

Branard, James (1889): "The Last Living Aboriginal of Tasmania", *The Mercury*, Hobart, September 10th

Bischopp, James (1832): *A Sketch of the History of Van Diemen's Land, also information on the Van Diemen's Land Company*, London

Bligh, W. (1792): *A Voyage to the South*, London

Bonwick, James (1870): *The Daily Life of the Tasmanians*, Sampson Low & Son & Marston, London

Braim, Thomas H. Archdeacon (1846): *History of New South Wales to the year 1844*, 2 vols., London

Breton, W. H. (1833): *Exploration in New South Wales, Western Australia and Van Diemen's Land during 1830–33*, London

Bunce, D. (1857): *23 years Wandering in the Australian and Tasmanian Outback*, London

Calder, J. E. (1875): *Some Accounts of the Wars and Habits etc. of the Tribes of Tasmania*, Hobart

Clark, C. M. H. (1968): *A History of Australia, Vol. 2, New South Wales and Van Diemen's Land, 1822–38*

Clune and Stephenson (1954): *The Viking of Van Diemen's Land, the life of Jorgensen, 1780–1841*

Collins, D. (1789): *An Account of the English Colony of New South Wales*, 2 vols.

Colonies and Slaves (1831): *Papers on them*, Vol. 19, London

Cook, Captain James (1780): *Round the World*, 4 vols., London
Crowther, W. E. L. H., D.S.O., M.B.: *The Passing of the Tasmanian Race*, The Halford Oration
Croxet (1753): *Nouveau Voyage à la Mer du Sud*, Paris
Curr, E. M. (1886): *The Australian Race*, Melbourne
Davis, Jas. Barnard, M.D., F.R.S. (1874): *On the Osteology of the Tasmanians*, Haarlem
Dixon, J. (1839): *The Conditions and the Capabilities of Van Diemen's Land as a place of Emigration*, London
Dumont, d'Urville (1837): *Voyage au Pale Sud et dans l'Océance sur les corvettes l'Astrolobe et la Zelee pendant 1837*
Fenton, James (1884): *A History of Tasmania from its discovery in 1642 to the present time*, Hobart, Launceston and London
Flinders, Matthew (1814): *Voyage to Terra Australis during the years 1801–3*, London
Flower, Professor W. H., F.R.S. (1878): *The Aborigines of Tasmania: an Extinct Race, a Lecture*, Manchester and London
Gervais, Paul (1876): *Zoologie et Paléontologie Générales*, 2 vols., Paris
Henderson, J. (1832): *Observations on the Colonies of New South Wales and Van Diemen's Land*, Calcutta
Hobart Town Almanack for 1836: contains Ross's *Fourteen Years Ago* with his account of the aborigines
Holman, James (1834): *Voyage Round the World*, 4 vols., London
Hull, H. M. (1859): *Experiences of 40 Years in Tasmania*, London
Hull, H. M. (1866): *Statistics of Tasmania from the year 1816 to 1865*, Hobart
Hull, H. M.: *The Aborigines of Tasmania*, MS. in the Royal Colonial Institute
Hutchinson (1910): *The Living Races of Mankind*, London
Huxley, T. H. (1870): *Journal of the Ethnographical Society*, Vol. 2, pp. 130–404.
Jeffreys, Lieut. C. H. (1820): *Van Diemen's Land, Geographical and Delineation of the Island*, London
Labillardière: *The Voyage of La Perouse (1791–1794)*, Paris
Laplace, C. P. T. (1855): *Voyage Autours du Monde*, Vol. 6 (1833–9), Paris
Lee (1912): *Commander Sir John Hayes*, Hayes, London
Man (August 1938, p. 121, Vol. XXXVIII, pp. 142–70): *The West Coast Tribe of Tasmanian Aborigines, Skulls & Implements and the Problems of the Australian-Tasmanian Descent. The Skulls coming from the Melbourne Museum*, J. Wonderley, Melbourne, pp. 121–7

Martiner (1791): *A Voyage in the Brig Mercury*, London

Meredith, Mrs. Charles (1852): *My House in Tasmania (or nine years in Tasmania)*, 2 vols., John Murray, London

Nixon, Francis, Bishop of Tasmania (The First Bishop) (1854): *The Cruise of the Beacon*, Bell & Daldy, London

Nixon, N.: *The Pioneer Bishop in Van Diemen's Land 1843–1863*, printed in Tasmania in 1953

Palmer, H. W.: *Van Diemen's Land, its Rise and Progress*, London

Peron, F. (1811): *Voyage de Découvertes aux Terres Australis*, 2 vols., Paris

Pruner, Bey: *Journal of the Anthropological Institute*, Vol. VI, 1877

Robson L. L. (1965): *Convict Settlers of Australia 1787–1852*

Rossel, E. P. E. (1808): *Voyage d'Entrecasteaux*, 2 vols., Paris

Roth, Ling (1890): *The Aborigines of Tasmania*, Kegan-Paul, London

Roth, Ling (1891): *Crozet's Voyage to Tasmania*, trans. by Ling Roth, Kegan-Paul, London

Royal Society of Tasmania: *Papers and Proceedings*, 1910–11, also 1925–6

Royal Society of Tasmania: *Papers and Proceedings*, The Food of the Tasmanian Aborigines, read July 1910 by Fritz Noetling, pp. 278–83, also further notes in the same volume on the habits of the Tasmanian Aborigines, pp. 102–19, also notes and queries on p. 231, p. 258 are also important

Scott, G. (1914): *The Life of Matthew Flinders*, Sydney

Sharp, C. A. (1956): *Letters of Anne Lovell, A Tasmanian Family 1846–1872*

Sharp, C. A. (1968): *The Voyages of Abel Tasman*

Smyth, R. Brough (1878): *The Aborigines of Victoria and Tasmania*, 2 vols., Melbourne

Strzelecki, Count Paul E. de (1845): *Physical Description of Van Diemen's Land*, London

Tasman, Abel Jansen (1642): *Journal van de Reis naar et Onbekende Zuiland in den Jone*

Topinard, Paul (1834): *Étude sur les Tasmanians*, Vol. III, Mémoires de la Société d'Anthropologie, Paris

Turner, Sir William, K.C.B., F.R.S. (1910): *The Aborigines of Tasmania Part II*, The Transactions of the Royal Society of Edinburgh, Vol. XLVII, Part III (No. 16), pp. 412–54, Edinburgh

Van Diemen's Land Manual for 1834, edited by H. Melville, Hobart

Weatherburn, A. K. (1966): *George Evans, Explorer 1780–1852*

West, John (1852): *History of Tasmania*, 2 vols., printed in Tasmania by Henry Dowling

Index